PERFORMANCES

PERFORMANCES

GREG DENING

THE UNIVERSITY OF CHICAGO PRESS

GREG DENING is Emeritus Professor of History at the University of Melbourne. His many books include *Edward Robarts; Xavier; Islands and Beaches; The Marquesas Islands; The Bounty; History's Anthropology; Xavier Portraits; Mr Bligh's Bad Language;* and *The Death of William Gooch.*

The University of Chicago Press, Chicago 60637
Melbourne University Press, Victoria, Australia 3053
Text © Greg Dening 1996
Design and typography © Melbourne University Press 1996

05 04 03 02 01 00 99 98 97 96   1 2 3 4 5 6

ISBN: 0-226-14297-3 (cloth)
ISBN: 0-226-14298-1 (paper)

A CIP catalogue record for this book is available from the Library of Congress.

This book is printed on acid-free paper.

For

RHYS ISAAC

The most generous man I know.
For many years he and I have celebrated
discovery and knowledge together.
He will celebrate this celebration of mine with joy.

CONTENTS

Acknowledgements   *xi*
Notes to the Reader   *xiii*

PRELUDE

Ethnography on My Mind   5

MAKING A PRESENT OUT OF THE PAST: HISTORY'S ANTHROPOLOGY

A Poetic for Histories   *35*
Sharks that Walk on the Land   *64*
The Face of Battle: Valparaiso, 1814   *79*

PRESENTING THE PAST: HISTORY'S THEATRE

The Theatricality of History Making
  and the Paradoxes of Acting   *103*
Possessing Tahiti   *128*
Hollywood Makes History   *168*
Inventing Others   *191*

Contents

RETURNING TO THE PAST ITS OWN PRESENT: HISTORY'S EMPOWERING FORCE

Songlines and Seaways   *207*
Anzac Day   *225*
School at War   *233*

POSTLUDE

Soliloquy in San Giacomo   *267*

References   *273*
Glossary   *285*
Index   *287*

IMAGES

Plates 1–12, between pages 144 and 145

POSSESSIONS HAWAI'I
POSSESSIONS TAHITI
POSSESSIONS TE HENUA
BOUNTY PERFORMANCES
SCHOOL AT WAR

Acknowledgements

THIS collection of new and old writings is dedicated to my friend Rhys Isaac, Professor of History at LaTrobe University, Bundoora, Victoria. Rhys, Inga Clendinnen and I shared the excitement of establishing core subjects in a history degree in a department newly founded by Professor Allan Martin. There is, in educational institutions, a special sweetness in not being bound by 'the ways things are always done' and by being free to follow one's own educational ambitions. We quickly found that we could not teach only what we used to know, but had to join our teaching to our research and to present ourselves to our students where we found ourselves to be at the time. We found ways to meet regularly and to read one another's work. Donna Merwick, soon to become my wife, joined us. All our fields were different—eighteenth-century Virginia, sixteenth-century Mexico, seventeenth-century Dutch-America, eighteenth-century Pacific. But when our writings began to appear, commentators, especially in the United States, dubbed us the 'Melbourne Group'. We would be hard put to say what it was that joined us together in other people's eyes more than physical location. But the denomination of the 'Melbourne Group' has always given me personal pleasure. It reminded me of days when esteem, affection and constructive criticism gave us the courage to write history as we felt history should be written. How could I not always make Rhys, Inga, Donna my first acknowledgement?

Performances includes some pieces that have been published before. In the way of things I should acknowledge the journals and publishers that gave them their first light, but my true acknowledgement is to those academic editors who gave their time and care to what I had written. So let me thank Dr Aletta Biersack (editor of *Clio in Oceania* 1991, Smithsonian Institution Press, 'Poetics of History'); Professor Fred Myers (*Cultural Anthropology* 1993: 8/73–95, 'Theatricality of History Making'); Dr Judith Brett (*Meanjin Quarterly* 1982: 41/417–37, 'Sharks that Walk on the Land'); Dr Peter White (*Archaeology in Oceania* 1986: 21/103–118, 'Possessing Tahiti'); Dr Donna Merwick (*Australasian Journal of American Studies* 'Inventing Others'); Dr Michael Roberts (*Social Analysis* 1990: 29/62–66, 'Anzac Day'); Dr Roger Thompson (*War and Society* 1983: 1/25–42, 'The Face of Battle').

Just as there are no performances without audiences, so there is no writing without readers. At Melbourne University Press, I have been blessed with my first readers—with that anonymous reader, first of all, who made such constructive comments on my drafts; then with Julianne Richards, the copy editor, who read every word several times over and saved me from myself many times; with Lindy Coverdale, in production, who marshalled the energies of editors, designers and typesetters to do their reading creatively and innovatively and managed my author's quirks; with Brian Wilder, Director of MUP, who offered me support and encouragement from the first moment I walked into his office. They all did their duties for me generously, not just for *Performances*, but for my previous publication at MUP, *The Death of William Gooch: A History's Anthropology*, as well. I thank them all greatly.

Notes to the Reader

AS it is for so many others, history is my passion. Writing it, teaching it, reading it fills the days and years of my life. In all passions, there is pain and pleasure. The pain is that of any artistic endeavour—the hours of engagement that any minute of performance takes. The pleasure is the exhilaration of feeling—occasionally—that the performance has worked.

'Performance' is a word of some ambivalence. 'What a performance!' we sometimes say, with more cynicism than appreciation, of behaviour that seems extravagantly out of place or over-acted. Striving for effect sometimes creates a sense of artificiality. Indeed our cultural prejudice is that understatement is the proper performance of those who are more self-confidently civilised. I cannot say whether these performances are over-written or under-stated. 'Sculpt' is a word I have used with my students when talking about writing. I would hope that a reader would find these performances sculpted. I never have been a devotee of my first drafts or even of my fourth.

'Performance' holds within it, too, an older meaning of completion. Performance is a duty or obligation done. It has long held the connotation that the qualities of the duty done were heightened by being public, by having an audience. A performance is a consummation. A performance stands by itself in some way.

These *Performances* of mine, then, stand by themselves, completed for different occasions and different audiences. However, like performances in an art exhibition, or in a concert, or on the stage in an evening of theatre, they stand together, too.

If I say here, now, in what way I claim these *Performances* stand together, be clear that I have no intention of cutting short any argument whether they do or they do not. The freedom of the audience to be the critic in the gallery or in the concert-hall or theatre foyer is something I treasure. I really have only one ambition for readers of these performances of mine. It is that at some moment the reader will say to her- or himself, 'That is just what I was about to say!' That, for me, the writer, is the true pleasure of my text, its erotics, as Susan Sontag and Roland Barthes would say.

Some people, however, like programme notes; many like tour guides; everybody feels that her or his goodwill as a reader in picking up a book should be matched by the author's sense of responsibility in using the reader's time well.

So let me make some sort of programme notes for my Performances. History as a form of consciousness is their constant concern. History—changing, enlarging, identifying; history—an everyday thing, saturating every moment of our cultural existence. Making sense of what has happened is how we live. We do it in all sorts of ways. We sing it, dance it, carve it, paint it, tell it, write it. We find different ways to make sense of what has happened according to the different occasions of our telling and the different audiences to which we tell it. We explain things to tax office clerks, give testimony in a law court, gossip at the dinner table, write a diary. The ways we make sense of the past are almost innumerable, but we are culturally astute in knowing how these different ways are to be interpreted, how what is true for one occasion is not true for another. We know instinctively that this consciousness of things past is, in fact, our present.

If my *Performances* on history as a form of consciousness were an art exhibition, they probably would be called 'Presenting the Past'. There is time and space in the word 'presenting'. Time in the sense that putting something into the present is to make it 'now'; space in the sense that to present something is to stage it in some way. 'Presenting the Past' will always imply bringing past and present together. It will also imply that the past will not be replicated or repeated, but represented, shaped, staged, performed in some way other than it originally existed.

Making a Present out of the Past: History's Anthropology—Part I—
is not a novel concept about history. That 'every generation writes its
own history' is a cliché of vernacular historiography. Perhaps the energy
with which I pursue the meaning of this cliché is novel, though. I am
saying that history—the past transcribed into words and signs—is the
way we experience the present. We make sense of the present in our consciousness of the past. I say this reflectively in 'A Poetics for Histories'. I
say it more concretely in my narratives of the historical consciousness of
two cultures in the death of Captain Cook and then in my story of how
dramatising the past allowed men to kill one another in 'The Face of Battle'.

Presenting the Past: History's Theatre—Part II—proceeds in the
same way: a reflection on the theatricality of history-making followed by
narratives of the ways I have discovered history being made into theatre—
in the possession of Tahiti, in the cinematics of the mutiny on the *Bounty*,
in the invention of others in ethnography. I am a supporter of Aristotle
in the area of theatre. Not just because he flouts the anti-theatrical
prejudices of Plato, but for his respect for the theatre and because of the
confidence he has in an audience's ability to abstract meaning—he calls
it *mythos* or plot—out of the trivialities of the stage. Everyday life, like
life on the stage, is talk and signs and significant action. Our ability to
make sense of this theatre is our cultural survival gene. Don't we say of
those who fail in this essential exercise, 'they lost the plot'? Isn't the least
theatrical of history-writing, and the least effective, that which pontifi-
cates on what the history means? The best theatre in historical writing is
that in which the Death of the Author is an exchange for the Birth of
the Reader. The story tells itself, I might have said, if it were not for the
fact that the story never tells itself. It has to be told.

**Returning to the Past its own Present: History's Empowering
Force**—Part III—does not concern so much bringing the past into the
present as returning to the past those qualities of the present that it once
possessed. That is not so easy a thing to do as it might seem. We are comfortable in our view of the past. The past happened in a totally particular way in time and space. That is its realism. All the possibilities of
what might have happened are reduced to one. The energies of historical
inquirers are focused on discovering what that one possibility was. But

by that we have not re-presented the past. To do that we have to enter into the experience of those actors in the past who, like us, experience a present as if all the possibilities are still there. If a historian ambitions to describe how people actually experienced their lives, then that historian has to slough off many certainties. To give back to the past its present, one has to be a little humble about what one can know. In Part III there are some efforts of mine to write history with the deference that the past deserves.

My *Performances* have a 'Prelude' and a 'Postlude'. These present/ pre'sent myself in these histories. Perhaps such personal presence may seem a little theatrical. Well, yes, it is. But it is the constant theme of these essays that any performance, in life or in theatre, produces performance consciousness. There is a realism in that, I think, that goes beyond self-indulgence.

Prelude

THE Prelude, or, Growth of a Poet's Mind was the title of an autobiographical poem by William Wordsworth begun in 1798 when he was twenty-eight years old and finally put aside forty years later. It was his attempt to discover what the poetical imagination might be, out of his own experiences. He saw the unhappy days of his education at St John's College, Cambridge University, with all its formalism of book-learning and trivial competition, as the counterfoil to the inner freedoms he was beginning to feel. Wordsworth had spoiled the ambitions of his family and friends for his career by being ranked in his final examinations at Cambridge only as *hoi polloi*. He thus had ruined his chances for fellowship in college, preferment in the church and a place in law. He thought that the reason for his failure was that he was 'not of this time, not of this place'. He was a 'freeman', 'ill-tutored for captivity'. Cambridge was a 'privileged world within a world'. Whereas he had a 'world about me, 'twas my own. I made it, for it liv'd for me'. He conceded, however, that in this memory of his, this history, this ethnography on his mind—as I am tempted to call it—he could not say 'what proposition is in truth the naked recollection of that time, and what may rather have been call'd to life by after meditation'. He was well aware that there might be 'self-conceit' in trying to discover what something like poetic imagination might be by looking at himself, but he felt that 'humility' and 'diffidence' might put a limit on his certainties.

As it happens, there was a contemporary of Wordsworth at Cambridge in whom I have an interest. It was William Gooch. He was a poor scholarship boy from the tiny Norfolk village of Brockdish. His education, unlike that of Wordsworth, was a triumph. He ended his career at Cambridge as '2nd Wrangler', second in the hierarchic grading of the year in which Wordsworth was hoi polloi. Gooch embraced the Schools with enthusiasm. Indeed if there was a personification of the *mentalité* of Cambridge of the day, it was William Gooch. His success caught the attention of the Astronomer Royal, Nevil Maskelyne, and earned him a position as astronomer on Vancouver's voyage of discovery to the Pacific. Sailing to join Vancouver on the supply ship *Daedalus*, Gooch landed at Waimea on the Hawaiian island of Oahu. There he and his companion, Lieutenant Richard Hergest, were attacked and killed by Hawaiian *pahupu*, warriors 'cut-in-two' by their tattoos. They were killed because they were 'gods', a later tradition—a later after-meditation—recorded. 'They had sparkling eyes'.

My interest in Gooch was in how to tell his story, how to tell the history of his death with its mysteries of cross-cultural perceptions and the anthropology of his life with its closed down system of education. I felt I had a lien on him and Wordsworth, too. For long years of my life I had experienced the 'Schools', the performance of scholastic philosophy in 'Acts' or defence of theses in formal syllogistic logic. And I had known, too, what it was like to be totally enclosed by rule and formality. I thought I knew both Wordsworth's frustrations and Gooch's triumphs. Certainly I thought I could write their history and anthropology the better for that shared experience. But I also thought I knew my own frustrations and triumphs the better for knowing them in theirs.

I have had a privileged life. The prelude to my academic teaching and writing career was seventeen years of study in which I had few other obligations than a student's responsibility to learn. My four years of philosophy, five years of history, four years of theology and four years of anthropology were for me a magical mystery tour of life. I have celebrated them ever since. I know with Wordsworth that it is a 'self-conceit' to think that by reflection on my experiences in these years I might add to any reader's understanding of what historical and anthropological imagination might be. But my Prelude on the ethnography on my mind is written, too, with 'humility' and 'diffidence'. We all have to live with our after-meditations, and make of them what we will.

ETHNOGRAPHY ON MY MIND

I SAW them, years after they had made indelible images on my mind, in a second-hand furniture store. Stacks of straight-backed chairs, felt-covered kneelers, prie-dieux, marble-topped wash-stands, small table-desks. I had sat on them learning the dog-Latin that filled my days, or 'did' my spiritual reading at them, or knelt at them, my soul squirming in 'desolation' or soaring in 'consolation'. I had washed and shaved at them, shivering behind the curtains of my small cubicle in a dormitory of six young men at some unearthly hour of the morning. I had stood beside them in these same cubicles on Tuesday and Friday nights, stripped to the waist, waiting for the 'tocsin', the bell that signalled the beginning of penances. Then, breathlessly answering the verses of Psalm 140, 'Deliver me, O Lord, from evil men', my companions and I would flog ourselves with small rope disciplines. I remember the fear and humiliation of these sessions. Some of those around me would flog themselves mercilessly and I, physical coward that I was, flinched at the pain and tried to temper the bite of the cords.

Hanging on the walls of this furniture shop or piled on its floors waiting for a sale were the props of twenty-two years of religious life. I had used them first when I was sixteen years old and last when I was thirty-eight.

In one corner of the store was another group of relics. There stood a collection of counter-like white tables. Their wooden facades were carved with blue and green grapes and gilded grape leaves. They were the side altars from a chapel whose every nook and cranny I knew. I had prayed long hours in it. I had made my vows there. I had dusted its every corner and waxed and polished its parquetry floor. Each altar still had the empty cavity on its top where the altar stone would have laid. They were selling well, the salesman said. They were much in demand as drink-bars. 'Look at the grapes', he said. 'Wine signs!'

Wine signs, indeed. I looked for other signs. There would be a famous signature on one of them. I would know it to see it—the scuff-marks of a kicking foot at the bottom centre of the altar. Father Newport used to kick the altar there every morning. Father Newport was an eccentric among many eccentrics at Loyola College, the Jesuit Novitiate and House of Studies for Philosophy from which all these furnishings had come. Father Newport was possessed of some mysterious disease which required him always to be in a sweat and for him to cook his own meals in his room. To keep up the sweat he would run everywhere inside and outside the house. Conversation with him was carried out at a gentle jog down the corridors. Whether his cooking did it or not, I do not know, but he was possessed of prodigiously loud stomach rumbles. To disguise them, while he said mass on the side altars beside an assembly in silent prayer, he used to kick the altar.

Yes, the signs of his scruffing were still there on one of these bars-to-be. 'La-di-da!', he would have said. 'La-di-da!' is what he always said. 'La-di-da! How are you? La-di-da! That's good'. He was college bursar, and therefore buyer. I remember once he bought out whatever had survived of a burnt-out jam and canned fruit factory. For years we ate sour gooseberries and jam that had sugared in the heat. We lived on the hope that the labelless tin we were opening for our weekly bread and jam picnic lunch would not be the peach jam we had grown to hate.

Father Newport was also the driver of the college's ancient green Ford. He believed that tyres wore more evenly if he drove in the middle of the road. He also believed that the amount of petrol he had in the tank should approximate what was needed for the trip in hand. He would fill the tank sparingly at the college drum of petrol at the beginning of each journey. Sometimes he miscalculated. I remember once when he collected from St Vincent's Hospital an assortment of casualties from a particularly vigorous football match between first- and second-year 'philosophers'. I had a wrist in plaster, another had a bandaged ankle, and a third had his neck in a brace. The green Ford did not make it home on its ration of petrol. The three of us in our clerical collars and varied bandages were left to push the car down the centre of the road while Father Newport steered.

For years I lived on the same corridor as Father Newport. He was my confessor. He was a kindly confessor, believing that most of the temptations of celibates came from herbs in the soup rather than from the Devil. But he always felt that he was particularly prone to whatever infections were around. So when I knocked on his door to go to confession, he would always say, 'La-di-da! Wait a minute'. Then I would hear a muffled 'La-di-da! Come in'. I would kneel at the prie-dieu beside his chair. He would have a penitential stole over his shoulders and a brown paper bag over his head.

There was a time, because I was attending lectures at the University of Melbourne, when I would be in my room when everybody else was in the dining room at meals. It was a time when Father Newport, doing his own cooking, expected to have the run of the college. The toilet he and I shared on our corridor always leaked from the ceiling when it rained. One rainy night I came in late from the University. As I entered the corridor, Father Newport came running out of his room to the toilet. He was stark naked. But he carried an umbrella in his hand. 'La-di-da! How are you?' he said as he passed me.

His room was over the front entrance of the college, beneath the high square tower which with its battlements could be seen for miles around. In the tower was 'Hell', a library storage room where all the books that were listed in the *Index of Forbidden Books* were kept. These were not so much salacious books—although there were always plenty worth a peek. They were books of philosophy, theology, history and social theory deemed to be adversarial to the matters in which we were being educated. Permission had to be obtained to enter this locked room. Permission was easily given, let it be said. The isolation of the books was more an obeisance to Canon Law than evidence of the Jesuits' fear of the books' corrupting influence. Nonetheless it was with some sense of solemnity that one climbed the narrow stairs with a key tagged 'Hell' in hand. It was a tempting room to dawdle in for all sorts of reasons. One of them was the view on all four sides. The mountain ranges that circle the plain on which Melbourne was built stretched around. This 'Hell' in a tower was enclosed with the silence of vast spaces, so that the sounds that broke it had a magical touch. I treasure even now the magpies' warble in that deep quiet. Even the mournful whistle of the Hurstbridge train as it rumbled down the gully below the college lingers in my memory. Anyway, I read William James up there in 'Hell', and John Stuart Mill, Henri Bergson, David Hume and many others. I hope that if I ever do happen to meet them in Hell I can tell them that their subversions were, and still are, more effectively counterpointed for me with silence than with argumentative noise. I would tell them, too, that Father Newport's perpetual sweaty condition required him to enshrine his thin body in red flannel longjohns. He would wash them in his room and dry them out his window. So this 'Hell' had its unearthly silence and a red flag too. Over the years I have always favoured a note-taking system which in its structure enabled me to recall the occasion and place of my reading. Now that I have *Varieties of Religious Experience, On Liberty, Creative Evolution* and *An Enquiry Concerning Human Understanding* on my own library shelves, I still cannot see their covers without being reminded of broad vistas, enclosing silence and red flannel.

Institutionally, at least, the Jesuits considered history more subversive than philosophy. There was a shelf or two in 'Hell' of polemical and critical histories of the Order itself. I was in the tower one day researching a paper I was to read to the Melbourne University Historical Society on Edmund Campion. It was 1958 and the student Historical Society was a vibrant part of the Melbourne History Department's intellectual life. Edmund Campion was the quintessential English Jesuit martyr. He had turned his back on a brilliant academic career at Oxford and secular ambitions in Queen Elizabeth I's court under the patronage of Robert Cecil Dudley, her secretary of state. Campion had gone to Douai in the Lowlands. Douai was the seminary of an expatriate English church. Thence he went to Rome and Prague, where he was theologian, Jesuit novice, Professor of Rhetoric and Philosophy, priest. From Prague he walked back to the English Channel. It was an 800-mile pilgrimage of the sort Ignatius Loyola, founder of the Society of Jesus, had made. But it was also a penance for having disobeyed his superior's instructions not to become involved in controversy when he challenged 'an old doting heretical fool' to a debate, the loser to be burnt. His secret crossing into England was followed by eighteen months of religious derring-do, as he escaped those searching for him. 'Campion is Champion' was the cry as he revived the waning spirits of English Catholics. It all ended with his capture, torture, trial and hanging at Tyburn.

Campion had been an important figure in my life. For many years as a boy I had prayed that I might have a 'vocation'. I knew I wanted to be a priest and Jesuit. I had wanted to be so since I was nine or ten years old. But was I 'called' by God? Catholicism may be satisfying in its sacramentalism: the institutional signs of God's working are all external and they 'work' whatever the frailties of the minister or the recipient. But finding whether the finger of God is on one's soul is altogether more personal and uncertain. Calvinists wanting to know whether they were 'saved' experienced the same. A care for the ways of discovering a 'discernment of spirits'—whether it was lowly human motives that were driving one or divine grace—was one thing, among many, that joined John Calvin and Ignatius Loyola. At a much later time I remember understanding intimately the feelings of a young missionary, William Pascoe Crook, whom I learned to know because he had sojourned for a brief and terrifying time in the Marquesas Islands, whose history and anthropology I was writing. Crook one day heard Charles Wesley preach in the Tottenham Court Road Chapel and knew he was 'saved'. He skipped home praying that in this moment of certainty he might die and resolve the problem of what he might do in the future to spoil it. My moment of sweetness and certainty came in my final year of schooling, 1947. I was a boarder at Xavier College, a Jesuit school whose history and anthropology, too, I was later to write. It was during the school Retreat, a three-day abridged and highly bowdlerised version of the *Spiritual Exercises* of Ignatius Loyola.

I had chosen for my 'spiritual reading' Robert Hugh Benson's novel, *Come Rack! Come Rope!* (1912), a story of Edmund Campion's life and death. I felt a little guilty doing so because it was not likely to have been the 'spiritual reading' encouraged by the retreat master. I seem to remember he was hawking a collection of Catholic Truth Society Pamphlets, but Hilaire Belloc or G. K. Chesteron would have been encouraged too. Even C. S. Lewis. Anyway the romance of Campion's adventures as told by Benson suffused my soul with sweetness and I knew I had a 'vocation'. I remember especially passages from Campion's letters written in the midst of his flights and subterfuges. Later when I became a Jesuit novice and we were being practised in our preaching by being made to learn dramatic and/or pious passages by heart and to perform them publicly, I chose this passage from Campion:

'I cannot long escape the hands of the heretics: the enemies have so many eyes, so many tongues, so many scouts and crafts. I am in apparel to myself very ridiculous: I often change it, and my name also. I read letters sometimes myself that in the first front tell news that Campion is taken, which, noised in every place where I come so filleth my ears with the sound thereof, that fear itself hath taken away all fear. My soul is in my own hands ever. Let such as you send for supply premeditate and make count of this always. Marry, the solaces that are ever intermingled with the miseries are so great, that they do not only countervail the fear of what punishment temporal soever, but by infinite sweetness make all worldly pains, be they never so great, seem nothing. A conscience pure, a courage invincible, zeal incredible, a work so worthy the number innumerable, of high degree, of mean calling, of the inferior sort, of every age and sex.'

That one should make sense of life by sublimating the trivial to some higher plane is not unusual. Identifying the heroics of Campion with the 'sacrifices' I would have to make was, in a sense, easy.

Self-denials were a constant symbol of commitment in our lives. There were self-denials demanded by Church rule and custom that gave us identity—no meat on Friday, fasting before communion, lifting one's cap as one passed a church in a crowded tram. These showed us to be

Catholic, indeed persecuted Catholics in a Protestant world. There were extra self-denials that identified us with a religious elite and stood as measures of our holiness—morning mass every day, visits to the 'Blessed Sacrament' after meals, membership in a variety of religious groups— Pioneers (a total abstinence society), Crusaders (where one rose in rank by commitment to an ever increasing use of the sacraments), Apostle-ship of Prayer (daily prayers for a specified monthly purpose), the Sodalities and the saying of the Little Office of the Immaculate Conception. Oppor-tunities to test oneself by 'doing more' abounded. I have to say that the perceived larger sacrifices of religious priesthood—Chastity, Poverty, Obedience—never loomed high in this painful hierarchy of denials, although the loneliness of religious life was patent enough to a young boy. I never did cope with the stripping of the affectionate side of living, the replacement of the love of family and friends with 'charity'. When I was to leave the Jesuits twenty-two years later, I did so because I felt that there was too much distance between my personal beliefs and values and those I was required to give witness to by institutional role, but I remember saying to myself that when someone asked why I was leaving I should really say 'because I wanted someone to weep at my funeral'. 'Like Jesuits at a funeral' was one of those ironic catch-phrases meant to describe the cheerfulness of those celebrating a new and eternal life in the presence of death. The many burials we attended at the Kew Cemetery were rather distracted dispatches. 'Particular friendships' were forbidden by rule and, when observed to be developing, perfunctorily dealt with. I suppose a fear of homosexuality was behind this, but more real, I think, was the fear that close friendships would threaten to break up the social fabric of community. The result was that relationships were stripped of everything feminine or soft. For me, the fact that 'no one would weep at my funeral' was in the end a sacrifice too great.

Let me take you back to 'Hell' where I began this reflection on Campion. I am after all presenting an 'ethnography on my mind' not an autobiography. I am teasing out what I call later in these essays my 'songlines', deep-rooted understandings of my experience. I was reading in 'Hell', in preparation for my paper on Campion to the Melbourne

University Historical Society, René Fuelhop-Miller's *The Power and Secrecy of the Jesuits* (1932) with its thesis on the 'brainwashing' effected by the *Spiritual Exercises* of Ignatius Loyola and its closeness to Nazism and Fascism. I did not feel 'brainwashed' but I knew without him telling me how totally saturating and internally consistent the *Exercises'* strategies were for re-making the 'old man' in each of us. I do not have many advantages over Roland Barthes, a scholar whose work I greatly admire and who has influenced me deeply, yet I think I have one. Where he was literary critic (Roland Barthes, *Sade, Fourier, Loyola*, 1976) to the *Spiritual Exercises,* I have been 'exercitant', not once but many times. True, his distance from the *Spiritual Exercises* gave him brilliant understanding. But my closeness to them gives me something he could never share. I experienced the full thirty days of the *Spiritual Exercises* twice, once as a boy of sixteen years on the threshold of religious life in the first year of the novitiate, and then again as a priest, thirty-eight years old and at the end of my twenty years' education in Jesuit spirituality, scholastic philosophy, theology, history and anthropology. Every year between these two experiences of 1948 and 1968 I experienced the shorter eight-day version of the *Exercises.* Every day of those years—well, most of them—I did my hour's prayerful meditation out of them. Counted generously, that is a year and a half out of twenty years in which I engaged my mind, body and spirit as totally as I could in the *Spiritual Exercises.*

The *Spiritual Exercises* will surprise those who see and read them for the first time. As a text they are slim and sparse, trimmed by the genius and experience of Loyola as he made them himself and gave them. They are in no way discursive. They can be read in thirty minutes: but they need thirty days to do. They are all design and structure, not substance and content. They need to be read in a special way. Their reading is controlled by an elaborate poetics in which the body itself and the space around it become an ambience of invention and reception. They are divided into what are called four Weeks, like acts in a drama that does not end till the plot is resolved. And the days between the Weeks, days of rest from the intensity of prayer and meditation, days of ordinary but separated living, are like intermission times, moments in which to be critics of the theatre of one's soul. The central point of the *Exercises* is decision. All the individual exercises before the decision—meditations on the developing drama of Christ's life, death and resurrection and a number of set pieces of constructive imagination about the exercitant's relationship to Christ—are directed to making a determination: rationally but informed by faith. Once the decision is made, the exercises are directed to commitment and fulfilment. Before the decision the mood is collected and measured. Afterwards it is free, pentecostal and celebratory.

Since the decision to be made in the *Spiritual Exercises* inevitably involved some disturbance of an ordinary or self-satisfied existence—to leave one's worldly ways and to commit oneself to religious life, or once committed, to put ideals into practice—one soon discovered over the years the rhythms of exultation and lethargy that accompanied engagement in the *Spiritual Exercises*. Inevitably one created a certain relative comfortableness, and discovered short cuts in the hardship of religious life. Inevitably an adolescent body—or even an adult one—created crises of conscience over what was sinful and what was physically natural. 'Retreats' were the time to restore one's fervour. I remember the 'dryness' of the first days of retreat when one resisted the decision to be made until one made a 'confession' to one's spiritual adviser that went beyond whatever one had previously revealed. Then there was an overflowing 'consolation' in which one felt that one had a touch of mysticism, when prayer shook off its narrative form and one could float in some inexpressible thought. These hours were sweet indeed. One did not want them to end. They did end, of course, in the return to ordinary living as one retreated from the heights of 'Retreat'.

The notion that there should be a methodology by which a relationship could be established between the natural and supernatural was anathema to many in Loyola's time and since. Both those who believed that any mystic experience was altogether outside human manipulation and those in authority who feared the freedom that Loyola's methodology gave to individuals—freedom to guide themselves rather than be guided—condemned the notion of 'exercises'. In the *Spiritual Exercises* Loyola provided a methodology for all the ways we have of making contact with God: meditation, contemplation, mental and vocal prayers, examination of conscience. They were, he said in a 'First Annotation', just like the bodily exercises of strolling, walking and running. The text of the *Exercises* is, in its simplicity, like a manual. It is a manual for two people, the Director who guides some person, or persons, through the *Exercises*, and the Exercitant, the person performing them. Like all manuals, the *Exercises* are directed to giving the exercitant control over his or her experiences. It does this by categorising the experience and giving names to its parts. The exercitant is given the means to recognise one category against another. The exercises themselves are divided into Weeks, Days and individual exercises. States of spirit are typologised and defined in terms of which one is to be achieved before progressing to another. All these divisions and distinctions give progressive order. They also give a language and a conceptual framework for communicating with the Director.

The key to Loyola's methodology was his insistence that every prayer event should have two preparatory steps. He called them 'Preludes'! They had to do with the imagination. The First Prelude was a 'Composition of Place'. This was the careful construction of an ambience that corresponded with the goal of the particular exercise, using darkness or sunlight, closed or open spaces to create a reflectiveness. The body itself could sometimes be used as a stage, by syncopating the rhythms of breathing and the movements of thought. Most importantly, Composition of Place was the first step in focusing the mind. Composition of Place is a 'mental representation of place', Loyola wrote in the *Exercises*. 'Attention must be called to the following point. When the contemplation or meditation is on something visible, for example, when we contemplate Christ, Our Lord, the representation will consist in seeing in imagination the material place where the object is that we wish to contemplate. I said the material place, for example, the temple, or the mountain where Jesus or His Mother is, according to the subject matter of the contemplation'. Where the object of meditation was not visible but an abstraction, say sin or divine goodness, the imagination was to focus on the individual's 'whole composite being, body and soul'. Loyola added that one method in evoking these images was the 'Application of the Senses' by which one intruded oneself into the scene that one was constructing by successively 'seeing', 'smelling', 'hearing', 'touching' everything in it. Every moment of reflective prayer was like the construction of a 'Memory Palace', that famous Jesuitical technique of enfolding vast quantities of information into places architected in the mind. We made 'Image Palaces' for the stage of our prayerful performances.

If the First Prelude of the Composition of Place fixed the mind's attention by creating the stage props for the events to be meditated upon, the Second Prelude made theatre of it. The exercitant in the Second Prelude was asked to define the cathartic point of the narrative to be constructed, the enlightening point of the meditation. Mostly the meditation to be performed concerned the events in the life and death of Jesus Christ—his Baptism, the Temptation, Choosing Disciples, Conversion of Mary Magdalen, the Sweat of Blood in Gethsemane to name only a few. Identifying the significance of the narrative required the creation in one's mind of a mini-drama, a division of the event into scenes or acts which would come together in one whole.

These preparatory steps were entry points into the hour of meditation begun daily at 6 a.m. They were also the subject of fifteen minutes preparation the night before. 'Points of Meditation' they used to be called. They were in fact moments of art: of creative thinking and writing. Often they were performed to others, often listened to as others performed them. Generally they were privately written down in note form to oneself. They were balanced by a fifteen-minute reflection after the meditation in which each one became a critic of his personal performance in preparing the meditation and in the meditation itself.

These were ideals given to us. Practice inevitably was somewhat less. How laziness, carelessness, sleepiness frustrated the ideals is another set of stories. But in the conditions of our life, failure to live up to ideals was a matter of guilt and penance and of constant effort to reform.

'Look at your navel long enough, in the end you'll only see a belly button'. I think I invented that epigram to persuade my students over the years that if they wished to write reflective history and anthropology they needed some experience outside themselves. In our *Spiritual Exercises* at Loyola, we needed images from outside ourselves to make our 'Composition of Place'. They came from extensive 'spiritual readings', constant exhortation and repeated practice in displaying the images and their significance to others. In my case, they also came from a wide range of readings of an historical or geographical sort. There was a vast literature of a semi-polemical nature on the historicity of Jesus and the scriptures—H. V. Morton's series *In the Steps of Paul, Peter, Christ* . . . among them: I still have the mood and timbre of his pictures of Ephesus and Galilee in my memories. I remember, too, volumes, but not their names, on the Passion of Christ, blow for blow, nail for nail. One learned to know how and why water came from the thrust of the soldier's lance on Golgotha, what happened to the scalp under a crown of thorns, what were the effects of a leather thong lash laced with bones. Above all, I and others were experiencing the beginnings of a remarkable development of scriptural analysis that was suffusing back to us from the Catholic academies of Europe. It liberated us from the pervading fundamentalism of Australian Catholicism. In 1944 Pope Pius XII had written the encyclical *Divino Afflante Spiritu*. It was no radical document, but it was freeing nonetheless. It insisted that the Bible was not one literary form. The Bible was a whole library of literary forms—poetry, drama, epic, parable, preaching. Each part had what we would now call distinct poetics. Each part was to be read in a different way. Only a small part was 'historical'. Immediately, questions of the factuality of the Bible became subsidiary to discovering what meaning was being purveyed. Was Jonah swallowed by a whale? Did Peter walk on water? Did Jesus feed thousands from a few loaves and fishes? The questions did not seem to matter. But the inspired meaning of the narratives did. The texts had a never ending capacity to be enlarged. That was their strength.

Suddenly, too, everything about them was human. They were products of scribes, writing out of their own times to their own times. Suddenly to represent the figures and events in their texts required the discovery of their humanity. To make a Composition of Place, required some sort of ethnography. Jesus was a Palestinian Jew. He lived and died in his own present moment. If he lived like us in our present moments, he lived like us in the present participle—hoping, fearing, loving, apprehending what is to come only vaguely. I don't suppose I shall ever be able to convey how that bland discovery enlightened me and was my cathartic moment. I clung to it for a long time. I still do. I felt and would feel ever more strongly that to write the history of men and women one has to compose them in place and in their present-participled experience.

The discovery that the truths of natural and supernatural living are all mediated by texts that should be read by re-composing them into the present participle is saying what every historian should know. To know a past as past is beyond our immediate capacity. We only know a past through the histories made of it, by the past becoming in some way a text which we must read not just for the story it tells but also for the occasion of its telling and the mode of its expression. These texts in which the past is present to us are mostly past-participled, hindsighted, stilled, closed. The texts are always 'after-meditation'. They order the past and give a comfortable sense of control. All the possibilities are reduced to one in such a hindsighted view. But that is not the way we experience our present moments. The present for us is always filled with possibilities, is always processual and unfinished. How can we say we are writing what men and women actually experienced if we dehumanise them into a past-participled world? By that we disempower them, make them our puppets.

I remember that when I came to study history at the University of Melbourne in 1955 I experienced another cathartic moment in my intellectual life. I had been reading Thucydides, mesmerised by what I took to be his 2500-years-old modernity. I picked up F. M. Cornford's *Thucydides Mythistoricus* (1907). 'By *Mythistoricus*', Cornford wrote, 'I mean history cast in a mould of conception whether artistic or philosophic, which long before the work was even contemplated was already wrought into the structure of the author's mind'. Cornford's presentation of what that structure was for Thucydides—Greek drama and mythology— 'blew my mind'. I think it 'blew my mind' because it enlarged forever my understanding of the way texts represent and shape our living.

The principal theatre of our intellectual as distinct from our spiritual life at Loyola was the *Disputatio*, the performance of scholastic philosophy. *Disputatio* was the adversarial debate of a 'thesis' in strict syllogistic form. It was in Latin, of course. All our lectures were in Latin, all our textbooks, all interpersonal communication outside of set recreation, all notices and instructions from superiors, all our rules and regulations were in Latin. Classical scholars no doubt would shiver at the thought of calling what we did with the Roman tongue, 'Latin'. Living in a modern world required rich invention of vocabulary and much 'pidgin'. The thesis defence was a closed form. We would have a hundred of them to defend in each subject—Epistemology, Ontology, Cosmology, Ethics. The thesis defence was closed in the sense that it required an enunciation of its propositions, an identification of the principal adversarial arguments, a discursive presentation of its significance in a broader field of philosophy, a 'proof' in logic. Then there was a response to the syllogistic arguments of two adversaries who would offer 'objections' to the thesis. These adversaries had to offer 'strings' of syllogisms. The defender or 'Act' would have to offer distinctions in the major and minor propositions. The adversary would live in the hope that he could predict these distinctions. If he had not, he likely had to pursue a string invented on the spot. Every Saturday was repetition day. The defenders and objectors were picked at random from the class. Once a month, and more importantly once a term and once a year, there would be public disputations before the whole of the philosophy school. A 'Grand Act' would be held sometimes when there was thought to be a particularly brilliant student. He would be open to challenge on any thesis by any visiting professors from other seminaries. There was much myth about these occasions and we held those who had performed in them in some awe. Monumental failures were also the stuff of tradition. The three years philosophy were reviewed in one final hour-long oral examination in which we had to defend a selection of theses out of all our subjects. It was an important occasion and one which would be repeated at the end of the four-year theology course. On the results of these two separate examinations depended whether one would become a 'professed' Jesuit, that is, one who could participate fully in the government of the Society of Jesus and hold its principal offices. Being professed depended, scholastically, on achieving an 'honours' result in these examinations.

There was much formalism in all this, and many cribs collected and handed down over the years helped make short cuts. But the ethics and the competition of the Acts required that there be no collusion between defenders and objectors. Both on the occasion were very dependent on their wits. If there were crashes there were also triumphs. I have to say that often it was only many years after completing philosophy that I was able to recognise the significance of the issues we were debating. But I also have to say that the discipline of putting one's mind around the different requirements of these hundreds of theses and performing them both publicly and on paper in one's notes stood me in good stead. When in later years as Professor of History at the University of Melbourne, I became frustrated at the destructive effect of the photocopier and the highlighter on my students' minds and saw how note-taking had become a lost art, I would sometimes look at the shelf in my study that held the fifteen or so bound volumes of my notes from my four years undergraduate studies in history at Melbourne. I suspect that in these volumes are the true ethnography of my mind. I was always loathe to open them to my students. There was too much of a gap, I felt, between us, in the ambitions these volumes represented to me and the sense of reward they gave me. Certainly there is a tidiness in them that surprises me now in my daily messiness and when the recovery of anything seems to be another sort of performance altogether. These volumes of my notes look to me now like 'Points of Meditation' on any historical question I studied, or scripts for performance of these same issues.

The Jesuit tradition of theatre is long. In the sixteenth century when the Jesuits were founded, their enemies were anti-theatre. Anti-theatre has a long history. Plato was anti-theatre. The Church, the Puritans were anti-theatre. Any authority, really, that is disturbed by the possibility that there is some independence between outer show and inner reality; any authority that is convinced by religion, politics or philosophy that realism is not of their own making, any authority uneasy at an audience's freedom to interpret a drama is anti-theatre. The Jesuits themselves were not unconscious of the dangers of theatre, but Loyola was confident that soul and body, mind and imagination, physical environment and human feelings were bound together. The best teacher was performance. The best way to 'discern spirits' was to perform.

Risk is at the heart of performance. That is obvious in the suspicions we express about performance. 'What a performance!' we will say disparagingly. 'Give him an Oscar!' we will shout across the boundary fence at some footballer's feigned collapse looking for a 'free kick'. 'Putting on an act', 'playing to the gallery', 'making a spectacle of oneself', all are notions associated with performance. We are comfortable enough with the notion of practice. Practise the guitar, practise maths, batting practice. There is a great deal of judgement in practice, but it is self-judgement. Performance, however, is public. We have an audience for performances. There is something out of our control in a performance. We have to catch an audience's attention. An audience does not owe us anything, except perhaps a general politeness. True, we sometimes have captive audiences who will endure much to be supportive. But performers quickly have to be good readers of an audience's reactions. It is difficult to fool oneself as a performer. We recognise restlessness, boredom, silent disapproval in an audience too easily. We know what we do not achieve in performances. Performance also inevitably involves the whole person, all the senses, all the emotions, memory, a sense of presence, co-ordination of mind and body. We give our special signatures to performances. We have a sense of mastery which enables us to put our personal stamp on them. Sometimes our performances will be so perfect that they will remain in our memory our whole lives long. I have a memory of fifty years that teases me. I was a schoolboy testing for opening bat in the School XI. I glanced a fast bowler who was terrorising me to leg. I can remember the perfection of that stroke to this day, its timing, the co-ordination of wrist and body, the feel of the meat of the bat. I probably never did it again. I certainly did not get into the team. I suspect that is why sports persons have such sharp memories. The sense of stylish perfection imposed on some bodily movement is imprinted on their minds forever.

By 1928 the Australian Jesuits had cut their umbilical cord from Ireland. They became an independent Vice-Province instead of an Irish mission. They were now responsible for their own education and training. Instead of sending their young men to Ireland, England or continental Europe for philosophy and theology, they had to establish their own institutions here in Australia. They began their own College of Philosophy at Loyola College, Watsonia, Victoria and of Theology at Canisius College, Pymble, New South Wales. There is always a special feel in the foundation days of an education institution, a sense that one can create structures and syllabuses in relationship to one's educational ideals rather than in obedience to 'what has always been done'. The young Jesuits who experienced these early years at Loyola and Canisius inevitably enjoyed the freedom from the restraints of being Irish—even English and European—and in some excitement explored what it meant to be both Australian and Jesuit. This was a generation of Jesuits just ten or twelve years older than myself. I had experienced their excitement and professionalism at their new school, St Louis' in Perth. They had experimented there in making St Louis' a truly Jesuit school in the tradition of the *Ratio Studiorum*, the Jesuit constitution and model for all the Society's educational institutions. These Jesuits were a generation, too, who were to be given their chance at postgraduate education in philosophy, moral theology, scripture and dogma in a post-war Europe that was enjoying the spring time to Vatican Council II's summer.

The mood this generation left us at Loyola and Canisius was one of discovery. Above all it was a sense that we could revitalise what we called our 'apostolate', the sort of labours that we would undertake in response to our religious ideals—teaching in schools, educating seminaries, spiritual counselling to lay people, pastoral work in parishes, chaplains to universities, giving the *Spiritual Exercises* to lay and religious alike, editing, writing and publishing a range of pious and intellectual journals, adult education in Catholic theories of social justice. This revitalisation was to come about by recovering the roots of our Jesuit tradition. We would go back to times when the spirit of prophecy inspired the Order, before the overlays of later routine smothered the life out of it. I should stress that this was not a conservative movement. It was very liberating. It was not the replication of a Golden Age. It was theatre enacted to catch the spirit that would infuse new and changed conditions. There was a feeling of playing a new–old role, of being at the forefront of something new rather than of guarding some museum-like treasure.

In scholastic philosophy, for example, it was not the romanticists that influenced us. Not Etienne Gilson, not Hilaire Belloc, not even Jacques Maritain. We felt more professionally engaged. We felt that we were taking scholastic philosophy where it had never been. Jesuits like Joseph Maréchal in Louvain and Bernard Lonergan in Rome were making discoveries of method and conceptualisation that were to be the ground-swell for a theology of process and hope. Maréchal was recently dead, embattled philosophically in the Church for his supposedly Kantian tendencies which had been condemned by Vatican Council I. He was the teacher of Karl Rahner, the Jesuit who would be the theological giant of Vatican Council II. Lonergan was yet unpublished but available to us in lecture notes and an oral tradition already spread abroad by his early students. All three, Maréchal, Lonergan and Rahner, became label-led with the name Transcendental. Yet from this distance, I think I was excited by their trust in human experience. At that time their intellectual integrity made them champions of freedom of inquiry. There is great risk in such championship. Deep in Jesuit tradition has been a trust in rationality. Their great heroes, Peter Canisius and Robert Bellarmine, were as learned as they were saintly. Yet education to rationality demands a freedom that is sometimes corrosive of certainties. Rational history, rational theology, like rational science, is a great relativiser. The sure hand of God in institutions is less clearly seen when the foibles of being human are understood, whether they be popes or politicians. In discovering the rhetoric of power, one discovers it in evil and good alike. The Jesuits' abiding gift to the world in the last four hundred years has been the wit-ness men of faith can give when they stand on the frontiers of know-ledge. Questioning but sure, they walked a dangerous past; free but unfree they lived a paradox; learned and believing, they spoke to the real conditions of all who felt a tension and division in their lives. I suspect that the true romance of their lives for me was the gamble they were prepared to take. They would allow us to commit ourselves totally to both secular and religious studies—to astronomy, geology, science, history, literature, anthropology, philosophy, scripture studies, moral and dogmatic theology. It is a risky business, this performance on the frontiers of knowledge. No one really knows if either belief or doubt will win out.

The tease of describing process in human behaviour has remained with me all my academic life. I remember in these years discovering a little known Belgian Jesuit philosopher, George Picard, whose trust in the '*Sum*' rather than the '*Cogito*' of Descartes' famous proposition '*Cogito ergo Sum*' gave me some presentiment of my own preoccupation with the present participle of experience—living—rather than the constructs of the past participle—lived, life. I suppose that I was coming down on the Jesuit side of the old Jesuit/Dominican debate about the 'real distinction' between Essence and Being. There was no 'real distinction'. When I came to read Herbert Marcuse many years later, I would think that he had it right: 'All reification [all essentialising, I would add] is a process of forgetting. Art fights reification by making the petrified world speak, sing, perhaps dance'. Essences are the Frankenstein monsters of religious and intellectual life. I hope it will become clear in the *Performances* that follow that I see the ethnographic mode as one means to dispose of these monsters.

The Australian Jesuits did not escape all Irishness in becoming a Vice-Province. They felt more secure in their intellectual liberalism than in their sense of how to train young religious spiritually. They had imported from Ireland all their ideas on how to shape a novice in his first two crucial years. Jansenism was imported as well. Jansenism regrettably had been the nursery of the Irish priesthood ever since the English forced the Catholic Church to send its men to France for their education. Jansenists and Jesuits were enemies opposed in the general Church, but the Jansenists' distrust of human nature and their sense that religious virtue was to be achieved by severe cruelty to the 'old man' in each of us imbued Irish spirituality nonetheless. Ironically, Loyola's ambitions to have the Jesuits break out of the monastic tradition of closed walls around the soul and the intellect were later overlaid with Irish

23

mistrust of human nature and a system of closed surveillance. Of the classic polarity of prophet and priest—prophets, those whose sense of direct relationship with God gave them freedom to reform and change tradition; priests, those whose sense of establishment made them guardians of how things had always been done—the Irish came firmly down on priesthood. Custom ruled. Commitment to a sacrificing life away from the 'world' was seen to be attained by imposing strict systems of identification with the institution. These systems were extraordinarily efficient. Anyone familiar with studies of how military institutions socialise their members to act instinctively, by *rites de passage*, uniforms, close drill and the creation of a special language; or anybody familiar with Irving Goffman's studies of total institutions and their power to expunge 'eccentricity' from ordinary standards of behaviour, would recognise how totally and masterfully the Irish Jesuits incorporated these systems into their novitiate training. I cannot say that this was done with any directed consciousness. But it was certainly done with constant reflection on 'what worked' in relation to their goals of remaking their candidates in their own image.

It would take a better pen than mine to describe in a few words how this was done in a Jesuit novitiate. But it turned around the creation of a completely new language with which to communicate shared experiences. 'Ours' was the way we identified Jesuits, and Our's was an experience coded in Latin and pidgin-Latin form. This language became the more real the more we were isolated from all other sorts of languages. There were no radios and no newspapers at all for the first two years. For the next six years only the front page of the Thursday *Age* was seen (Thursday was a 'villa' day, a day in which from 9 a.m. until 4 p.m. we were expected to go on long country walks. In the novitiate the length of these walks and the companion on them was determined by the Master of Novices. For my better spiritual growth he tended to pair me with the most vigorous walkers. A walk to Warrandyte by Eltham and home by Heidelberg was what he thought my 'Bodily Health and Spiritual Vigour' required). There was also a list of 'Forbidden Topics', subjects which must be excluded from conversation. Among the topics forbidden were women, family, outside friends, those who for some reason had left the novitiate, politics, wars and previous school life. Precedent ruled every aspect of life. Every office and role had its rules and always the first rule was that a journal must be kept. The journal, submitted for inspection to superiors at regular intervals, determined for the next officer what had to be done. '*Ex gratia*' was aways a suffix to a permission given to do something out of the ordinary, lest precedents be established. Any obligation that had to be done privately, such as daily meditation or the twice-daily 'Examination of Conscience', would be subject to surveillance by a 'visitor', a functionary whose role was to creep around, open doors and report on how obligations were being performed. The day itself was divided into a detailed timetable, each quarter-, half- or full-hour of which had its specific task and a way in which the performance of the task would be reflected on orally or in writing. The year was a detailed calendar of liturgies and pious practices, each one with its rubrics but each one, too, an occasion in which personal style could be imposed in the performance of them.

It would be wrong to think that this closed world was necessarily an unhappy one. I would find it unendurable now. Indeed the contradictions between the regimentation of the system and the flexibility encouraged by the spirituality that inspired a post-Vatican Council II Church were patent. The closed world of the novitiate as I experienced it often redeemed itself by being theatre to itself. It entertained itself with mimicry and reverse world rituals. Laughter at the ironies of fluffed lines or inappropriate gestures was constant. It was 'insider's' laughter. Not mocking or destructive: on the contrary, it was reinforcing. It was familial. It was the 'back-stage' of our theatre, that space we reserved for ourselves away from the intrusions of our institutions. I will come to recognise it, and you will see it in the *Performances* to follow, as the 'Paradox of Acting', that freedom we have in the processes of living to change the worlds that shape us so closely.

I entered the closed world of the novitiate on 2 February 1948. There were fifteen of us, boys mostly from Jesuit schools, but also a couple of men with more life experience, who would not complete the novitiate. At our entry, we each became *anima* (soul) to an *angelus* (guardian angel), a novice beginning his second year who would induct us in these first ten days of probation. That morning, 2 February, a group of young men completing the second year of the novitiate would have made their first vows of Poverty, Chastity and Obedience. They would have been dressed for the first time in clerical clothing and gowns, and have read their Latin vows from a page they would have written out themselves and signed. It was a moment of solemnity, and of much joy. Clerical dress was the badge of one's life of sacrifice. In these years the Catholic faithful, especially one's family, honoured it. They were mystified by the rule of life it signalled, but coming mostly from classes that had little or no opportunity for post-school education, they held the prospects of fifteen years and more Jesuit training before ordination to the priesthood in some awe. On this 'Vow Day' of 2 February, the Feast of the Purification of the Blessed Virgin—the feast of the 'churching' of women after child-birth, make of it what you will!—the next year of novices had become senior and guardians of tradition. Initiates are the best guardians of tradition. They ensure that what they have endured the new men will also endure. My *angelus* was a New Zealander from Queenstown. I was to learn that he slept all through the winter with only a sheet as bed cover. I always had the hope that that is what a Queenstowner, used to the cold, would do, but feared that he was setting the standard of penance. He was into penance. His task in the novitiate was to make the small rope disciplines with which we beat ourselves. He also made the small wire chains with sharp points that we used to wrap around our arms and legs. They were painful and would draw blood. Our *angeli,* as they induced us into the 'customs' that we were obliged to follow were under instructions to uncover the peculiar ways of the novitiate gradually, revealing the more bizarre of the customs only at the end. But, as we learned the freedoms we had lost one by one, we became apprehensively certain that there was worse, much worse, to come.

The Master of Novices was an Irishman. He was a bubbly man, rebel in his way, a sharp and humorous man—*after* and *before* he was Master of Novices. As Master of Novices he was austere and rigid in his observation of the rules. His room was the barest of cells with no mark at all of his personal history in it. No photographs. No untidy traces of himself. No superfluous furniture. He would pray long hours on the bare boards of his room, which was outside the novices' chapel and dark and cold. He was a kind man and always good to me, although I always lived in dread that he was the model for what we should be. The Jesuits had evolved a system, almost military in character, in which discipline and correction belonged not to the Master of Novices but to a sort of sergeant-major, the *Socius* or companion to the Master of Novices. The *Socius* would impose penances on us—'telling our faults' before the community, eating our meals kneeling. Spiritual counselling belonged to the Master. The truth is, I think, I approached the Master with more fear than the *Socius*.

I imagine that to the present-day young or to outsiders to this closed world, this exotic behaviour of ours would seem like perform-ances of some primitive tribe, a clan deserving perhaps of some anthro-pology, but puzzling and alien to more open sets of values. Whether I suffered irreparable damage from it I cannot, or am unlikely, to say. There were many rewards in it. Perhaps social alertness to all the signals around us is likely to vary with character, but it is also likely to be encour-aged by a system in which every action is subject to some reflection. I value social alertness both as an anthropological and an historical skill. I see it as an ethnographic skill that helps in the discovery of system in cultural behaviour. We spent much time in the novitiate in developing an alertness to every movement in ourselves and others. In fact each of us had pinned to the inside of his gown a string of ten beads by which he counted his commissions of some fault that he was trying to remedy, or registered some positive act of virtue which he was trying to encour-age in himself. We might be trying to eradicate some uncharitable thoughts, or some breaches of the 'Rules of Modesty' (the directions we were given on how to walk, our body posture, how we should manage our eyes), or some thoughts of rebellion against proper authority. Or we might be wanting to make some lift in our prayerfulness and 'recollection' by making 'ejaculations'. True, it was somewhat disconcerting to be in conversation with someone and to see his hand go inside his gown and pull down a bead. One wondered what uncharitable thought he had just had, or what sort of prayer one had induced in him. We each had a small printed card. During our twice-daily Examination of Conscience we would tote our beads and do our daily, weekly, monthly arithmetic. Then there were the weekly Quarters of Charity in which we would kneel before our community and hear one by one their comments and criticisms of our behaviour. Or there was a daily one-on-one exchange of exhortations and admonitions. The other side of this rather frenetic preoccupation with correction and self-reform was a sensitivity to our impact on others and of others on us. We did not lose anything by having that sensitivity. It fostered a high degree of altruism. It also gave us great theatre. Something of the ethnographic must have possessed me even then. I created an annual publication—we would call it a 'desktop publication' in these days of computers—called *Nostra* which was meant to be a description of these days in photograph and word–picture. Its volumes will be in the Jesuit Archives still. I like to think that it waits there for some ethnographer historian—images of our living in the present participle.

Offices and duties were distributed at Loyola less with an eye to talent than with an eye for the good of one's soul. One year I was appointed *Magister Equi*, Master of the Horse. The horse's name was Eustace. He was an enormous brute with great rolling haunches and a huge belly inflatable at any given point to frustrate tight girths. City-born, I was innocent of any real knowledge of horses. I thought they all knew some sort of farmland patois like 'whoa', or 'giddup'. Eustace only knew violence. He had come to Loyola from timber-haulers in the mountains. He was trained to give of himself instantly and totally, which was good for logs but bad for mowers and ploughs. One of the tasks of the Master of the Horse was to plough the orchard. My image of ploughing had come mainly from the Dutch Masters. I saw it as a serenely meditative occupation, tripping over occasional larks, lunching on bread and wine at the noon *Angelus*. I discovered that ploughs are heavy, unmanageable things. They required two hands just to hold them upright. Where, I asked, did the reins go? They went around one's neck. With Eustace streaming into the middle distance of the orchard, one had a poor choice. Pursue him at a breakneck pace with the plough, or break one's neck by dropping the plough. It was then, I think, that my scepticism for sacred scripture began. It sometimes takes more courage to take one's hand off the plough than to keep it on.

In 1971, I was appointed Max Crawford Professor of History at the University of Melbourne. I had left the Jesuits and the priesthood in 1970 after the encyclical Humanae Vitae (1968) on birth control. The History Section of the Australian and New Zealand Association for the Advancement of Science invited me to address their Plenary Session in Sydney, no doubt to see who I was. I addressed them on 'History as a Social System'. My experience in the prelude to my academic career had taken me across a number of disciplines, notably philosophy, history, theology and anthropology. Discipline was a discovery of the Enlightenment. The advantages of blinkering one's mind to see the world in some perspective were many. In the explosion of knowledge that followed, disciplines multiplied. My own University of Melbourne, founded in 1854 with four chairs, Law, History, Classics and Literature, by the time of my appointment had 135. The nineteenth century saw a frenetic claiming of this or that part of the environment and of this or that part of the human anatomy by groups of men and women (mostly men) who inevitably came to think of themselves as some sort of science. To see the world in a particular way 'below' the appearances of things required sustained effort. They needed special languages to describe and analyse what they saw. They needed rituals and mythologies to divide them from the competing others. They established induction processes which imposed conformity. They required all the cultural and social forms by which they could identify themselves—acceptable questions, acceptable forms of evidence, acceptable criteria of judgement, acceptable modes of transmission of qualifications. Inevitably the identification with one discipline was reinforced by caricature and vituperation of others and their worlds of discipline became closed down, self-satisfied, suspicious of change.

I feel that the great privilege of my life has been for most of it to have been a 'professor', 'one who makes open declaration of his sentiments, beliefs, etc.' (*Oxford English Dictionary*). For forty-six years I have been obliged by role and life style to give public witness to my personal knowedge and values, to be a professor. I have always preferred to celebrate the knowledge I have professed rather than to fight about it. If I have had a constant academic ambition, it has been to be subversive of polarities of all sorts, but especially of fundamentalism. So when I have been confronted with closed worlds and fundamentalist tendencies in departments, universities and disciplines, I have felt an urgent need to open them up. I think that my prelude taught me to open up closed worlds in two ways.

The one was by performance. Students had to be persuaded that writing history is a performance. They needed to be dissuaded from 'doing' history, serving it up to readers—their teachers and examiners—who were paid to read it. Students had to discover how a reader can be intrigued freely by one sentence to read the next. If students perform their history, they will have performance consciousness. They will be alert to all the ways in which they are distanced from what they perform. They will enjoy the 'Paradoxes of Acting'. They will know the ways in which they sculpt their narratives. They will be focused on the theatre of what they do.

More than performing, we history-makers must know ourselves. We must have an ethnographic sense of our cultural persons. The past is emptied of almost all its meaning by the selective texts that survive it. We realise that the meanings in the text are mere shadows the more we experience the fullness of the meanings in our ordinary living. All my academic life I taught history by first requiring my students to transcribe some event or ritual or drama in their lives into narrative. I called this ethnography. They soon discovered how difficult that was to do. They soon learned that there was nothing that they observed but was the subject of some reflective discourse by somebody else. Knowing what that discourse was, what questions shaped it and in what way their own ethnography added to it was to be the cultural persons they needed to be to write history.

In my lecture on 'History as a Social System' at ANZAAS in 1971, I told my professional colleagues all that. The lecture, I felt, was itself a Prelude to all my Performances still to come. At least I can say of it that ethnography was always on my mind.

Making a Present
out of the Past
HISTORY'S ANTHROPOLOGY

THE trouble with narrative—telling stories, making histories—is that it is so easy, but thinking about it is so hard. We are always narrating something—what happened in the supermarket, what we read in the newspaper, what we used to do in the 'good old days'. Narrating is universal, too, across cultures, across times. The Ancient Greeks did it stylishly. The Wretched of the Earth do it tearfully. Narrating is so easy and so universal, in fact, that there are inevitably suspicions about narrative when we have to 'do' something special, such as philosophy or genetics. In History, at least, some important scholars look down their noses at narrative—Fernand Braudel, Le Roy Ladurie, Jacques Le Goff—anyone really who thinks that history has to lift its game to where the big boys fly, and be a 'science'. On the other hand, there is a pretty determined bunch of historians who think that what's not narrative is gobbledegook—J. H. Hexter, Geoffrey Elton, Isaiah Berlin, Lawrence Stone. Just relating the facts is all an historian need do, they say. Leave the fancy stuff—like voices, authorial presence and politics of knowledge—to interpretation and all that waffle. Narration is what *we* do, just telling what happened. There was a time, too—mercifully brief in the order of things—when something called 'philosophy of history' made a play about narrative. There, there, the philosophers of history said to the historians you are actually doing something special when you narrate. You colligate this and configurate that; you provide an *explanans* for an *explanandum*. You're just not being nomothetic, that's all.

Meanwhile, Stravinsky has turned the world upside down in *The Rite of Spring*. Picasso has turned it inside out in *Guernica*. Wittgenstein is writing strange coloured books. There have been two world wars and a holocaust. Mickey Mouse has turned fifty. Goebbels blindfolds a whole nation. Advertising agents become the wink-wink, nudge-nudge cultural anthropologists of our times to sell us jockey briefs and fast cars. Dale Carnegie has put a sincere smile on every salesperson's face. Suddenly we know that our most vital social and cultural skill is our ability to read—that is, not just to be literary, but to see, hear, touch, smell all the signs around us with political astuteness. The real world we live in is an Outsider's world of observation and interpretation in the moment-after, of distinguishing the many meanings of apparently simple signs, of matching the tropes of all the narratives around us to the occasion of their telling, above all of catching the politics—the empowering and disempowering forces—that suffuse all our knowledge and representations. Suddenly, whatever our analytical and theoretical propensities, we are culturally postmodern. We might not have the labels—like fiction, trope, metaphor and metonymy—to be semiotically descriptive of how we read, but our cultural existence depends on our ability to recognise what these words actually mean in their daily expression.

Cultural living in its bare bones is talk, talk translated into all sorts of symbols. That's its realism. We make all our relationships by talk, all our institutions, all our roles. The theatre of everyday life is talk, and we are experts in reading the immediate meaning of our words, but more importantly what those words really mean. This talk is not just babble, not just stream of consciousness, though there is plenty of both. The talk is shaped in some way, given beginnings and endings, given dramatic form. The talk is not just talk. It is presentation. Timing makes it so; punchlines, too; ambience; gestures; silences; presence; rhythm; fast flows and discontinuities; engagement with an audience; rhetorical forms, sometimes as old as culture itself, sometimes raw and new.

Presentations are something crafted. We present our narratives with some theatricality. Our narratives also pre'sent something. They are ostensibly about something past, about something that has happened. But they are also the medium of our present relationships. Our stories are as much about us as about something else. Our listeners know that, and we, when we are listening, know that. That is why these performances of mine in Making a Present out of the Past say that histories—all the ways we transform lived experience into narratives—are metaphors of the past and metonymies of the present. Bear with the language. It is a seepage from focused analysis, the way all such words are seepage from special dialogues. Think of 'supply' and 'demand', 'id' and 'ego', 'highs' and 'lows'. Metaphor: history is metaphor of the past. History is not the past. It is the past transformed into something else, story. Metonymy: history is metonymy of the present. These stories in their telling *are* our present.

A POETIC FOR HISTORIES

POETICS are not poetry, but the suggestion that they might be is left with the breath of the word. I would not in any case be embarrassed to be thought in this to be writing a poem for history as well as a poetic for histories. There is much of life and living in history. Being a humanity is one of history's many graces. Poetics and poems are both concerned with the authenticity of experience rather than the credentials of the observer. In a Poetic for Histories I mean to free our discourse on history from any claim or presumption by historians or anthropologists that by our expertise we are directed to seeing history as having one form or another.

The histories I write of are mainly a human characteristic, not a technique of inquiry. They are the vernacular of our cultural and social systems. We all make histories endlessly. It is our human condition to make histories. No sooner is the present gone in the blink of an eye than we make sense of it as past. We tell stories about it. We interpret the meaning of gestures made, of words spoken, of actions done. We make a narrative of the past in our mind, in our conversations. We record it in some way—in a diary, in a letter, on a certificate, in a tax return.

Poetics are a serious business, a critic has told me. 'Use the word with respect for those who refined it.' I do. But I do not mean to puzzle over Aristotle's famous distinction between poetry and history. And Hayden White does not need my compliments for destabilising the Anglo-Saxon tradition in reflective history. Structuralists and literary critics expecting additional precision to their discourse on poetics can stop here. By poetic in Poetic for Histories I simply try to discover the most generous way to describe a reflective discourse on all the hermeneutic dimensions of histories as cultural artifacts. Poetics, like prose, are something we are always practising. Poetics are the relationships we have with the texts that suffuse our lives. Poetics are the facility with which we relate the systems of meaning in these texts to the occasions of their reading. In the poetics that I practice here, I pursue what Richard H. Brown has called 'symbolic realism' (Brown and Lyman 1978:14). In histories, object and subject, the known and the knowing, the said and the hearing, I and Thou and It are bound together. Our science will need an aesthetics to discover them all.

It is unimaginable that someone, 'primitive' or 'civilized', has no past; it is unimaginable that someone does not know some part of that past. 'Memory' is our everyday word for knowledge of the past, but memory suggests some personal or institutional immediacy in the connection between the past and those who experienced it. We need a word that includes memory but embraces all the other ways of knowing a past. We do not have such a word; but in this poetic for histories, let me declare that word to be *History*.

History/histories

History by this is public knowledge of the past: not public in the sense of being institutional, but public in the sense of being culturally shared, being expressed in some way. For an expression to have shared meaning, it must be possessed of some system which can be recognised. But this recognition will always hold the ambivalences of circumstanced exchanges. The systems in the expression will always be modified by being expressed and recognised.

History is a human universal. Knowledge of the past is expressed by all human beings according to their different cultural and social systems. History is a generic form of consciousness in which the past experience of oneself or of others in an environment outside oneself is transformed into symbols that are exchanged. Let us say there is History—as there is Culture, a methodological abstraction for talking about a perspective on human behaviour. There are histories, like cultures, that need an ethnographic description for their forms and structures and functions. A poetic for histories is that ethnographic description.

We each, no doubt, have a thesaurus in our mind of the different ways in which we and others make sense of the past—reminiscence, gossip, anecdote, rumour, parable, report, tradition, myth. We could probably fill a crossword puzzle with histories of different sorts—saga, legend, epic, ballad, folklore, annal, chronicle. We would recognise the distinctiveness of these ways of knowing the past, even if we would probably argue over what precisely these distinctions should be. That is, we have a practical sense of their different poetics. We know the different meanings we abstract from their different forms. We know how to behave on the different occasions of their expression. Maybe you are suspicious at this moment that I should collect all of these under the one analytic concept of History and call them all histories. You know History as something different and as yet owe my definition no deference. Hold your suspicions for a while. I am going to try and persuade you that your having them will lead to a discovery of how powerful poetics are.

HISTORIES' DOUBLE ENTENDRE

Histories, transformations of the past into expressions, clothe, constitute, *are* a present social reality. Histories always have this *double entendre.* They refer to a past in making a present. The knowledge of the past that re-presents the past in story or account makes the structures of the present—such as class or identity—in the expressing. So histories in our poetic are not just the stream of consciousness about the past but that knowledge made dramaturgical in its forms of expression. Histories are fictions—something made of the past—but fictions whose forms are metonymies of the present. Histories are metaphors of the past: they translate sets of events into sets of symbols. But histories are also metonymies of the present: the present has existence in and through their expression. The present—social reality, the structures of our living—has being through representations of the past in coded public forms. We read or hear histories in this double way. We know in them both a present and a past.

This should not be a disturbing statement. But it sometimes is. It is sometimes seen to plunge us into subjectivity and relativism. It is sometimes seen to leave us with the appearances of things and no underlying reality. But it was the young Karl Marx who said in *The German Ideology*: 'Consciousness can never be anything else than conscious existence, and the existence of men is their actual life process (Feuer 1969: 288)'. He puzzled how the most powerful structures have trivial, particular expression. I do not see myself as doing something very different from him. To write a grammar by which the past is transformed through histories, one need not do something new, only hold the middle ground between poles of every kind.

The founding fathers of sociology and anthropology did their sciences a disservice when they confused historical explanation with History and histories. In seeking their independence and separation from other sciences, they looked for ways other than historical to explain human events and actions. Their exclusivity distracted them from the discovery of how histories as everyday experience construct social reality. They equated a method of argument with a mode of consciousness and by that were unable to make a fundamental postulate about human social reality: it is experiential; it is constituted in and by presentations of the past. Put another way: praxis is histories. Histories are 'sensuous human activity' that make and unmake the structures of living.

Such declarations are solipsistic and not a little gnomic. I write a solemn little convention to myself that histories are public knowledge of the past that make a present. But we have everyday usages of words like 'history', and these are not changed by any definition of mine. In everyday usage 'history' is sometimes an account of the past and sometimes the actions and events of which there is an account. 'That's history', we say, meaning something is done with and is no longer relevant. 'Making history' is a phrase we use comfortably and ordinarily. Someone who has done something first, registered a record, been notably unique or inventive has 'made history', we say. Or something is said to be an 'historical fact'. There is no doubt that it happened.

Now I, wanting to persuade you to my conventionality, can point to all these everyday phrases and show how they hold a distinction, clear on reflection, between History as expressed knowledge of the past and the past as something that has happened. The careless presumption of everyday life, however, is otherwise: the past and History are the same. Or given the impact on our culture of one and a half centuries of higher education, the presumption of everyday life could be that History is a special sort of activity belonging to 'historians'.

Perhaps by the end of this essay I will have persuaded you to enter my conventionality. The likelihood, however, is that we will talk past each other. 'Real' and everyday meanings will constantly reassert themselves. Unless I invent some algebra—'X is ways of knowing the past'—critics of my conventionality will be distracted by the fact of it and fight my idiosyncrasy. Discourse never begins because we can never strike a bargain to agree as if 'history' means this or 'history' means that. We lack the discipline or social contract to see 'history' as if it meant something other than our taken-for-granted interpretation of it. Surrender to conventionality is always a socialising process. It is then that our 'as ifs' are real.

THE CONVENTIONALITIES OF DISCIPLINE

Surrenders to conventionality are what disciplines are. The disciplines are social systems that raise their partial 'as if' perspectives from mere conventionality to mythic proportions. In the language of semiotics, their models move from being symbols to being signs. They move from metaphor to metonymy. From being known to be conventional and partial, they are understood to be real and whole. All the boundary-making rituals of everyday life in which the conventionalities of class and sex and race and sect are transformed into social realities are the same rituals that make for powerful ethnocentricity of the disciplines.

We will find them all, these *rites de passages,* in examinations, in selection, promotion, and establishment, in the residence rules of departments and schools, in the special languages, in the professional taboos. These are ways of making a blinkered view of the world seem mythically true. No matter that every science properly protests its rationality, the mood and sentiment created by each science's social relations make the artificiality of its perspective as natural as good and bad manners. As social and cultural systems, disciplines move from their sense of the conventional and metaphoric quality of their models to a sense of their naturalness and reality. Their models become signs of the whole of reality, not just symbols of its parts.

With the rise and fall of their political and social power, disciplines transfer their own models to their culture's mythic understanding of the environment. 'Supply and demand', 'id and ego', 'survival of the fittest' move from being recognised analytical contrivances to being objective descriptions of what actually happens, and reliable predictions of what will happen as the models gain the strength to have an undeniable and cosmological value in the culture at large.

Let me put forward a thesis about the discipline of history. Our everyday usage of 'history' as equivalent to the past comes from the small hegemony that the 'as if' models of the discipline of history have had. A history of 'history' inevitably focuses on the development of national identities and bureaucratic mass societies and the institution-alisation of politics, religion, and the economy in the civilising process of the nineteenth century. All these processes demanded the ideology of the factual. Just as the myths of psychologists, sociologists, economists, and now, perhaps, of geneticists have become the myths of our culture, so previous to that the myth of historians that their history was the factual past has given a blinding clarity to our perceptions. It has been the myth of historians become the myth of our culture that the past is discovered objectively and factually by our being accurate about it. One symptom of that belief is the statement that 'primitive' societies have no history. That statement should be: 'primitive' societies do not have the systematic conventionalities—rules of inquiry and evidence—that allow them to historicise in ways recognisable and persuasive to us; nor do they have the infinitude of institutional support systems (from archives to *The Guinness Book of Records*) to persuade them that accuracy is the truth, that History is the past. I trail my coat. Let me show that being accurate is a fetish of a very special sort of history. A poetic for histories will show histories' more varied concerns. Let me show also that an ethnography of History as a mode of consciousness is History's anthropology even as it is anthropology's History. Historians cannot escape a theory of how the past is in the present any more than can anthropologists.

Histories are ways of knowing what happened in the past. The qualities of histories are different from the qualities of the past. Ways of knowing are described by their systems of expression, their processes of communication, their relationship to shared experience. Ways of knowing can be called among other things objective, metaphoric, romantic. On the other hand, all that has happened is almost indescribable. The moment we give it distinguishable characteristics, we transform it, we know it, we make of it a history. Yet in our culturally mythic view of it, this past of which we make a history has two characteristics: it happened independently of our knowing that it happened—we are not its creators—and it happened in a specific way, in specific circumstances; its specificity is its objectivity, independent of the narrative or the meaning we make of it.

HISTORIES ARE THE TEXTED PAST

We cannot describe the past independently of our knowing it, any more than we can describe the present independently of our knowing it. And, knowing it, we create it, we textualise it. That is the circle, hermeneutic if you like, of our human being. Nonetheless, we have a sense that the past is text-able. The past is everything that has happened—every heartbeat, every sound, every molecular movement. This totality is both objectively specific (it happened in a particular way) and infinitely discrete (the happenings are not connected). Mozart writes a sonata on a cold day in a spiteful mood; Pomare, high chief of Tahiti, at the same moment distractedly 'eats' the eye of a human sacrifice. Yet we have a common-sense confidence that the 'real' past, like the 'real' present, is much more connected and ordered. We have a confidence that the past is ordered in itself in such a way that we can make a narrative of it. It is text-able. We are confident that our selection is an exegesis of an order already there. It is the same common-sense confidence we have in the cultural systems of our present.

This mythic confidence in a text-able past is the ambience in which histories are made. The past itself is evanescent: it has existence only in histories. Histories are the texted past.

What happened in the past inevitably leaves sign-bearing relics: in personal memories first of all, but, more importantly, in memory translated into its public social forms—gossip, legend, story, myth, anecdote, parable, sermon, speech. It leaves relics, as well, in transcriptions of all kinds—in memory written down, in the registers of institutions, in illustrations and depictions, in all the material things of the cultural environment. These oral, literary, material relics are extraordinarily complex in their sign-bearing characteristics, although there is an everyday common-sense prejudice that they are simple. The oral and the literary relics bear a message; they inscribe language; they convey information. Inevitably the inscribed language is stripped of the context of speech, the eye-to-eye exchanges that catch the mood, the nuances, the tropes that condition the signs. Already the relics of the past in their messages are transformed simply by being read. Already the past is as much created as preserved by readings which must invent the circumstances that give meaning to words. Our ordinary histories, double texted as they usually are, contain all the inventions of readings divorced from immediate experience.

Most relics hold a message: they all hold a code. They all encapsulate their cultural forms. Precisely because they are cultural artifacts, they hold within themselves their ordinary significance as things that are beautiful or sacred or useful or precious or manufactured. Those who use these artifacts know them in their ordinariness. They know when and how to use them and with what proprieties. These cultural things make a symbolic environment that show sex in a colour, status in a type of wood, class in a design. Even those relics that we would count more traditionally as documents—diaries, letters, logs, books—are cultural things as well and have encoded in their forms, materials, and shapes expressions of meaning beyond their messages.

The complexities do not end there. Relics of what happened in the past are cultural artifacts of the moments that produce them, but they also become cultural artifacts of all the moments that give them permanence. In a familiar Pacific metaphor the relics of the past are always cargo to the present. Things that cross cultural boundaries lose the meaning encapsulated in them and are reconstituted in meaning by the cultures that receive them. Relics of the past cross all the cultural boundaries that lie between past and present, and when they do they are reconstituted in the relations and means of production of each cultural zone they enter. We say that relics of the past 'survive the accidents of time', but it is only the destruction of these relics that is accidental. Their preservation is cultural. I think of institutions: archives and museums are mirrors of power and cosmologies. I think of roles: bards, priests, and journalists protest that they convey what is given them by inspiration, God, and events; but they make their news anew nonetheless. I think of class and sex: they own both the past and the present who own the means of preserving what has gone. I think of souvenirs and memorabilia, national trusts and heritage commissions. I think of Daughters of the Revolution, conservationists, and environmentalists. Relics of the past come directly from the past but they are reconstituted in their meanings by all the cultural systems that give them meaning. They gain meaning out of every social moment they survive.

Teasing Moments Make for Histories

The past, which we are mythically confident is knowable as such, is only known through symbols whose meaning is changed in the reading of them and in the preserving of them.

Histories are the product of that dialectic between discovery and invention. That does not make histories different from everyday experience. Everyday social reality is a product of the dialectic between the given of its systems and the creations of our interpretations. We are not the less realists for accepting histories' processual fictions any more than we are relativists for seeing that human culture is a balance between the predictability of socialisation and the creativity of interpretation. Even in the most mundane circumstances we are forced to invent because our rules never quite fit the idiosyncrasy of the circumstances, because the circumstances are always changed by our previous interpretations. The ordinariness of everyday life is always disturbed by the extraordinariness of a misread cue, or a *bon mot* become *faux pas*, or a novel combination of personality and role. I would say that every day we are confronted by some otherness that teases us to interpretation. When that otherness is outside our cultural system, we call those moments of interpretation ethnographic moments. But we have those moments within culture as well. In times of conflict or social ambiguity, we make a ritual of interpretation. We carve out a social space, make boundaries around it with language and protocol, the better to convey the simplicities of our interpretations. I think these teasing moments are made for histories. Anyway, that is my thesis. In the strangeness or novelty of the circumstances, we are teased to understand, to rationalise, by looking back. We present ourselves by making histories.

Past and present are bound together in an interpretive act we call History. The character of that interpretive act and its varieties we will return to later in this poetics. How social reality is constructed by and in these interpretive acts is an anthropological concern. Speaking now of the special conventionality of academic history, I have to say it is also a historian's concern. What anthropologists do of present cultures historians do of past cultures. They ask how the past is in the present. French revolutionaries made a revolution looking backward. 'Reformations' were re-formations. Whatever the differences of methodology and evidence between anthropology and academic history—and they are only differences of degree, not of kind—they each cannot describe the other or the past without asking how the praxis of culture is made up of interpretive acts. I call discourse on that shared concern 'ethnohistory'.

Ethnohistory is the focused conversation we have about the ways in which historical consciousness is culturally distinct and socially specific and how, in whatever culture or social circumstance, the past constitutes the present in being known. Ethnohistory, anyone who reads this will know, has had other meanings. Ethnohistory has meant 'history of primitive or traditional cultures'; it has meant the 'anthropology of past primitive or traditional cultures'. But 'ethno-'does not mean 'primitive' any more than 'anthro-'does, and I have objections to being thought to do ethnohistory of the 'primitives' and history of the 'civilised'.

I do the history and the anthropology of 'primitive' and 'civilised' alike; and insofar as there are those who would join me in understanding the nature and function of historical consciousness, I do ethnohistory both of 'primitive' and 'civilised' and of cultures in the past and in the present. So I think I am 'doing' ethnohistory and inviting my students to 'do' ethnohistory when we ask why it is that Australian schoolchildren are likely to say that the aborigines, rather than the Hawaiians, killed Captain Cook. We are curious how the history of the death of a hero has become entangled with home fears of what is strange and dark. I think I am doing ethnohistory when I puzzle why sailors might think that the mutiny on the *Bounty* was caused by Bligh's bad language, while admirals thought it was because he was not a gentleman. Sailors make history out of their experience in total institutions and know what sort of impersonal language gives them privacy and what sort of personal language exposes them to the intrusions of power. Admirals know that anyone who has to say he has authority has not got it, and they see how a gentleman is born to it in his deportment and etiquette. They write their reflective histories telling stories at the wardroom table about the gaucheries of nongentlemen. I think I 'do' ethnohistory when I try to describe Strangers in contact with Natives and Natives in contact with Strangers, interpreting what is new in the light of what is old and, in that, remaining the same and changing. Indeed, I do ethnohistory wherever the ethnographic moments of everyday life make cultured being.

As it happens, however, I find that ethnographic moments are never so piquant for a poetic of histories as they are in the contact of Natives and Strangers. The compounded nature of histories, the self-images in the cartoons of the other, the processess of culture and expressed structures are simply writ large in circumstance of extravagant ambiguity.

CARGO

It is an old joke that the world will not end with either a bang or a whimper. It will simply sink under the weight of old *National Geographic* magazines. The cargo of even that small universe of ethnographic experience is large. The sum total of the cargo of all the interpretive encounters of our world is immense. One lifetime would not be enough to read all the interpretations that were the product of ethnographic moments in Polynesia alone. One could write of the Pacific what Edward Said wrote of the Orient in *Orientalism*. Europe invented the East in its ethnographic encounter and then, possessing the inventions, added invention on invention. European inventions of the Pacific, to be discovered wherever there is an academy or an archive or a museum or a library, are beyond measure. And one must add to them all the living inventions not written down but which survive in lore, in shared images, in cannibal jokes, in fantasies about sarongs. It would be a brave man who would say he could write the ethnohistory of these encounters and have reflected on all the inventions of Native Polynesians as well as Stranger Europeans.

I like the metaphor 'cargo'. The relics of the past, the only ways in which the past survives, *are* cargo to all the present moments that follow. We all stand on the beaches of our present and make of our past, even of our past person, an object. The past is me; the past is it. Probably every person who reads this will be actively involved, individually or institutionally, in preserving some of that cargo. Like myself you might have a souvenir of an ethnographic experience, an artifact, the proof of some fieldwork, a memory of boundaries crossed. It might be a statue, a bowl, a stone adze that was the cultural currency in one symbolic system translated now into an instrument of teaching, a status symbol, a badge of anthropological interest. Like myself, you will be on some committee to discuss the cost of conserving somebody else's souvenirs or to discover the institutional will to keep something or to throw it away, to fathom the morality of owning the loot of ages. All relics of the past, even if they disappear with the note of a song or the sight of a mime, have a double quality. They are marked with the meanings of the occasion of their origins and they are always translated into something else for the moments they survive. Historical consciousness is always built out of that double meaning. History is always the past and the present bound together in the sparse and selected symbols that time throws up.

James Boon began some years ago consideration of 'cultural operators' (Boon 1973: 15). He was curious about the mechanics of interpretation in which we know the simple point of complex actions laid out for us in a sequence of time in drama or in opera. We catch the moment around which all else seems to turn. We entrap the whole in an instant. Imagine we go to the theatre to see *Death of a Salesman,* a part of life and life's relationships and structures, set out, like life itself, in a series of conversations. We hear the sentences of the conversation on the stage— about baseball, about dingy hotel rooms, about careless children and too careful wives—and we transform all the sentences, reduce them to one principal significance. We know the sentences in their unity to be concerned with coping or not coping with the emptiness of public presentations of self. Let us say we go to the theatre. The curtains are pulled back. There is Arthur Miller sitting on the stage. '*Death of a Salesman*', he says 'is about Everyman, Willie Loman, in an entrepreneurial society, and Everyman's inability to cope with the emptiness of the public presentation of self. That will be $10 please.' We would not know it at all. We would not be entertained by it. The medium of most of our living is conversation, of texted narrative. The clothing of our structures is the trivialities of everyday existence. We nonetheless have the poetics to make such theatre of this 'sensuous human activity' that captivates us, not by its parts, but by its whole.

Entertainments

I want to say that in history we are *entertained* by the meanings we put on the past. And Strangers are entertained by Natives.

'Entertainment' may seem a frivolous word. Clearly we are often more than amused or agreeably engaged by the past. Indeed, no matter what hegemony the entertainment industry has given to its meaning of amusement, 'entertainment' still keeps its more primary meaning of being engaged, having attention focused, being held to something. Victor

Turner attracted me to the word (Turner 1977), but Clifford Geertz (quoting Northrop Frye) attracted me to the notion. We do not go to *Macbeth* to learn the history of Scotland; we go to see a man lose his soul for the sake of a kingdom, Frye says—and Geertz approves (Geertz 1975: 450). In entertainment—on the stage or in our mind—we set up conditions to distill meaning. Out of complexities we make simplicities. We put round a boundary, we hold varied words and actions within a convention. Out of conversations on a stage, we abstract a dramatic unity. Out of images on a screen, we draw significance. In the theatre, of course, we are conditioned to act as interpreters. We are cut off from our ordinary social acts to enter the conventionality of being an audience. We are cued to the beginning and end of the drama with lights and curtain and silence. The noise of ordinary life is quieted so we hear the sound of play. We will weep or laugh in the space of the theatre, as we pray or know a presence in the sacred space of a church. We are unfettered by the ambience, by the rubrics, by the expectancies within us to respond.

I suspect we all can write the poetics of the theatre: we are all theologians of our own entertainment. We are participant-observers of the action on the stage and of ourselves as audience. In the foyers we discover we were 'only entertained' because we discover the conspiracies of directors and actors to make 'as if' what we saw was real. We do not play the critic so readily in ordinary life. It is another quality of the hermeneutic circle that ordinarily there is the difference between entertainment and reality.

I argue in what follows that historical consciousness finds expression in different forms of dramatic unity, that those forms have different conventionalities, that they make the past meaningful both in the conventionality of their textual nature and the conventionality with which they are received and heard. The past is constitutive of the present in the entertainment that histories give. Histories are the theatre of this entertainment. Rather, histories are the varied theatres of this entertainment. That is, histories are not just the content of a story or an interpretation of the past. Histories are not just a message. Histories are the mode of the story's expression, the public occasion of its telling. That is why histories are an anthropological concern. Ordinarily, one would call this understanding of history hermeneutical and acknowledge the influence of giants like Wilhelm Dilthey, R. G. Collingwood, Max Weber, and all the commentators on them. But inevitably in the formalist hermeneutics of such scholars as Paul Ricoeur and H. G. Gadamer, history is reduced to a sort of 'high history' that is the practice of historians, set apart like priests to do something special. Anthropology has the patience that hermeneutical philosophers do not have to see and describe the everyday nature of special histories and the historical nature of everyday life as well.

Types of Histories

The forms and structures of histories differ with different expressions. A history recounted at the family dinner table is different from a history told in religious ritual. A history recited in political parable is different from a history written in a doctoral dissertation. Each type of history will have its own social rules of expression, its own criteria of objectivity. Each type of history will balance past and present in different ways. The participants in each entertainment will know fairly exactly the reactions expected of them. There will always be some claim that one type, say academic or sacred history, is 'real history'. There will always be some jockeying for the exclusive use of the ordinary word 'history'. Sometimes some social group might win or nearly win and 'history' is declared in, some fundamentalist way to be only this or that transformation of the past. But such definitions are rarely descriptions of what is, only declarations of territoriality claimed.

The transformation of the past that is History is always made in social circumstances. Take the story told at the family dinner table, no doubt repeated a thousand times, leached in the telling to its essence, creating laughter and tears in the hearers in its almost coded phrases. What it loses in accuracy it gains in truth. Its truth concerns the bonds of familiarity. Insiders know their closeness in the shared humour at a social disaster or impropriety. The circumstances of its telling—acceptance, affection, expectancy, openness—make a boundary about the group and intensify their understanding that the story about the past describes the present. Maybe someone will correct an inaccuracy about a date or a place or a person, but usually so as to enlarge the meaning with a savoured relevance, not in the name of facticity *per se*. Response and reaction are almost studied as in a script, especially if some outsider is present to whom the family performs. They will bow to the one who 'tells it best'; they will groan with exaggerated boredom at yet another repetition of the story; they will interject on cue. It is an invitation to see family members as they 'really are', with their social screen lowered and their proper social selves put aside, confident that their bonds will not be loosened by a peep at their ignorance or their gaucheness or their social pecadilloes. These are the rituals of transformation. The past is thus made over into the present. The history cannot be divorced from the circumstances of its telling. The very pointedness of selection in the story, the caricature of its exaggerated drama—all the marks of its inaccuracy—are what make it true for what it does in representing the family as they 'really are'.

Take sacred history read in religious ritual—the 'Gospel according to St Matthew', the 'Epistle of Paul to the Romans'. There is never so strict a fundamentalism that accuracy is not subservient to truth. If one made an ethnography of a Christmas service, how would one describe the reading of the gospel? The 'Infancy Narratives' of the gospels have been subjected more than any other passage of Christian sacred scripture to reformed reading and modernist scrutiny. They have also been overlaid with apocrypha and nearly 2 000 years of cultural interpretation. They are now texts that contain overlay upon overlay of metaphor and mood that would be impossible to describe fully. Painters, poets, musicians, cribmakers, and house decorators have imprinted myriad images on our cultural consciousness, let alone preachers and theologians. What happens in time in culture happens in time in a person. There is no easy shuffling off the fundamentalism concerning cribs, angels, animals, and snow with which one was indoctrinated as a child.

Standing in a Christmas service listening to the gospel being read, an adult believer will be touched by the moods engendered by childhood fundamentalism even if he or she hears the reading with a post-modernist ear. As believer, his or her credulity will not be strained by the realisation that angels' messages to shepherds, kings following a star, even virgin mothers are metaphors for the deeper, more mysterious truths the sacred history contains. They do not need the sophistication of the scripture scholar to move deftly between a demand that things be 'historically' accurate and an understanding that the mythic clothing of truth can be contradictory and even 'untrue'. As parents, they will happily convey a literal truth to the child at their knee and not be disturbed at their own divided understanding that angels, kings, and virgin mothers might really mean something else. The firmness of faith binds them not to the historicity of detail but to the meaningfulness of the whole.

I make no point that this imagined believer is typical or that all of us are relativists now. I make a point about the ritual as of the trans-formation of the past. Sacred history, especially, but all history as well, is no inert text. The past is transformed not once and for all, in a simple act of historical expression. The meanings in the expression are never stable or frozen at their moment of expression. They are always added to and embroidered by the very continuity and preservation of the text. Their continuity and preservation is always a cultural act in itself, done in institution and ceremony, done in technology, done in the very forms and structures of the text as a cultural thing. But the transformations are more multiple than even in their expression and their continuity. Our imagined Everyperson at the Christmas service, however slightly touched with the fire of the great contemplatives, will have made his or her own distracted meditations on the 'word made flesh'. The meanings he or she will see in the text will come from self as much as from the text, but never just from self or just from text. The hermeneutics of such a transformation have long been a science. I think of Ignatius Loyola and his *Spiritual Exercises*; I think of John Wesley. The essence of that science surely has been to discover both the spur and the curb to enthusi-asm. The spur has been to see the timelessness, the eternally renewed relevance of the sacred work. The curb has been to see that meaning has nonetheless some authoritative, institutional definition. If we would understand the transformations of the past that histories are, then we must describe as well the tension between the creative thrust by which personal meaning is implanted in the text and the authoritative demand, whether sacred or secular, that the meaning be public and conventional. Sacred history is entertainment in its essence. The text is neither totally inside nor totally outside the reader. The meaning is both changing and unchanging. The reader will be fully absorbed in the particularities of its expression and know it in its reduced simplicity. The history is received and made at the same time.

Political parables recite history for the lessons it contains. I think of election speeches, party nominations, manifestos, celebration of some public metric moment. Hearers are invited to bridge the past and present in the identification of similar conditions or motivations. The thrust is to put aside the differences of time, the nuances of change, and to motivate the hearer with clearly perceived similarities. There is little effort to persuade to the truth of the interpretation of the past: the truth of the interpretation is presumed. The effort is directed at evoking mythical metonymies, likenesses that are seen immediately to be true and are sustaining not because they are new, but because they are old. They call on the way the world is known to be from some perspective of class or race or sex. To be a cliché is a virtue. Given the right circumstances, this clichéd history gets renewed meaning, just as a national anthem gets its strength from the circumstances in which it is sung. The goal of history in political parable is mood, sustained righteousness, or anger, or pride. The understanding it gives has the completeness and indivisibility of an emotion and comes from the ambience of experienced signs in the medium, not the reasoning in the message. Hearers are expected to make their rationality subservient to a *realpolitik*. To question whether the history is correct, to quibble about its certainty, would be like giving a medical report in answer to the everyday question of 'how are you?' The history in political parable is sacramental: it makes the reality in its signs.

Even 'Scientific Histories' have an Anthropology

One has to understand that 'scientific history' or 'academic history' is as cultural and as social as a dinner-table story or scripture or a political parable. The rhetoric about these logical systems of 'academic histories' and the declatory definition of what they are and are not sometimes hide what disciplines share with everyday cultural phenomena. Indeed the vested interest in making them seem different and above culture is the very quality that makes them the same. The most remarkable development over the last century in Euro-American cosmological systems has surely been the evolution and division of innumerable sciences. Each one claims to be distinct from all the others; each proclaims its difference from common sense; each is jealous that its partial, unreal bit of reality should belong to somebody else. My own university, established in 1854 in a raw colony fired to some delusions of grandeur by the discovery of gold, created four founding chairs, of Modern History, of Classics, of Law, of Literature and Language. It was a fair, if compromised, map of an educated man's cosmology. Now the university has 117 departments. For 134 years it has boiled like some symbiotic brew primed by the politics of knowledge to divide and subdivide. The process at the University of Melbourne by which groups of men and women (mostly men) grabbed this or that bit of the human anatomy and the physical environment and said it was theirs is only a tiny part of the fractionalisation of systematic knowledge. One almost needs an ethnoscience to see the categories of the world as 'scientific man' sees it. The begetting of science by science produces as many kinship and residence rules and boundary-maintaining mechanisms as any clan or moiety. The *rites de passage* that give entry and status in the discipline mark the mind like circumcision marks the body, so that historians do not 'understand' sociologists, for example, and each enjoys its caricatures of the other. The reifications by which some object is separated out of the continuity of experience—say a gene or a neutron or a psyche or even a 'renaissance'—are established as so really distinct from everything else that it needs a different language to describe it, a different system of evidence and discourse to analyse it, a special sensitivity to see it. Virtually as much social energy is put into the support of differing reifications of the sciences as is put into the central reifications of our social system, such as the Law, the State, the Church. We are socialised to their real distinction by examination, promotion, residential requirements, associations, conferences, publications. C. P. Snow was satisfied to discover two cultures. At the University of Melbourne, he might have discovered 117 if his measures were those we make for race or class or sex.

The transformation of the past in 'academic history' is set in different social circumstances and performs different functions from other sorts of tranformations of the past. That it does have a social set and performs social functions needs to be explored a little, because many academic historians would be uncomfortable with the notion. The very idea of 'scientific' or 'academic history' would seem to take that sort of history out of the social circumstances that relativise it. Indeed, the nineteenth-century Euro-American society invested extraordinary social energy in inventing a history that was supposedly divorced from its social circumstances. For a brief span in the middle of the century, when philosophy and religion had lost some of their cosmological hold, 'academic history' took their place. The growth of nations, the development of mass society and of massive institutions to control it, the bureaucratisation of empires encouraged a faith in a science that told 'what actually happened'. Scientific history was seen to be different from romantic legend, sacred text, and political manipulation of the past because it demanded accuracy. It also defined what accuracy was and provided an open discourse in which accuracy was measured.

Scientific history was admirably suited for government, law, education, bureaucracy—everywhere where the transformation of the past had to be seen to be reliable, measured by the same criteria, true. The rub, of course, was in being true. Scientific history, by definition, was accurate. The opening of national archives, and then of special collections, the growing cultural realisation that the ordinary national and political past as distinct from the cultural past of classical antiquity was worth observing, the emergence of new histories out of new sources, the creation of reviews in which the amateur was flogged into line for his faulty references and the professional waited in terror for the recluse who knew it all and had not told—all gave practical definitions to what was accurate history. Accurate history was what could be attested to by appeal to some 'primary source'. Inventiveness and imagination in discovering new primary sources became a mark of an historian's genius and good luck. In a joined-together world of historical societies, academies, publishers, libraries, archives, reviews of all sorts, an historian's finickiness toward accuracy was a public possession. Under the circumstances, it is not surprising that being accurate became equated with being true and that history became equated with historical facts.

It would be difficult to exaggerate our own Euro-American culture's preoccupation with the past as historical fact. Every day, it seems, some athlete 'makes history' somewhere in the world with another record. The industry of revising the past by the discovery and publication of some 'startling fact' is beyond measure huge. We are bombarded with quizzes, with calendars of people and events, with celebrations of metric moments. We are entertained by our own historicity: accuracy is truth. I remember a newspaper reporter, who, goodwilled and wanting people to hear me lecture, but frustrated by my reflexivity and my bland relativism, did his best with me with a headline: *Bligh, A Real Nice Guy*. It was up to me to make history news with an 'exposure', a 'revelation'. The past entertains us, romantic positivists that we are, by being rendered ever more accurate.

It should be clear that in calling academic history entertainment I do not mock the seriousness or the good intentions of the pursuit of meaning in disciplinary ways. I only mean to indicate that pursuit of meaning never was a privileged position outside of culture and society. I equate different types of meaning pursuits—from gossip to the recitation of myth to systematic inquiry—in their dramaturgical quality. I do not equate them for what they are or what they do or for the worth of investments we put in them. We are entertained by the past in our different histories under their different conventionalities. No one form of these histories is truer than the others *because* it is unconventional. Our poetics for all of them allow us to read the 'truth' in all of them. Objectivism and relativism are both unreal, unhuman perspectives if being objective is thought to be unconventional and being relative is thought to be maverick. Our poetics allow us to share our entertainment by the past under different conventionalities.

The conventions of that dramaturgical entertainment include not just the text and its structure but the reading and the cultural rules of reading as well. The presentation of 'academic history' and the reading of it—that is, the living discourse that is the response to the written down text and the then continued tradition that is the context of reading—these correspond to my notion of entertainment. I should add, without wanting to raise another hare, that the seriousness of the intent of the author of a text does not preclude an audience being amused by it, and being amused, like having a joking relationship, can establish realities in turning them around.

CULTURE AND THE STRANGER'S EYE

It should be clear by now that this essay will not offer a poetic of 'Polynesian' historical consciousness, nor indeed of the historical consciousness of Native Polynesian and Stranger European, each in the environment of the other. The 'ifs' and 'buts' of such an exercise offend my sense of economy for this piece. I have tried it elsewhere and I invite you to taste its ambiguities there. The truth is that I have been so preoccupied with the dead Polynesians of the past that I have little expertise to talk of a poetic of historical consciousness of the living Polynesians of the present. I watch with interest the efforts of the new nations of the Pacific to produce their own histories, and I note the pressures on them from their own institutions of power to produce histories in an acceptable Western idiom. I watch the movements for ethnic and cultural identity in the various Polynesian islands, and I note in the poetic of their histories their distrust of their processual selves, as if they think being Hawaiian or being Tahitian is some positive, unchanging essence that is now lost but is somehow recoverable. I watch the ever more self-conscious dialectic between living cultures and ethnographic descriptions of their past. I think of the debate over Margaret Mead raised by Derek Freeman (Freeman 1983). But all around the Pacific it is the same. Cultures cannibalise their own images. It has happened often enough in our own culture, this dialectic between living and reflections on life, but is happening all around the Pacific starkly now. What a complicated two-way 'Mirror for Man' anthropology has turned out to be, once we understand the poetics of an ethnographic moment.

A poetic for histories of the dead Polynesians will overwhelm anyone who tries to do it unless he or she has a pragmatic confidence in only doing what can be done. The relics of the Native Polynesian past have all been transformed into relics of the Stranger European past. There is nothing—not a written down experience, not a myth, or a legend, not a material artifact, not an archaeological site—that does not, by the expressions of it, by the collection and preservation of it, and/or by the interpretation of it and inclusion of it in a Stranger's discourse, require critical reading to separate the Stranger's cargo from the Native's past. There is no need, because of that, to adopt a know-nothing silence about a poetic of histories of past Polynesians. Both European Strangers and Polynesian Natives of the past are distant from us now. At a distance history's ironies are to our advantage, and we can catch a glimpse of their different taken-for-granted worlds.

Roy Wagner has offered us the disturbing notion that culture belongs to the stranger's eye—to the professional stranger, if he or she be an anthropological observer, say, or to the person who is distanced by reflection or role from what happened around him or her. Culture is a stranger's invention: it is the sense of wholeness and integration an outside-outsider or an inside-outsider develops. In a poetic for histories, one has to describe this same invention of the past. Whatever the different social expressions of historical consciousness, they are all born of the irony that things are never what they seem. Irony is history's trope. In the space between the meaninglessness of the present and the unknowable past is the entertainment of history. The artifice of history's words is to give historians, whoever they are—gossips, priests, academics—

control over the past in a way participants could never control their present. Historians, again, whoever they are, are outsiders. They always make a drama out of what the participants experienced as one damn thing after another. Historians always see the past from a perspective the past could never have had. They are like meteorologists predicting yesterday's weather today. They get their certainties from consequences.

'Auto-History'

For more years than I care to remember I have read and written about the relationships of history and anthropology. I, who thrive on anthropology's generous spirit of discourse, have sat in a chair of history; and in a university that has had no anthropology, I have been the anthropologist. Beached in this way by the politics of knowledge, I have a jaundiced view of the boundary disputes of disciplines, and I would turn reflection on history and anthropology away from them. I see the cartoons and caricatures disciplines draw of one another as symptoms of a territoriality that is human enough, but dangerous when it masks a claim for power based on the partiality of each discipline's view. Kings as philosophers amuse me, but philosophers as kings frighten me. Now that my liberalism is more radical and my pragmatism more certain, I have little patience when the question 'Who are you who say that?' precedes and precludes the question 'What is it that you say?'. Yet I am impatient, too, with the false consciousness that separates ways of knowing from ways of being. This is why I have written of a poetic for histories.

In a period now when anthropologist-historians such as Clifford Geertz, Marshall Sahlins, Renato Rosaldo, Rhys Isaac, Barney Cohn, Natalie Zemon Davis, Robert Darnton, Valerio Valeri, James Boon, and Richard Price have consciously blurred genres, my old concerns may seem somewhat dated. Maybe. Boundaries, I suspect, like the poor, are always with us.

Back in 1966, feeling professionally competent as an historian but in the middle of the tortuous initiation rites of being an anthropologist at Harvard, I wrote 'Ethnohistory in Polynesia' (Dening 1966) to make two pragmatic points: a priori definitions of what could or could not be done in history and anthropology were irrelevant; each inquiry stood on its own persuasiveness as to what could be done. And, since the history of Polynesian cultures could only be written out of sources that were European, one would always have to know who the Europeans were before knowing the Polynesians. I was disturbed at what I thought was a flaw in Pacific anthropology. It was ahistorical, it pursued the Polynesians in a time out of time. It was not truly ethnographical of the present nor of the past. Even in the fieldwork of the 1920s to the 1930s, the cultures described were not so much what was observed as something that belonged to an imagined moment before the Europeans came.

Twenty years later, I am not comfortable with the term 'ethnohistory' if it is thought to be a special sort of history that one writes of non-Western societies. I now think of myself as an ethnohistorian only when I am distinguishing systems of historical consciousness across cultural time and space and when I am describing the ways historical consciousness creates present cultural moments. The realization in Pacific studies that 'fatal impact' is an unhelpful analytic concept in describing cultural processes has reinforced my earlier postulate that the relationship between Native Polynesians and intruding Euro-American Strangers has been symbiotic.

In 1973, I wrote an ethnography of the demarcations of disciplines, 'History as a Social System' (Dening 1973), part of which has been referred to in the Prelude above. Philosophers had usurped discussions of the disciplines and what they said about the logic of explanations was of little relevance to what actually happened in the systematisation of knowledge. Scholars were divided, I argued, by their tropes of understanding, 'prudence' on the historians' part, 'scanning' on the sociologists' and anthropologists'. They were all socialised to the acceptance of the limitations of their own tropes and the foreign qualities of others' tropes by all the ways social boundaries are made. For some time I had engaged my history students in ethnographic descriptions of their own and present social milieu, the better to interpret the symbolised past and the better to sense how sparse and disembodied of context were these transformed experiences. 'History as a Social System' flew the kite that trailed the banner 'History is ethnography'.

In 1974, I edited the *Marquesan Journal of Edward Robarts* 1797–1824 (Dening 1974). The journal had been written by a beachcomber who had lived seven years in the Marquesas at the end of the eighteenth century. Robarts' account was a remarkable ethnographic moment become cultural artifact. In his personal experience, Robarts showed how the native Marquesans were invented and then possessed by stranger-societies and stranger-scholars once the inventions were written down. There was an extraordinary osmosis, which I cannot describe here but only wonder at, whereby one small man's personal experience was registered in the experience of explorer-visitors, raised through them into literature in Herman Melville's *Typee*, and came to affect and condition twentieth-century anthropology of the Marquesas. Everything I have said in 'A Poetic for Histories' is exemplified in Robarts's journal.

There was a more important point conceptually to which I was led in editing Robarts. Robarts' journal described the actuality of Marquesan society: it told of Marquesan persons doing things, conditioned in their roles and their obedience to their cultural roles by their personalities and by the chance and circumstance of living. Against a structured view of what he thought the Marquesans thought they *should* be doing typically and culturally, Robarts also told whom they actually married and with whom they were in conflict and why. It is in describing what actually happened that I find history (the discipline of history) and ethnography joined. I see a distinction between actuality and reality. By 'actuality' I mean what happened as it is known in its balance of the circumstantial and the determined, in its typicality as well as its particularity, known for its multivalent meanings. By 'reality' I mean what happened as it is reductively known, by its determinants, known in its simplicity of meaning, set in some hierarchy of acceptability. History and anthropology are joined by the common humanism of their interest in the actual. They both deny themselves the fundamentalism of reality-construction. Their tolerance in seeing and describing things as they actually are is self-denying of the power to make things really something else. I like the shared poetry of their vision: they know their own ambiguities and cannot see 'reality' for its ironies.

In 1978, I wrote an ethnographic history of a school, *Xavier, A Centenary Portrait* (Dening 1978). It was a long way from the Pacific, but not from 'primitive' cultures. Schools are as good a place as any to describe the dialectic between *langue* and *parole*. They are marvellous places to see the symbolic environments that histories make. In itself, the celebration of a centenary, the writing of a school history by a socially prestigious 'old boy', the decisions that needed to be made as to the style of entertainment a school history should be and the debates that were raised around breached conventionalities, all made for my personal experience of the public nature of history-making. Susan Sontag ended her essay *Against Interpretation* (Sontag 1967) with a call for an erotics (in place of a hermeneutics) of art. Certainly ethnography is a celebration of the pleasure of being and history will never escape its own antiquarianism. But then again, I do not think that being guardian of the signatures human beings make on life is antiquarian at all.

Xavier—and the erotics of writing history—liberated me to write *Islands and Beaches: Discourse on a Silent Land, Marquesas* 1774–1880 (Dening 1980). I felt liberated from the need to disguise the pasts of Marquesan-Natives and European-Strangers 'as if' they were free from each other or from me or from all that intervened between me and them. As strangers and natives were bound together, so were present and past. *Islands and Beaches* was an effort to show what that binding-together actually was. It was anthropological history in that 'I', the author, enlarged the past by being enlightened by the snatches of anthropological discourse I had caught. It was historical anthropology because it reflected the ways in which historical consciousness constituted the present moments of 1774 to 1880 in the Marquesas, as well as the ways in which historical consciousness constituted all the present moments that joined the then of 1774 to 1880 to the now of 1974 to 1980, the period of my writing. Writing history is inevitably an exegesis of an exegesis. I speak of what I thought I did. What I did is to be found in all the varied readings of *Islands and Beaches*.

I have been teased in recent years by how one could better do this anthropology of the past. I cannot escape the consequence of the directions I have already taken. Anthropology's vision is built not on the 'primitiveness' of the native but on the advantage of the dialectic between distance and familiarity. The symbolic environment of an eighteenth-century missionary chapel is as revelatory of the nature of religion as the symbolic environment of an eighteenth-century Tahitian *marae*. The ritual space on an eighteenth-century British naval vessel, like the *Bounty*, is as much a stage for the performance of authority and power as is a Tahitian *marae* and its spaces for sacrifice. The triangle of distances and lines between between Strangers and Natives and between now and then is still the advantage and frustration of historical anthropology.

In the years that have followed *Islands and Beaches* I have tried to narrate these abstract theoretical issues through anthropological histories of particular events. You have some of my efforts before you in this volume: 'The Face of Battle', 'Sharks that Walk on the Land', 'Possessing Tahiti', 'School at War'. They are each written with the conscious effort to unwind the double helix of past and present that was life then as it happened and is now as I make history of it.

I do not believe that I have moved far from my initial belief that in academic history and anthropology it is better to do what can be done than to declare what cannot. I made an effort to display what can be done in a small monograph called *History's Anthropology: The Death of William Gooch* (Dening 1988 and 1995). I do not believe that we can escape Pablo Picasso or Albert Einstein or Roland Barthes or Michel Foucault any more than we can escape Jesus Christ or Buddha. What they have spoken cannot be unspoken. We are all plagiarists on life and living. *History's Anthropology* is ultimately an ethnography of an historical act—mine and all those that made the life and death of William Gooch. All writers, all scholars, must make some surrender to the systems that allow their thoughts and images to be shared. I wish now of *History's Anthropology* that I had plagiarised the courage of Picasso or Einstein or Barthes or Foucault to test the vulnerability of these systems a little more. There is much of the liminality of ritual in writing. It has an in-between quality that I value most as a professor of history, a declarer of histories. It is a space for knowing oneself, bonded and free at the same time.

Ten years is a long time in anyone's intellectual life, when the pace of research and publishing is so furious. Since completing 'A Poetic for Histories', I have written *Mr Bligh's Bad Language: Passion, Power and Theatre on the Bounty* (Dening 1992). It won me that fifteen minutes of fame that Andy Warhole suggested we each might ambition. *Mr Bligh* won me a prize. It won me some opprobrium, too. I was cited, because of it, as one of the principal agents in Australia for the 'killing of history'. I thought that a little unfair. I am not really into killing anything. But when the reviews of one's book begin to number hundreds, one learns to be choosy. Someone else said that I was a 'magical realist'. I liked that. It is nearer to where I have come in these past few years, and where I ambition to go in the years to come. Writing *Mr Bligh*, I discovered theatre, theatricality and the anti-theatrical prejudice. What that meant to me is displayed in some of the pieces below. What it means for me now is a supreme confidence that the realism of history lies in its theatre. In that sense the realism of history, not of the past, will always be somewhat magical.

SHARKS THAT WALK ON THE LAND

THE Polynesians are those people who, some two or three thousand years ago, spread to all the islands of the Pacific through the great triangle that reaches from Hawaii to New Zealand to Easter Island. That was their great cultural triumph. They had mastered the immense ocean. They had discovered all the islands of the Pacific and then in turn were discovered by European explorers from the sixteenth to the eighteenth centuries of the Christian era.

In their different island worlds the Polynesians developed separately, playing variations on their common cultural themes. They held in common, however, an understanding of themselves—call it an historical consciousness—expressed in the mythical opposition of 'native' and 'stranger'. This opposition of 'native' and 'stranger' was prior to and independent of the European intrusion. The Polynesians were native and stranger among themselves and to themselves. They saw themselves as made up of native, those born of the land of their islands, and stranger, those who had at some time come from a distant place. 'Tahiti' is the Hawaiian word for 'distant place'. Strangers came from 'Tahiti'. Or they came from 'Havaiki', the more general Polynesian word for a place of origin. Typically in their myths the first stranger, a chief, came many generations ago in a canoe from a distant place. He found the natives on their island and either overthrew the existing chiefly line by violence or married the highest born women of the natives and established his strangers' line.

In myth and in ritual this opposition of native and stranger was a constant metaphor of Polynesian politics and social organisation. Political power was thought to come through usurpation by the stranger and was given legitimacy by the native. A reigning chief would trace in genealogy his line to a hero who would have come from a distant place and conquered the native inhabitants of the island and their chief. It was not just an event of the mythical past, however. The reigning chief, even if he had come to power by the natural death of his father, would have played out a usurping role in the rituals of his accession and would have married into that line which connected him most closely with the original natives of the land. So the opposition native and stranger was both history and cosmology. It offered an understanding both of the past and of the present: the conqueror, the stranger, came from the sea; the conquered, but founding force, the people, were of the land. So Land and Sea had the oppositions of Native and Stranger. And because Polynesian cosmology imaged the sky as a great dome reaching down all around the island to the circle of the horizon, those who came by sea came from 'beyond the sky'. They were *atua*, gods. Being called *atua*, as they almost universally were, the European Strangers who came to Polynesian islands from beyond the sky, were both flattered and reinforced in their judgements of savage simplicities. We might hazard a guess that the Polynesians, just as they saw in their own Stranger Chiefs the incarnation of usurping power, so they expected the European Strangers from beyond the sky to play out their mythical usurping roles. Native–Stranger:Land–Sea. There are other associations as well. Strangers from the Sea, from Beyond the Sky, Usurping Power, were chiefs; they were also man eaters, sacrificers. There was a Hawaiian proverb that caught it all: 'Chiefs are sharks that walk on the land'.

In Hawaii, as elsewhere in Polynesia, the structural opposition of Native and Stranger was played out in an annual cycle of rituals. Eight months of the year belonged to the Stranger Chiefs, and were the ordinary time of human sacrifice and war, the time of *kapu* (taboos), and of those protocols of the dominance of chiefly power. It was the time in which the chiefs walked on the land like sharks and the people of the land, the commoners, obeyed all the *kapu,* or suffered death as *kapu* breakers. These eight months of the year belonged to Ku, the god of war and sacrifice, the ancestral deity of the Strangers.

These were the ordinary months of the year. But there were four months beginning October–November that were a sort of carnival time, when the ordinary was overturned, when the temple rites of Ku were suspended. In these four months the ritual focus of the island was on the fruitfulness of the land and the sea rather than on the power of the chiefs. It was the time of the year in which the god of the land, Lono, returned to the islands. At the end of these four months there were twenty-three climactic days. The highest ranked of the chiefs or 'king' temporarily lost his sovereignty. He and other chiefs went into seclusion, locked themselves away on their individual lands. The time of Lono was called *makahiki* and it followed a strict calendar. In the second month, there began a procession of the priests of Lono right-handedly around the island. That is, the land was always on the right and the sea on the left. Right hand, life, land: left hand, death, sea. The procession of Lono was a symbolic act of his possessions of the land. At the same time there were left-handed processions, counter-clockwise, around the lands of the chiefs, symbolic acts of dispossession. In the time of their seclusion they lost that power which they had usurped from the people of the land. Lono's procession was led by Lono's symbol, a cross-like piece of wood from which hung banner-like pieces of white cloth made of bark. At all stages of the procession the common people came forward with abundant gifts. It was a time of feasting and games. There were great boxing matches, sledding, running races, javelin throwing and dancing. Like carnivals everywhere it was a time of freedom, sex roles were reversed, *kapu* were overthrown and none were sacrificed for breaking them. When the island was encircled, the procession ended at Lono's temple. During the four months of *makahiki*—ideally at the time of the winter solstice—there was a conflict ritual called *kali'i*. The 'king', coming from the sea, confronted Lono and was 'killed' in his usurping power. Then his sovereignty was returned in the name of Lono. At the end of *makahiki,* Lono's temple was dismantled and the new year of Ku was begun with a human sacrifice. Once again the sharks walked on the land.

In November of 1778 James Cook's *Resolution* and her consort the *Discovery* appeared off the north-west coast of the island of Hawaii. It was Cook's third voyage. He was a world famous man. His voyages of discovery had captured the imagination of Europe and America. He was also a tired man. It was his tenth year at sea on Pacific explorations. Historians on Pacific explorations in hindsight, and indeed Cook's colleagues in reflection on what happened on this third voyage, have agreed that even at this stage all was not well. Cook's temper, never good, was less in control, and he flogged more than forty-five per cent of his crew, and many of them more than once. Cook's cool judgement with native peoples seemed awry and his patience thin. He was sick with years of the strain of leadership in dangerous places and the horrendous food of voyaging. His poor stomach, kidneys, bowels and lungs would offer a grim picture for any 'Body Programme'. Sir James Watts, a medical historian, has played on the irony that in saving himself from scurvy and a Vitamin C deficiency, Cook lost out on Vitamin B, and he may have had worms which deprived him of niacin and thiamine. For those who do not read boxes of breakfast cereals seriously, Sir James has a grim warning what a lack of niacin and thiamine can bring: fatigue, headache and insomnia, breathlessness, irritability and depression, painful mouth and tongue, digestic disturbances, loss of interest and initiative, constipation or diarrhea, loss of concentration and memory, psychoneurotic personality change, sensitivity to sunlight. 'Historians,' Sir James warns, 'have ignored for too long the serious effects on decision making from Vitamin B deficiencies, which could help to explain some otherwise inexplicable actions of the great naval commanders'. Be that as it may, the *Resolution*'s men went to the north-west coast murmuring among themselves at their commander's ill temper and wondering at his imprudences.

Indeed as the *Resolution* approached Hawaii he was crankier than ever, because his crew, conservative as ever, would not drink the spruce beer he had substituted for their grog for the sake of their health. And his crew were cranky at him, spoke 'mutinously' as the phrase went, because instead of stopping at anchorage where they might enjoy the pleasures of the islands, he had, for the sake of manipulating the market on supplies, decided to keep at sea off Hawaii and to drop in only at selected bays. They had spent hard months mapping and surveying the north-west American coast in a vain effort to find a passage through to the Atlantic and had comforted themselves with dreams of wintering in the islands. Instead, for nearly two full months in the winter seas of December and January off Hawaii, since made famous for their enormous surf and commented on by Cook as the largest he had ever seen, they made their slow clockwise voyage around Hawaii, beating constantly against the wind, tacking endlessly, the whole crew angry at Cook and he at them.

When they came close to land to do a little marketing, they noticed several things: on the north coast only commoners, and no chiefs, visited them; the offerings made were extraordinarily generous; the islanders all called Cook 'Lono'. Finding that none of the usual versions of Cook's name—Tuti or Kuki—would satisfy the Hawaiians, Cook's officers also began to refer to him as Lono when they spoke of him. The two vessels with their cross-pieced masts and sails proceeded on their right-handed procession around the island, until on 17 January they anchored at Kealakekua Bay on the south coast of Hawaii. They received a welcome there the like of which they had never seen in the Pacific, a thousand canoes and ten thousand islanders in complete jubilation.

Kealakekua is a large sweeping, half-moon bay. High cliffs in the centre drop to the water's edge and divide the low-lying point on the western edge, where there were the many huts of a settlement, from a shallow valley in the south-east corner, where there was a large stone structure and a few huts. This last was a temple or *heiau*. It happened to be Lono's temple at which the annual *makahiki* procession began and ended. It came as no surprise to the priests of Lono and all the people of Kealakekua that the two vessels with Lono's symbols displayed and seen off shore early in the *makahiki* season should have slowly made their way to where it all began and ended.

It was not the chiefs who welcomed them, but priests. They led Cook immediately to their temple where he let them do with him ritually what they wished. They took him to each of the images of lesser gods and he heard their denunciations of them. He let them hold his arms like the cross piece of Lono's symbol and offer him sacrificial food. He sat through their long litanies and heard them address him again and again as 'Lono'. He then asked the priests whether or not the small enclosure beside the temple might not be his to erect a tent for astronomical observations, sailmaking and a hospital. He needed to watch the stars. So the sailors erected a strange little temple of a tent and talked stars and sun to the priests of Lono who knew all about stars and were watching them themselves because the *makahiki* feast was determined by the rising and setting of the Pleiades and the setting was nearly upon them.

The high chief of Hawaii, Kalaniopu'u, did not appear for several days. When he did come on the twenty-fifth he came with a ceremony and majesty that the sailors had not seen before. He came in the great feather cloaks of Hawaii and invested Cook in one of them, which is still in the British museum. Kalaniopu'u would not meet Cook on the *Resolution.* He circled the *Resolution* in a large sailing canoe, the priests chanting and displaying their feathered gods. Then he met Cook on the beach in front of Lono's temple. On 2 February, Kalaniopu'u began to ask anxiously when they were going. The Englishmen left on 4 February. It was, as far as computers can calculate it, the last day of *makahiki* in that year. They did not go before two more unnerving coincidences. The Englishmen wanted firewood and asked for the fences, scaffolding and wooden images on Lono's temple and were surprised that the priests of Lono readily agreed. The priests demurred only at one statue. It was the image of Ku. That one stayed, the priests said, and watched the sailors dismantle Lono's temple at season's end.

Also, a much loved gunner on the *Resolution,* William Watman, had a stroke and died. The chiefs asked that he be buried in the temple. Old William Watman was buried with ceremony he could hardly have foreseen. 'As we were filling the grave', the *Resolution's* journal reads, 'and had finished reading the ceremony (during which they preserved the most profound silence and regard) they would throw in a dead pig and some coconuts, plantains, etc; and indeed were inclined to have shewed their respect for the dead by a great quantity of these articles, they also repeated some ceremonies, and although they were in some measure stopped from going through their funeral prayers, yet for three nights and in one it lasted the best part of it . . . [they] surrounded the grave, killed hogs, sing a great deal, in which acts of piety and good will they were left undisturbed: at the head of the grave a post was erected and a square piece of board nailed on it with the name of the deceased, his age and the date, this they promised should always remain and we have no doubt but it will as long as the post lasts and be a monument of our being the first discoverers of this group of islands'.

So the Hawaiians made the Englishmen's sacrifice their own. And while the season of Ku was thus begun, they had no qualms that it be marked with the cross and sign of Lono. As it happens, William Watman's death is remembered there still with a sign that has lasted longer than his wooden cross. There is a plaque there now celebrating this as the first Christian service on Hawaiian soil.

Makahiki was over and on those last days the people constantly asked when Lono was going. When Cook said his goodbyes and said he would be back next year in the winter from his search of the north-west passage.

So Cook went and he would have been back next year, except that a few days out the foremast sprung on the *Resolution* and he was back in seven days. There was no welcome this time. 'It hurt our vanity', the Englishmen said. The people were insolent and the chiefs sullen and questioning. There were immediately thefts and confrontations. The Englishmen could not believe that the atmosphere could change so rapidly and put it down to the strains that nearly three hundred extra mouths brought. Truth was they were out of season and out of role. They were not of the land: they were of the sea. They were not Native come to power for a season: they were Stranger, usurping power, sharks that walked on the land. The change in the Hawaiians brought changes in the English, and they say as much in their journals—that they displayed power and violence to get their way much more overtly. There were several incidents of violent clashes and on 13 February Cook himself was involved in a strange pursuit, alone except for a marine, running several miles, pistol in hand, after a thief. That night a cutter was stolen and on the morning of 14 February Cook closed the bay with armed men and went ashore looking for Kalaniopu'u to take him hostage for the return of the cutter. Kalaniopu'u was asleep and was obviously ignorant of the cutter's theft. He came willingly enough with Cook down the pathway in his settlement till some of his relatives said something to him and he looked frightened and sat down. Then came news, first to the crowd and then indirectly to Cook, that another chief had been killed in a clash on the other side of the bay. The crowd around Kalaniopu'u became threatening and Cook fired shot out of his double-barrelled gun at a man who was about to strike him. The shot was ineffectual against the warrior's protective matting, and when Cook fired a ball to kill another assailant it was too late. The crowd rushed forward and, with daggers that the Englishmen had given them, killed six marines and Cook at the water's edge. There was nothing that the waiting boats and the more distant ships could do. They saw their captain lying face down in the water. The Hawaiians were beating him about the head with rocks. Then they carried off the body in triumph.

The English were enraged and dismayed, unbelieving that they could have shared in so awful a moment for a man of destiny like Cook. They looked for a reason for it all, and found it in the cowardice of Lieutenant Williamson who they thought had withdrawn the boats too early, or in the imprudence of Cook in carelessly exposing himself and being too precipitate, or in their own carelessness at not having demonstrated the power of their guns before it was too late. Clerke, Cook's successor, acted calmly enough and refused to allow wholesale retribution, but there was fighting and slaughter nonetheless. They do not describe in their journals acts which they say are better not described. But the sailors mutilated those they slaughtered, carried back their decapitated heads in the bottom of their boat, hung them around the necks of those they captured. It is difficult to know whether these actions were shocking to the Hawaiians or whether they fitted fairly exactly the expectancies of those who knew that in the time of Ku there would be sacrifice.

Certainly everything that the Hawaiians did was a mystery and a contradiction to the Englishmen. They could not reconcile the savagery they had seen with the nonchalance with which many of the Hawaiians now treated them. Cook's body had been carted up the cliffs to a temple of Ku where it had been ceremonially divided among the chiefs. It is something a conqueror would do to the defeated or the successor to his predecessor—bake or waste the flesh from the bones so that the bones could be distributed. 'Every chief acts as a conqueror when he comes to power', the Hawaiians say. The priests of Lono who had been so friendly got their share of Cook's remains and brought a parcel of flesh to the ships to placate the Englishmen. When would Lono come again, they asked as they gave over Cook's flesh. Return, of course, he did. *Makahiki* came every year and for forty years and more the right-handed procession of Lono at *makahiki* time was led by a reliquary bundle of Cook's bones. It did not mean that the annual coming of Lono was more real because of it: Lono's coming was always real. It did mean—it is Marshall Sahlins' point—that god was an Englishman.

E. H. Carr has scandalised his historian colleagues by enunciating the principle that an historical fact is not what happened, but that small part of what has happened that has been used by historians to talk about (Carr 1961: 12). History is not the past: it is a consciousness of the past used for present purposes. In that sense the death of Cook immediately became historical. Those on board his ship began to write down what they thought had happened. An interpretation of what had happened mattered to them. They blamed one another for negligence or incompetence or cowardice. They examined the inconsistencies of their most consistent captain to excuse negligence, incompetence and cowardice on their part, to find a cause of his death in his weariness, his bad health, his crankiness. They searched their understanding of the uncivilised savage and of the treachery of natives. Clerke and King, at least, if not the rest of the crew who thirsted to be savage to the savages, sensed that what they had seen in their way the Hawaiians had seen in ways incomprehensible to them. None of them could comprehend why the Hawaiians seemed to presume that nothing had changed. The women still came to the ships at night even after the slaughters of the day. Old friends among the priests and chiefs and people came forward, and inquired for Lono as if he had never died.

There were two strange scenes in those confused days after the killings. One, on the side of the mountain in the temple of Ku, Cook lying there dismembered but resurrected in those who possessed him. The other, in the great cabin of the *Resolution*, the gentlemen of the two ships observing the proprieties of the navy in dividing up the clothes and possessions of their late commodore and buying them in a small auction.

We will never really enter the minds of those in the temple of Ku. It is hardly likely that they had killed Cook in order to make actual the ritual death of Lono at the hands of the high chief Kalaniopu'u. But when it was done they understood what had happened because their myths gave them a history and that history was necessary for the maintenance of all that they were. They were Native and Stranger to one another: Kalaniopu'u was the greatest Stranger of them all, the usurper, shark that walked on the land. He was who he was because in the season of sacrifice and war, in the season of Ku, he was conqueror of the land, of the people, whose god was Lono and whose season was *makahiki*. All Cook's gestures and threats, done in his eyes for the sake of property and discipline, were gestures out of season. It was as if the right order had not been played out and Lono had not been conquered for the season. Cook was not Native now, but Stranger, a shark that walked on the land. In those circumstances the killing was easy and the death made everything come true again. So they kept asking when Lono would come again.

The gentlemen in the great cabin auctioning their captain's goods had their own proprieties. They had to find the correct balance between the pragmatism of navy men a year and more from home, making use of things their owner no longer needed and making sense of their own emotions. They had to cope with wearing the captain's shirt and britches and the growing realisation that they had lived with a hero. They had difficulty in knowing the line between their own experience and the growing reality of their myths. They knew they had been present at a moment of some destiny. And they tried in their journals and logs to make sense of it. They cursed the corruption of the Deptford naval suppliers who gave them a bad mast whose splitting brought them back.

The venality of some small merchant had killed Cook. They remembered all the imprudences of Cook—in landing at low tide when the boats could not get near, in not listening to his marines who told him to get out, in not showing the Hawaiians the real force of their arms. They blamed Lieutenant Williamson commanding the boats for not doing something, anything. Williamson was disliked; they easily made him something of a scapegoat. The gentlemen auctioned off Cook's clothes in the Great Cabin as the chiefs divided up his bones in the temple of Ku. They all—gentlemen and chiefs—had some sense how great men find resurrection in their relics. Even the lower deck had their eye on the value of souvenirs. All the Hawaiian artefacts they had collected went up in value and you can find them now in the museums of the world—spears, axes, feather cloaks and beads—marked with the note that they belonged to the men who had belonged to Cook and had seen him die. They all had a clear sense that they were making history. And they knew that making history is a very schizophrenic thing. They knew all the chances and circumstances of the event—they knew crankiness, cowardice, carelessness; they knew the accidents of timing. They knew the inscrutability of heathen savages and their own civilised ignorance. They knew that if they had *not* done this or *had* done that, it would not have happened. But they knew, or they were coming to know, that what really had happened was that a hero had died. How it happened was not the accidents of it at all: how it happened was the heroic meaning of it. All the rest of their lives in wardrooms, at dinner tables, in pubs, they would be asked how it had happened. It would not matter that they were like valets who have no heroes. Whatever they said about what actually happened, what really happened was that Cook had died a heroic death.

If Captain Cook found resurrection among the Hawaiians in the spirit of Lono, he also found resurrection among his fellow countrymen in the spirit of hero, discoverer and humanitarian. It did not matter whether he was really Lono for the Hawaiians. It did not matter whether he was truly hero, discoverer and humanitarian for his fellow countrymen. When news got home to Britain, the British, the continental

Europeans and the Americans made myth of it in poetry, drama and paintings. And the myth has had a sustained relevance in continually changing environments for two hundred years. This has been not just in a proliferation of histories, but in continual rounds of as many metric moments of centenaries, sesquicentenaries and bicentenaries as the birth and death and all significant moments in between can provide.

Two hundred years of celebrating Captain Cook might seem a lot of hero-worshipping, but it is not enough. 'Ways of seeing' Captain Cook in libraries, articles and museums have taken on a life of their own. Exhibitions and publications become a performing art in themselves. Why Captain Cook became a hero will not necessarily be the reasons why he remains one. The greater the value of the cargo of his relics the more sustaining his cult.

But Cook has touched some other cultural nerve as well. If the myth of Lono sustained the realities of chieftainship and power, the myth of hero, discoverer and humanitarian expressed in rituals monuments and anniversaries, sustains our own image of who we are and who we should be. How the civilised mythologise themselves in possessing the Native, and how the British did this in Captain Cook, is the point of the essay below on 'Possessing Tahiti'.

One can walk from the water's edge where Cook died, through the tangle of undergrowth that covers Kalaniopu'u's village, along the path they both walked on 14 February 1779, up to the temple of Ku. Here in 1825, Lord Byron set a monument when he brought back the bodies of Liholiho and his queen from Britain. They had gone to secure the aid of King George IV but had died of measles. Liholiho was laying claims on a special relationship that had begun with Cook's death and resurrection. Lord Byron set a cross on a cairn in Ku's temple. Its replacement is there still, always the double entendre that it ever was when different eyes see the same symbol as sign of the cross and sign of *makahiki*. When the world is full of sharks and gods as well as heroes and discoverers, who can write the history of them all?

Well, no one can certainly end the history of Captain James Cook. In 1992, a Sri Lankan professor of anthropology at Princeton University,

Gananath Obeysekere, wrote a book entitled *The Apotheosis of Captain Cook: European Mythmaking in the Pacific.* He challenged the idea that the Hawaiians believed Cook to be the 'god', Lono. Such a view, he thought, was culturally offensive and a product of a Euro-centric history that demeaned the Hawaiians' rationality.

Obeysekere's target was Marshall Sahlins, a professor of anthropology at the University of Chicago. Sahlins is a world-scholar by reputation, and has written books of genius on the Pacific for nearly forty years. In *Historical Metaphors and Mythical Realities* (1981) and *Islands of History* (1985) he puzzled over the death of Cook. His interests were not so much in writing a history of the events, as providing a reflection on the ways that a totally foreign and particular experience (the arrival of European strangers) was absorbed into the structural understandings of the Hawaiians of themselves. Although there are few more empirical scholars than Sahlins in either anthropology or history, and none more exhaustive of every line of inquiry than he, his reflections were focused on enlarging anthropology's theoretical understandings. He has a sense of and a pride in the discourse of his discipline that is as passionate as it is complete. He was mightily offended to be accused by Obeysekere of being a tool of European cultural imperialism. So, of course, he responded. *How "Natives" Think. About Captain Cook For Example* (1995) has been his answer.

I am unlikely, even now, to say that the history of the death of Cook has ended. I can invoke whatever authority the reading through forty years of the published and unpublished sources of the Polynesian/ Euro-American encounter has given me to say that Sahlins has his 'facts' right and Obeysekere has them wrong. I need, however, to pull out of 'Sharks that Walk on the Land' something that I know has always been there, but, as the Obeysekere/Sahlins debate has shown, not always seen.

Of course the Hawaiians did not call the Euro-American strangers 'gods'. They called them *akua*. Tahitians and Marquesans called them *atua*. I should have written 'Hawaiians', 'Tahitians', 'Marquesans', of course. In the years of the first encounters, these islanders knew themselves as something else—*kanaka, maohi, enata*. That is the problem of cross-cultural history. Both sides experience one another in translation.

I, for one, believe that cross-cultural history should be written in such a way that the reader is aways reminded of strangeness by leaving key words untranslated, and by attempting to describe more discursively what is the cultural experience behind the word. But I have been castigated many times by reviewers for doing that and making things so difficult for those who just want to know the 'facts'. Indeed, when one writes the history of mythologised figures such as Cook and Bligh, what the 'natives' think is often counted irrelevant and beside the point.

The islanders I know about, the *kanaka, maohi* and *enata,* had no difficulty in calling beings *akua* or *atua* in ways in which offends my Euro-centric rationality. They called wooden statues, birds, sharks, chiefs and sorcerers, among many other things, *akua* or *atua*. The strangers, Cook among them, who described these categories of *akua* as 'gods' and reported the islanders behaviour towards them, were often much offended. They thought, indeed, that the islanders were irreligious, because they did not give the reverence that 'gods' in the Euro-centric perception deserved. William Bligh, especially, was offended at the distracted nature of Tahitian prayers. Perhaps if these strangers had been a little more ethnographically sympathetic, they might have understood that what was contradictory to them was not contradictory to the islanders. Obeysekere has won some praise for being politically correct enough to decry the notion that the 'Hawaiians' could be so primitive as to divinise a cranky, violent, aggressive Cook. Of course, the 'Hawaiians' did not divinise Cook. They called him *akua,* as they did their petty, violent, greedy, very human 'chiefs'. Not to explore what they might have meant by *akua* is a very self-centred sort of anthropology.

How to induce skepticism in deeply held cultural beliefs has long been a study of those institutional forces that have sought to change native cultures, notably Christian missionaries, but also empires and merchants. Missionaries had a translating problem. They could not call their God *akua* for all the reasons that might alert cross-cultural historians to the fact that *akua* were not 'gods' in a Euro-centric way. They usually created an out-of-language term, 'Yahweh' or 'Jehovah', to describe the out-of-cultural experience they were inviting the islanders to have. Mostly they were resigned to the fact that cross-cultural ideas change very little. They evolved proto-Marxist strategies instead. The natives would not be converted, they argued, unless they were first civilised. They would not be civilised until they wanted the material goods of civilisation so desperately that they would change their means and relations of production to create the surplus to buy them. That work, and above all that sense of time with its division of labour, leisure and worship, would give the natives the discipline to change their decadent life style. Or the missionaries invented horrific rituals destructive of the strongest *tapu*. The demoralised lethargy among the islanders that followed primed the awakenings to come.

Novel experience itself does not create skepticism, or another culture's rationality, unless it raises questions that need radical answers. All over Oceania, the 'Ecological Imperialism' (as Alfred W. Crosby (1986) has called it) which destroyed hundreds of thousands of lives with its waves of infectious diseases reinforced cultural beliefs rather than changed them. Islanders understood disease and death in the ways they had always understood them, as coming from sorcery or breached *tapu,* even though they also associated the epidemics with the coming of the Euro-Americans.

I have no difficulty in seeing that Cook was killed by 'Hawaiians' who were frightened of him or who were angry at him, any more than I have difficulty in seeing that they welcomed him and his ships as hungry, lustful, ignorant, culturally deprived, linguistically poor, absurdly behaving men 'from beyond the sky'. Their mythic consciousness gave them no programme of action. They were not slaves to the structures of their minds. Their stories and rituals of Lono did not predict how they would act. But when they explained to themselves what was happening, and then what had happened, they had nowhere else to turn but to their own mythic consciousness. The meaning of what happened then became more important than their experience of what happened. That I suggested in 'A Poetic for Histories' is nearly a cultural universal. How that mythic consciousness is transformed into something else and yet remains the same is the ultimate question of cross-cultural inquiry. I would rather try and answer that, than blind myself to the independence and creativity of native thinking.

THE FACE OF BATTLE:
VALPARAISO, 1814

THE Face of Battle, any reader of military history would know, is a stolen title. John Keegan's book used it first and inspired me to borrow it. Military history is not my chosen field of professional historical interest, but I confess that the terrible experience of men in battle in World War I has mesmerised me all my life. I have no memory of battle and have stood outside the cultural experience of it. Books like Keegan's *The Face of Battle* (1977) and Paul Fussell's *The Great War and Modern Memory* (1975) stir a sort of scholar's envy in me, but more, a gratitude for the understanding they give. Keegan's challenge to historians to reconstruct the real experience of battle, and Fussell's thesis that men made sense of the senselessness of horror out of their deeply felt cultural metaphors, inform this small study. It is part of a larger cross-cultural interest that I have: to understand the cultural experiences of native and Euro-American strangers in the Pacific in their differences and in their bound-together relations.

The battle I want to describe only lasted two hours and twenty minutes: actual fighting lasted only about an hour. On a world scale of things it was hardly an important battle, although for the sixty-five who died in it and the fifty-odd who were crippled for life because of lost limbs, it was important enough. The battle was between the USS *Essex* under Lieutenant David Porter and the HMS *Phoebe* with HMS *Cherub* under the command of Captain James Hillyer. It occurred off Valparaiso, Chile, late in the afternoon of 28 March 1814. The battle belonged to the War of 1812 between Britain and the United States.

'Mr Madison's War' it was called. It had begun while Napoleon was on his way to Moscow and Wellington was on his Peninsular campaign. The United States was caught between the posturings of both Britain and France, as those two warring nations tried to wound one another by destroying the advantage of the United States in being neutral, if unfriendly, to them both. Historians seem fairly agreed that the war was at one and the same time inevitable and a mistake. *Realpolitik* made it inevitable. Britain could not afford to let her sailors desert to American ships and therefore had to insist on the galling right to board American vessels and impress her own nationals. Yet Americans could not and would not suffer this national indignity and had been outraged when the British boarded and even humiliated one of their own naval vessels, and at all times controlled the free seas to snatch whomever they thought might be their men. Nor could Britain ignore the subterfuges by which neutral vessels carried contraband to French ports. Yet the Americans could not afford to let their trading die. Poor communications and Madison's desire to wrest the foreign policy initiative from an opposition faction within his party, pushed the American president to a war when he might have won all he was to win by negotiation (Horsman 1962; Egan 1974: 72–5; Stagg 1976: 557–8).

The war was begun by the American government under the motto of 'Free Trade and Sailors' Rights'. It was to be a motto inscribed on great banners on the *Essex* as she fought the *Phoebe*. This same motto was reported on the lips of dying men in heroic poses during the battle. There is the first puzzle about the face of this particular battle. 'Free Trade and Sailors' Rights' seems a strangely esoteric cause for which men should die. That is, of course, a dangerous sort of judgement to make. One man's esoteric cause can be another man's reason for living. But in this particular battle in this particular war there seems little proportion between the trivialities of the cause and the depth of the gamble men were prepared to play with their lives. 'Deep play', Clifford Geertz has called it in the entirely different context of a Balinese cockfight. The bet that men might lose was out of all proportion to the gamble that they might win. I ask, in an ethnographic way, how this could be (Geertz 1975: 412–53).

Lieutenant David Porter, captain of the USS *Essex* and instigator of this battle of Valparaiso, was a man of madcap adventure, full of extravagant gestures and hyperbole. He lived life as if the rhetoric of war and the cant of nationalism was a description of reality. Yet in the disordered years between the American Revolution and the War of 1812 the narrative of his life was hardly hyperbole. In his very first cruise as a boy of sixteen years he saw a man killed beside him as they both tried to drive off a British press-gang. In his second, his vessel was looted by a French privateer. Two other efforts by the British to impress him were a prelude to his joining the American navy. When he did, he sailed under the mythically authoritarian Captain Thomas Truxton. On that voyage on the *Constellation* in an engagement with the French, the only American sailor killed was one who was run through with a sword by his own lieutenant for panicking in action. 'We would put a man to death for even looking pale on board this ship', was the lieutenant's comment. And so it went: Porter holding 173 French prisoners with matches lit over a loaded cannon pointed down a hatchway; Porter wounded by pirates in the Caribbean; Porter in battle with Barbary privateers winning against unbelievable odds; Porter killing a man in a Baltimore tavern; Porter, most dramatically, a prisoner along with 300 other Americans, of the Bashaw of Tripoli, almost but not quite rescued by the marines, as is remembered in the marine anthem 'To the Shores of Tripoli'; Porter in wild forays among smugglers and Spanish adventurers off Florida and out of New Orleans. A small pastiche of his life hardly catches the sense that, for Porter, what was ordinary was to play out the structure of his life in dramatic caricature (Long 1970; Porter 1875).

The air of unreality that surrounded the American declaration of war against Britain in 1812 was not relieved by the unexpected defeats the tiny American navy inflicted on the mammoth British fleets. In a series of single ship combats, the supremacy of the American frigates and the superior seamanship of American sailors won over the smug and surprised British captaincy. Theodore Roosevelt has claimed that self-reliance brought on by republican democracy played out its role as well (Roosevelt 1882; James 1817; Brannan 1823; Bowen 1816). The sweetness of victory, however, was doomed to become the bitterness of frustration as the British navy inevitably blockaded the east coast ports and closed in all American fighting ships. Porter in the *Essex* escaped that blockade. With a plan that was tactically and strategically brilliant, even if accommodating to his privateering derring-do, he ran for the Pacific in December 1812. He hoped to do havoc and make profit among the British whalers unprotected by their navy in the Pacific. This he did splendidly. He captured fifteen whalers, by his own calculation making a paper profit of $6 000 000 in prizes and cargo. After eleven months of raiding off the South American coast and around the Galapagos Islands, he sailed to the Marquesas in October 1813 to rest his men and refurbish the *Essex* and her captive ships. The violence he did there is another story, as is his claim of empire, the first made by an American, unsupported as it happened by President Madison. In the new year of 1814 he got word that the British were after him and that they had sent the *Phoebe,* the *Cherub* and the *Raccoon* to take him. He had all the Pacific, indeed all of the China Seas and the Indian Ocean, both to hide in and to disrupt British trade, but he itched for glory and he sailed directly to Valparaiso. It was a strange decision. Valparaiso was the first port of call round Cape Horn. It was post-office to the Pacific. Meeting with the British was inevitable, and they had three ships to his two (he had converted a captured whaler into the *Essex Junior*). Porter himself had long ago warned the Secretary of the Navy that the *Essex* with its thirty-four 32-pound carronades and its six 12-pound long guns was dangerously vulnerable. Carronades, powerfully destructive, firing heavy shot, were for close combat. If the *Essex* were in any way disabled, the enemy could stand off with long guns and destroy her at will. In the neutral port of Valparaiso Porter inevitably would fight in circumstances determined by his enemies who would blockade him. It is hard to imagine that these paradoxes were not clear to him. Yet amidst the realities of life and death, Porter set the stage for a play (Porter 1822; Dening 1980: 26–31).

Porter knew the *Phoebe,* and he knew her captain, Thomas Hillyer. Hillyer had been in the British Mediterranean fleet when Porter was fighting Barbary pirates. Porter and Hillyer had enjoyed a navy gentlemen's very civilised life in Gibraltar, often in one another's company, often guest and host in turn. Now in Valparaiso, Porter pined for a civilised fight, a duel with ships rather than pistols, the disorder of blood and hate overridden with rules and niceties (Marshall 1825: 2/26–31).

The duel is an apt metaphor for what Porter seemed to have in mind. American naval officers were still precise enough about honour and insult to kill one another. Indeed, as late as 1848, they had killed thirty-six of one another while their enemies had killed only fifty-four of them in all their wars. One of the officers of the *Essex* had been left buried on the Galapagos, killed in that freakish spot by some freakish preoccupation with honour. Precision about the boundaries of honour and even greater precision about the circumstances in which one could kill and be killed were the essence of duelling. There were duels at this time so nicely balanced that one participant's known skill as a marksman was offset by having the pair stand just ten feet apart. The duellists' outstretched pistols reached nearly chest to chest for courage or madness to have their full play. The duelling code, even nicer than parlour etiquette, defined class and group membership powerfully. The code legitimated the highest gamble of all—with life as the stakes—by raising the trivialities of honour above any other obligation or right. Motivation for this apparent extravagance came from socialising forces of enormous strength, the same sort of strength that transformed hesitant human nature in the face of battle into carelessly courageous fighting men (Paullin 1909: 1155–97).

More than seven hundred men in Valparaiso were about to gamble with their lives. From this distance, it seems to make little sense that men should gamble so deeply in a war someone invented, in a battle that did not matter, in a place at the end of the earth that nobody cared about, in circumstances that were so careless over what was worth dying for. Bear with me for making clear what I am saying. I am not rationalising away courage: I am not sceptical of high ideals as determinants of men's actions. I am curious about the sort of social rules men submit themselves to in killing and being killed. Battle, as Keegan helps us understand it, is quintessentially the tension between action; that is, behaviour guided by intention, motivation, plan, and event—behaviour determined by natural conditions, the unforeseen, chance. That is also the stuff of history: it is the start of a philosophy of history writing. (Catch the tension between action and event, between what is universal, repeated, and what is particular, unrepeated, and you have history.) Battle is plan—organisation of bodies of men, scheduled sequences of action, rational exploitation of the environment; but battle is also circumstance, wild instability, unexpected emotional disorder. Battle is the highly formalised, ordered reality of commanders and officers; battle is the boredom, exultation, panic, bewilderment of men. In terms of a present discourse about history and its relationship to the other social sciences, battle is both 'language' and 'speech', system and praxis, structure and form. In their oppositions and combinations these all make history. On the face of it, battle is mad, irrational. There is no communicating its experience, save by living it. Yet there is some understanding of it in the rules that enemies, like duellists, impose and obey.

As an extension of that reflection, let me say with Keegan: 'Battle . . . is essentially a moral conflict. It requires, if it is to take place, a mutual and sustained act of will by two contending parties, and, if it is to result in a decision, the moral collapse of one of them' (Keegan 1977: 296). Keegan, in an effort to describe the dimensions of that moral conflict, offers a list of its qualities. 'What battles have in common is human: the behaviour of men struggling to reconcile their instinct for self-preservation, their sense of honour and achievement of some aim over which other men are ready to kill them.' In this deepest of deep plays that battles are about, in this gamble with death that men undertake in fighting for honour and a goal, in this ultimately asocial or anti-social act of killing one another, they manoeuvre with one another to make a common social stage on which they can do the totally unacceptable in an acceptable way. Battles are filled with plays to make the totally irrational proper.

'The study of battle is always a study of fear and usually of courage, always of leadership, usually of obedience; always of compulsion, sometimes of insubordination; always of anxiety, sometimes of elation or catharsis; always of uncertainty and doubt, misinformation and misapprehension, usually of faith and sometimes of vision; always of violence, sometimes of cruelty, self sacrifice, compassion; above all it is always a study of solidarity and usually also of disintegration' (Keegan 1977: 297–8).

Battles are messily human: it will be a good historian who understands them, a better one who can describe them.

Porter arrived at Valparaiso from the Marquesas on 3 February 1814. In the fourteen months between this visit and his first, the fortunes of the Chilean revolutionary forces under Jose Miguel Carrera had waned a little. Valparaiso, which had excitedly welcomed Porter before— when he seemed to bring American aid to their independence—was more muted now because Spain, with British aid, might win out again (Merrill 1940: 218–23; Rippy 1964; Evans 1927). However, Porter played out to the full his expectancies and theirs as to the proper relations between a navy gentleman and high society. He had misgivings about the Valparaisan ladies' bad teeth and sweatiness when they danced, but invited them nonetheless to dinner on the *Essex*. As luck would have it, Hillyer arrived with the *Phoebe* and the *Cherub* early in the morning after this gala occasion. Wrongly informed at the harbour's entrance by the British consul that the Americans were in disarray, Hillyer blustered into the neutral harbour and almost collided with the *Essex*. Porter and he shouted compliments at one another, to which Porter added a threat that if the *Phoebe's* spar so much as overshadowed the *Essex,* he would blast the *Phoebe* out of the water and board her. Hillyer, though he did not know that the *Essex's* cannons were loaded and boarding parties hidden and ready, had the good sense to back away. Porter grumbled ever after at his own restraint in a neutral port and complained that Hillyer did not show similar gentlemanly restraint when he caught the *Essex* in neutral waters seven weeks later.

Between Hillyer's arrival on 8 February and their battle on 28 March were seven weeks of manoeuvring in which both men tried to set the social environment in which they would fight. The mood between the crews at first was not one of hate. It was rather jolly and competitive. They made extravagant, half-humorous aggressive gestures at one another, done for the sake of supporting spectators more than for their opponents. They paraded on the hulls; they decked their liberty boats; they flew motto flags; they wrote challenging letters. In the evenings they sang 'Yankee Doodle Dandy' and 'God Save the King' at one another.

In keeping with Porter's plan to meet the *Phoebe* in a duel, the crew of the *Essex* wrote a challenge to the crew of the *Phoebe*. They called themselves 'The Sons of Liberty and Commerce'.

'The sons of Liberty and Commerce on board the Saucy Essex whose motto is Free Trade and Sailors' Rights present their compliments to their oppressed brother tars on whose motto is [*sic*] too tedious to mention and hope they will put an end to all this nonsense of singing, sporting and writing, which we know less about than the use of our guns. Send the *Cherub* away. We will meet your frigate and fight you. Then shake hands and be friends and whether you take us or we take you, either will be to your advantage, as in the first case, you will not doubt, for the service you render in a cause every brave and free man detests, be turned over to Greenwich Hospital or to a new ship, on your arrival in England; and if we take you we shall respect the rights of a sailor, hail you as brethren, whom we have liberated from slavery, and place you in future beyond the reach of the press gang.'

The letter inspired a reply in verse:

> To you Americans who seek redress
> For fancied wrongs from Britons you've sustained
> Hear what we Britons now to you address,
> From malice free, from blasphemy unstained.
> Think not, vain boasters, that your insidious lay
> Which calls for vengeance from the Almighty God
> Can from their duty Britons lead away
> Or path of honour which they have always trod.
>
> We love our king, our country, captain too.
> When honour comes, we'll glory in his name,
> Acquit like men and hope you'll do the same.
>
> (*Niles Weekly Register*, 20 August, 1814: 420)

It seemed all froth and unreality, either in innocence or a professionalism that divorced any personal engagement from the deadly seriousness of the occasion. Actually they were not being flippant, or if they were, the mood was changing. Porter fussed about who had written the British verse and implied that it was not quite proper if Hillyer or one of his officers had done it. Hillyer, on the other hand, later referred to the 'Sons of Liberty' letter as 'Porter's insidious effort to shake the loyalty of thoughtless British seamen' (Graham and Humphreys 1962: 132). He did not altogether trust his men to be immune from thoughts about the justice of being pressed. He had had trouble at Rio de Janeiro on the way out. His crew had suffered heavily in a recent engagement in Java and they were fearful of the top-heavy crankiness of the *Phoebe*. He had them under tight discipline. So he began to fly a more ominous motto flag. In reply to the American motto flag, 'God, Our Country and Liberty, Tyrants Offend Them', he flew a motto which said 'God and Country, British Sailors' Best Rights. Traitors Offend Both'. It was ominous because it played on a dangerous ambiguity. Since the beginning of the American Revolution, and especially in the navies, it was not always clear who was British and who was American. Anyone could buy a name and a certificate to it in a United States port, and become by that an American. Yet one of the niceties of naval war at this time was that when the killing was done and that moral submission that Keegan wrote of was made, prisoners were a prize and as a prize had some security in their capital value. The ominous note in Hillyer's motto was the word 'Traitors'. Traitors, like mutineers, could be hanged. Suddenly there was an insecurity in the possibility of being a prisoner, if one could not prove to a sceptical British eye that one was American.

There are larger forces here at work than one might suspect and they have a bearing on the face of battle. In one respect Britain and the United States went to war over an ambiguity. As Europe in the Napoleonic era entered into a bloody redefinition of the nature of war, as production and trade became weapons just as important as soldiers and arms, the problems of making nations' cultural realities seen and accepted became paramount. It is an old sociological adage that violence is the last and least effective instrument of social control, coming after all the other socialising forces have made the social realities more effectively natural and imposing. Nations in the War of 1812 were trying to make a new order with a place for neutrality and citizenship and rightful ownership: they did it violently, trying to make new social realities by force when the ordinary cultural processes would not work. But in these decades there was also an old order of naval warfare that was going. There had been a fine distinction between piracy, privateering and naval action, a marginal area between law and lawlessness, private and public, that was always dangerously ambiguous. The letters of marque that distinguished privateering from piracy legitimated private violence by putting the distribution of profits into public courts. The paraphernalia of trade—shares, stocks, partnerships, auction—might have given privateering the appearance of legitimacy, but the violence actually done in the capture of vessels was hardly distinguishable from piratical violence. There was masquerade and subterfuge and trickery whose uncertainties and ambiguities were hardly wiped away by a few legalising papers (Garitee 1977). Naval action itself had its ambiguities. The prize system meant the crews had a private interest in warlike activity supported by the state. The state's monopoly of power and the clear claim to it was clouded by private claims that in any other guise would have been robbery and mayhem. Porter himself continually likened his activities in the Pacific to Lord Anson's, whose *Centurion* had captured a Manila galleon and had made his private fortune. The *Essex* had collected $50 000 in gold specie from her first capture and by the time she had reached Valparaiso carried a fortune. She was rumoured to have landed $2 000 000 in gold at Valparaiso before the battle. Porter's getting of his fortune had been by all the subterfuges of ambiguous identity, showing wrong colours, disguising the *Essex*, masquerading as British. He had arranged with his subordinates to show false colours if they came across the *Phoebe* unexpectedly until they could get close enough to destroy her with carronades. That 'all is fair in love and war' might be proverbial, but in fact, Porter invested great effort in trying to show that the British had not been fair, and just as much effort to catch his own unfair advantage over them.

Sent home after the battle in a cartel, that is, in the *Essex Junior* under his command with papers from Hillyer allowing him through the British blockade, he was so offended by a British captain's suspicions and search that he declared himself a prisoner not a prize and became thereby freed of his gentleman's agreement not to escape. He daringly rowed to freedom to the New Jersey coast and spent long hours writing up the rights and wrongs of the incident.

Establishment of the correct rubric under which the crews could do battle in ambiguous circumstances was a trial, and in the ambiguity the jolly mood between them changed. Hillyer took the *Phoebe* and *Cherub* out of Valparaiso, away from the challenges, and then blockaded the port. After the battle when he had nothing but praise for Porter's gallantry, he had one complaint. Porter had allowed his men to jump overboard and swim ashore. More than fifty did. To Hillyer they were lost prizes and he demanded careful accuracy in the accounting for them. For the escapees the incident ended their uncertainty at the changed rituals of being beaten.

The checks and counterchecks of chivalry and the search for rubrics under which to do battle were more numerous than can be recorded here. It was reported to Hillyer that Porter had called him a coward, so he sent a messenger under a flag of truce to inquire if it were true. Did a signal from the *Phoebe* mean that the challenge of the duel had been accepted? And would a gentleman have allowed the ambiguity? Prisoners, prizes from captured whalers, escaped from the *Essex*. Would not a gentleman on the *Phoebe* have returned them? But would a gentleman on the *Essex* have kept them in irons? Does Porter's burning of two captured whaling ships in the harbour constitute a breach of neutrality? The weeks went by. Porter was conscious that the *Raccoon* would be back from the north-west coast and there was news that other British vessels were on their way around Cape Horn. Soon Porter's position would be hopeless. In the end an accident made him quickly decide to gamble. In a brisk breeze, his cable broke. The *Phoebe* was downwind on her blockade. Porter unfurled sail and made a dash. As he left the harbour a sharp gust of wind snapped his main topmast. Four or five men spilled into the sea. There was no stopping to rescue them, but his own chance of escape was gone. The topmast was his key to fighting manoeuvrability. He desperately made for the shelter of Chilean waters, not to Valparaiso harbour, but to a small bay outside it. He was at pains afterwards to show precisely where he was: half a pistol shot from the shore, within range but not within sight of the harbour fort. Was it a neutral place or was it not? Hillyer thought not, and the *Phoebe* and *Cherub* closed in on the *Essex* with *Essex Junior* standing a little way off. The *Essex* was anchored under the bluffs of a high hill on which thousands of Valparaisans began to collect to see a battle.

The fighting was in two parts. The first began at 4 p.m. and lasted for thirty minutes when the *Phoebe* withdrew from the *Essex's* damaging fire. The second began again at 5.35 p.m. and went on till 6.25 p.m. when Hillyer realised that Porter had lowered his flag. In the first phase the *Essex* was anchored into an offshore breeze. Porter's chief efforts were to pull the *Essex* round on 'springs' to bring his broadside to bear on the *Phoebe*. His carronades were all broadside. He had only three long guns in the stern and three in the bow. Hillyer, knowing the *Essex* very well, angled himself to the *Essex's* stern and sent the Cherub to an equivalent post at the *Essex's* bow. Porter's efforts to bring the *Essex* around failed. The 'springs' put up with great courage by the carpenter's crew were three times shot away. Porter was justly proud of those first thirty minutes of battle (*Naval Chronicle* 1814: 32/168–71; Kemble 1931: 199–202; Smith 1974: 198; *Niles Weekly Register* 16 July, 1814: 340–1).

The *Essex* was raked by broadsides of thirteen 18-pound, one 12-pound, one 9-pound long guns from the *Phoebe* and two 9-pound long guns from the *Cherub*, while she could only bring three 12-pound long guns on the *Phoebe* and three (perhaps only one) long guns on the *Cherub*. In the language naval historians like to use in balancing the odds, the *Phoebe's* 320 men could throw in broadside 254 pounds of shot at the *Essex* from her long guns. *Essex's* 255 men could only throw back 66 pounds from her long guns at the *Phoebe* and *Cherub*. The *Essex*, of course, had a massive 504 pounds in her carronade broadside. (*Phoebe* had 242 pounds of carronade as well.) Hillyer stood off at what he described as half-a-gunshot distance, probably seven or eight hundred yards. It was just beyond the practical range of the *Essex's* carronades on the angle they were being forced to fire. The killing on the *Essex* was frightful, yet the *Phoebe* was punished enough to make her withdraw. It was the *Phoebe's* rigging and sails that were damaged. Only four British seamen were killed in the whole battle, and only one seriously wounded. It would have been Porter's tactic at this time not so much to kill as to damage (James 1817: 312–14; Roosevelt 1882: 307).

Hillyer described this stage of the battle as a 'little inauspicious'. A shot had passed through his half-furled mainsail, and his jibboom and mainstay were down. A half an hour was enough to restore order on the *Phoebe*, and he wore back against the breeze to the *Essex's* port quarter where he held the *Phoebe* broadside on springs. The *Essex* was already a near wreck. When Porter cut his cable to ride down the wind on to the *Phoebe,* the only sail left to raise was a flying jib. No sooner had he done that than the wind shifted and he was driven away. What he had described as a 'hot raking fire' before he now called a 'most galling fire', as nearly every shot from the *Phoebe* fired home on the smooth seas. His officers were gone, two blown overboard by splinters. His whole carpenter's crew had been killed. After a half hour he reckoned that only seventy-five of his men were capable of fighting. Never one lacking in a dramatic gesture, he decided to blow up the ship. The crew, he said, entreated him to surrender. They had some cause to believe he might end it all dramatically: he had once shot a sentry in the thigh when he found him asleep: he had tarred and feathered a sailor who did not want to take the oath of allegiance; he had held a match to a gunpowder barrel when threatened with mutiny. He listened to their entreaties, however, and made an effort to drive the *Essex* ashore. The winds were not with him on this day and they changed again to leave the *Essex* at the mercy of the *Phoebe's* 18-pounders. He ordered the colours to be lowered. For ten minutes the *Phoebe* kept firing. Hillyer said later that they had been slow to see the flag lowered and slow to hear the command to cease fire. In fact both ships had gone to battle with all their motto flags flying and their rigging alive with jacks. In the middle of the first part of the battle and seeing Hillyer's 'ridiculous' display, Porter ordered more jacks fixed to the mast. No doubt fighting commanders have a careful eye for each other's ensigns, even in the tangle of wrecked rigging. A British midshipman said that they saw the man sent aloft to get the *Essex*'s colours carried away by a shot, colours and all. A man might die putting symbols up: a man might die pulling symbols down.

When the firing stopped, Hillyer sent a boat 'to take possession of the prize'. The first aboard the *Essex* described the scene:

'I was in the first boat that broached her. Nothing was to be seen all over her decks but dead, wounded and dying . . . One poor fellow had his thigh shot off, managed to crawl to a port and tumble himself into the water which put an end to his misery . . . Captain Porter was in tears when he went on board the *Phoebe* and gave up his sword and he told Captain Hillyer that there were fifteen of his brave fellows killed after she struck' (Henderson 1970: 167).

Porter was more composed the next morning over breakfast with Hillyer. They compared notes and logs and had a solemn little debate as to whether the battle had begun at 3.50 or 4 p.m. They fussed over the number of prisoners there should be. No doubt Hillyer would have let Porter see the carpenter's report on the *Phoebe*. She had taken seven 32-pounders 'between wind and water' and one 12-pounder three inches under water. Thirteen 32-pounders had gone into her waist as well as some grapeshot and musket balls. Four men were dead, including Lieutenant Ingraham, who had been popular with the Americans and who, they said, had not agreed with the propriety of his captain standing off to slaughter the enemy. There were many more conversations and letters. Porter's son later wrote:

'It is pleasant to see the courtesies of life maintained even between the citizens of nations at war with one another, for there is no reason why gentlemen bred to arms should not practise these little civilities which tend to soften asperities, and often ameliorate the conditions of capture' (Porter 1875: 222).

The first thirty minutes of the battle were a lifetime for many on the *Essex*. That we cannot say precisely how many is symptomatic of the difficulty in describing the face of battle. Hillyer on the *Phoebe* had his secretary at his side, watch in hand, and noting every order and its time. Hillyer had a practised eye for history. The face of *his* battle had a bureaucratic look. He was careful for what he would have to say in the face of either victory or defeat. Porter, at least in the battle, was more naive and had enough to occupy himself in the present without worrying either about history or the future. In the battle he had stood in an exposed position, yet only received a bruised arm and a headache when he was pounded into the deck by the windage of a cannonball close over his head. David Farragut, a future first admiral of the United States navy, but then a fifteen-year-old midshipman and Porter's foster son, reported a quiet concerned conversation he had with Porter in the midst of this mayhem. Farragut became covered in blood when a seaman was decapitated on the stairs above him and the corpse crashed down on him. As he came somewhat dazed on to the deck, Porter asked him whether he was wounded and when he said he was not Porter suggested that he should have the tubes of gunpowder he had been fetching and that he should go and get them (Lewis 1941: 99). The face of Porter's battle is hard to catch. He had done his fighting, as it were, in the months before, in the drilling of his crew. Now the minutes of the battle do not seem long enough to allow him to do what he did—ordering changes of sails, setting springs, moving guns, clearing debris, extinguishing fires, supervising discipline. He fought now by being unflinching and by personifying them all in his symbolic acts of authority and patriotism.

It is difficult to catch the face of battle of all the rest. David Farragut remembered that it was the first death that left its imprint on his mind:

'It was a boatswain's mate, his abdomen taken entirely out and he expired in a few moments, but they soon fell so fast around me that it appeared like a dream and produced no effect on my mind. I well remember, while standing near the captain just abaft the mainmast a shot came through the waterways which glanced upward, killing four men who stood by the side of the gun, taking the last man in the head, and his brains flew over us both, but it made no such impression on me as the death of the first man. I neither thought of nor noticed anything but the working of the guns' (Lewis 1941: 99).

'Fighting' on a 'fighting' ship was not doing violence to a person or target seen. It was total preoccupation with particular tasks. These were regular tasks to which they were drilled—loading, priming, sponging, running back the guns, carrying balls and powder. The seaman beat known paths, probably not moving more than a few steps out of their drilling territory. But then there were extraodinary things to do—clear the tangle of rigging, move heavy spars, extinguish the fires that carronade wads made, remove the dead and wounded that fell around them. Behind the screen of smoke and noise, which they themselves made, everything else was blotted out. Occasionally they saw a ball coming at them, even dodged it. Mostly the violence intruded unpredictably on them. Cannonballs did not explode bodies into nothingness, they ploughed through men and things with terrible effect, leaving a carnage of limbs and bodies, blood and all the dread detritus of those violently killed.

David Dixon Porter reported later, no doubt out of reflective conversations, that his father believed the *Phoebe* fired 700 rounds of her 18-pound long guns in the battle (Porter 1875: 259). Only thirteen of her twenty-six would have been firing. Naval gunners of the time calculated that the fastest rate at which cannons might fire would be three rounds in five minutes (Padfield 1973: 111). Whirling through, then, ten and more at a time or coming through seven or eight in a minute, the *Phoebe*'s ball swept the upper decking, bursting through the canvas and hammocks that were hung in the rigging against sharp shooters. Or they splintered through the 1 foot 5 inch thick wooden sides into the decks below. The cockpit of the *Essex,* the traditional place deep in the ship for surgeons to treat wounded, was quickly filled. But the cannonballs burst through even here and men were killed while in the surgeons' hands. Porter himself in trying to convey how fierce the action was, said that fifteen men on one gun were killed, its crew replaced three times over.

It was a gunner's art not to charge his gun so much that the ball would smash through the ship's side cleanly at high speed. He would want it to penetrate slowly enough to do the greatest damage (Douglas 1851: 84–5). Splinters did the killing. Like shrapnel, they cut swathes through crowded bodies. There were 255 men aboard the *Essex*. They fought on two decks, about 140 feet long and at their widest 34 feet (Smith 1974; Toner 1906: 1/1136–9). What that meant in real space, that is, space diminished by forty-six guns, as well as hatchways and masts, is difficult to imagine. At any time she was crowded. Fighting, the *Essex* must have been a tangle of activity. To those closed in on the gun-deck, just as much as to those squeezed into her open waist and surrounded in the end by more than a hundred mutilated dead and wounded, splinters and cannonballs must have taken those around them in some lottery of death. In the way of reticent memories of battle, the survivors did not talk of the smells and sights and sounds, and they had not time to reflect on the mystery of such lotteries that took a face or a stomach or a leg that by any other accident could have been theirs.

It is no discovery of this study that so much of the face of battle goes unrecorded or, if recorded, is coded in the formal language of battle. A British midshipman's report that after the battle there were forty-four amputations by the surgeons leaves questions almost too prurient to ask as to how high a pile of forty-four lost limbs might be or how men behaved in ridding the ship of them (Henderson 1970: 167). The same midshipman reported that the British threw sixty-three American dead overboard. Like the slops of life? How did the treatment of the dead relate to the grand rhetoric that was soon to describe their reasons for dying? Did they see any contradictions between their banners of 'Free Trade and Sailors' Rights' and the things they saw in the tides the morning after?

Memories left to us of this battle are few—Hillyer's log and letters, Porter's official report, memoirs of an older David Farragut, stories in newspapers of the time cannibalised of other newspapers, snippets from various witnesses that contemporaries collected. These memories are the past written down, history. They are texts that have their own literary form. They shape the face of battle in their own structures. Hillyer's told of his realism in not throwing away the advantages he had, and the sensible things he did in backing away and fighting with his long guns from a distance. He was generous in victory, returning Porter his sword, full of praise for the *Essex's* crew's courage. He was matter-of-fact in reporting damage, understating in his complaints that Porter had let prizes escape. The face of his battle in his memory of it was what an Admiralty would see. Porter's was blustering, full of what-might-have-beens if only he himself had been more ungentlemanly and Hillyer more gentlemanly. He was proud of his crew and blamed circumstances not them for their defeat. The face of his battle was the roles he properly played. Admiral Farragut's memories were clear, honed to the didactic purposes to which they had been often put, wise in their hindsight view of mistakes and better tactics. The face of his battle was his eternal advantage of having been there.

Memories made sense of the battle: that was their function: that was their literary form. The senselessness of the battle experience is excluded from memory and therefore from history. There was a public memory of the Battle of Valparaiso created in the instant legends that were made of it. They were the stories of the battle published in *Niles Weekly Register* and repeated in newspapers all around the United States. To remark that they were instant legend, of course, is to prejudice an answer to the question whether they were legend or memory or experience. Perhaps it would be better to remark that they were experiences abstracted in memory for their heightened meaning and made legendary by the expectancies that they described what should have been. The stories concerned acts of sacrifice and acts of cowardice.

John Ripley, after losing a leg, said 'Farewell boys, I can be of no use to you' and hopped out of the bow port. John Alvison received a cannonball (18lb) through the body; in the agony of death he exclaimed, 'Never mind shipmates, I die in the defense of 'free trade and sailors' r-i-g-h-t-s' and expired with the word 'rights' on his lips. John Anderson had his left leg shot off and died animating his shipmates to fight bravely in defense of liberty. After the engagement, Benjamin Hazen, having dressed himself in a clean shirt and jerkin, addressed his remaining messmates and telling them that he could never submit to be a prisoner to the

English, threw himself into the sea (*Niles Weekly Register*, 20 August, 1814: 420).

There were other stories: of Lieutenant J. G. Cowell with a leg shot off above the knee dying of loss of blood but refusing the privilege of rank to get precedence with a surgeon—'Fair play's a jewel, doctor. One man's life is as dear as another's. I would not cheat any poor fellow of his turn.' Of Bissley, leg shot off near the groin—'I left my own country and adopted the United States to fight for her. I hope I have this day proved myself worthy of the country of my adoption. I am no longer of any use to you and I will not be a burden to her, so goodbye'. On the other hand, William Roach was found 'skulking' on the berth deck. Young Farragut went after him with a pistol to execute him, and William Cole, weltering in his own blood, his leg hanging on by its skin, dragged his shattered stump along the deck, pistol in hand, to get a shot at Roach as well.

The stories hold the inaccuracies that might be expected of such newspaper reports. Names are wrongly spelt: some are untraceable in the ships' muster rolls. They are all that is left of the face of battle of so many, however. Whether one accepts the likelihood of them being true will depend on the degree of one's scepticism. Suicide in one's best shirt and jerkin might seem an extravagant gesture against becoming a British prisoner. Pursuit of a coward to kill him when the British were doing everything in their power to kill them all, on the other hand, might ring true. Putting fine phrases on dying men's lips might belong to a vision of what dying properly should be more than a description of what actually happened. On the other hand, it is a quality of symbolic human behaviour to translate what is untranslatable into a slogan or a gesture.

I find these 'instant legends' very revealing. I began with the puzzle of the triviality of the cause and the unreality of the circumstances in this deep play of the Battle of Valparaiso. In one respect it is a false puzzle because I cut the seamless web and separated this moment of battle from the social context of the sailors' lives. We know the names, at least, of every man who participated in the battle. Of some of them we have bits of information—what they had done or what had been done to them—enough of what they were in order to know something of who they were. Of all of them we can give a social history of their public roles and relations, enough to sense the total institutions of their ships. By that we can gauge the processes by which in such total institutions where the public domain is total and private boundaries tiny, perspectives on what is trivial are lost. To understand the deep play of Valparaiso, go to the institutional relations that ensured that the sailors were all preoccupied with themselves. On ships there was no outside world. On ships in battle there was hardly even an enemy.

But that deep play has an historical as well as a structural explanation. History feeds on its own meaning. A slogan 'Free Trade and Sailors' Rights', senseless at first, becomes history as it is seen to give meaning to all that is happening. Hillyer and Porter sculpted their battle. Their posturings with one another made them champions. Porter, certainly, in the battle had more authority to be the *Essex* than he had ever had. In the battle his men kept urging him on, as if he were they. 'Don't give up, Logan', they shouted above the din. 'Logan' was their nickname for him. In all the seven weeks of manoeuvring, as they made their rules, as their mood changed, their slogans became history, mythical. 'Free Trade and Sailors' Rights' became not so much a cause of war as a means of identity. It is altogether believable that they would die with it on their lips. It was true because it encoded all that had happened to make them who they were.

Presenting the Past
HISTORY'S THEATRE

T HEATRE is a fearsome thing for fundamentalists of every sort. For those who believe that the truth is on the surface of things, there is no comfort in having to work for it. To discover, too, that love and hate, good and bad, and all of living can be represented, is to set the mind wondering whether all the world is a stage. Worse, to turn oneself into something else by acting, raises the question what else do we have in our power to transform.

'Tell me, sir', Herman Melville has his *Confidence Man* ask his mark as he sets him up with feigned innocence, 'do you really think a white could look the negro so? For one, I should call it pretty good acting'. 'Not much better than any other man acts', the mark replies, displaying his worldliness. 'How? Does all the world act? Am *I*, for instance, an actor? Is my reverend friend here, too, a performer?' 'Yes, don't you perform acts? To do, is to act; so all doers are actors'. And how is sham evident?, the *Confidence Man* asks. 'To the discerning eye', the mark replies, 'with a horrible screw of his gimlet eye'.

Melville, in this the most despairing and skeptical of his novels, sets 'wink upon wink upon wink', and has us believe there is no 'discerning eye' good enough to see what is really happening in the global Bartholomew's Fair that is commercial capitalism. The fundamentalists have no trust either in anybody's discerning eye other than their own. So they are forever telling what the good discerning eye should see.

I think that we never know the truth by being told it. We have to experience it in some way. That is the abiding grace of history. It is the theatre in which we experience truth. But we have to work at it, because the truth is always clothed in some way by story. History is always parable to the truth. The truth is always there but in some other form than we might expect. The truth is there with the same qualities with which we experience it in everyday life—sometimes uncertainly, sometimes contradictorily, sometimes clouded by the forces that drive us to it, sometimes so clearly that it blinds us to anything else.

Of course, it is only the romantic and the totalitarian who believe that the theatre of their histories drives a reader to the one truth and the one meaning they want to display. Reading and interpreting is much more roguish. Some years ago, the Commonwealth Government tried to educate the Australian public to the dangers of AIDS by creating some theatre in a television clip. Death, the Grim Reaper, was shown as a figure playing ten-pin bowling. The bowling pins were men, women and children. They bounced and clattered away randomly as Death scored. There was some alarm expressed at the time at the brutal starkness of the advertisement. Many felt it was too shocking. It was overkill, some said. Then we learned in the weeks that followed that the chief effect of the advertisement was a sharp drop in the membership of ten-pin bowling clubs.

It is a depressing story for anyone who thinks that writing history is theatre. How does one produce the effects one wants in one's stories? Presumably, if one knew that, one could rule the world or at least sell a lot of something. Maybe the answer is that one can never be sure of producing the effects one wants. Maybe Roland Barthes was correct: the reader is the true writer of the text. Maybe a history writer should think of him or herself as a composer. That way it is the reader who is the performer and the thing performed, the history I write, is the score for all sorts of flights of the imagination. I think I can settle for that. A book on a shelf has a sort of immortality. And if I could use my experience as a reader to buoy my spirits as a writer, I know that the text of even the most forgotten book can make the imagination soar.

'Nothing is more free than the imagination of man', David Hume wrote—a little too exclusively for our current linguistic tastes—in his *Enquiry Concerning Human Understanding* (1748), 'and though it cannot exceed that original stock of ideas furnished by the internal and external senses, it has unlimited powers of mixing, compounding, separating and dividing these ideas, in all the varieties of fiction and vision. I can feign a train of events, with all the appearances of reality, ascribe to them a particular time and place, conceive them as existant, and paint them out to itself with every circumstance, that belongs to any historical fact, which it believes with the greatest certainty. Wherein, therefore, consists the difference between such a fiction and belief?'

Wherein, indeed?

The Theatricality of
History Making and the
Paradoxes of Acting

Prologue (Playful)

M T HELICON, we must assume, was the original Humanities
Research Centre. At least the nine Mousai or 'Mindful Ones'
had tenure there. They began in a fairly undifferentiated, we might
almost say interdisciplinary, way, but visiting scholars introduced a little
entrepreneurial competition. So the nine daughters of Zeus were made
to fit, if not into departments, then into specialised consultancies:
Calliope (Heroic Epic), Euterpe (Flutes), Terpsicore (Lyric Poetry—
Dance) and Erato (Lyric Poetry—Hymns), Melpomene (Tragedy),
Thalia (Comedy), Polyhymnia (Mimic Art), Urania (Astronomy) and,
of course, Clio (History). Naturally they were judges and examiners in
most of the important international competitions and prizes. They
kept standards high, and some competitors suffered from their objectivity, notably the Sirens, who were obliged to re-tool or become
redundant.

Originally the Muses were associated with springs and pools.
Running water inspired: still water reflected. But with specialisation
came institutionalisation and they ended up in museums. Consultancy
outside museums had its problems. It usually ended up in a blank
stare, which was called 'being amused'. At the other extreme was the
intense young man Narcissus. He actually went to Mt Helicon, trying
to escape a pretty young plagiarist called Echo, who had the annoying
habit of repeating everything everybody said. He paused by the still

waters, made a reflection, fell in love with it and was transformed into a flower. Reflexivity can do that.

Clio, being first-born, always had a superior air. She was depicted crowned with laurels and usually held a trumpet in one hand and a book in the other. References, it seems, have always been important. Clio's name meant 'Glory'. There has always been an expectancy that history blows somebody's trumpet.

Prologue (Even More Playful)

History-making—transformations of lived experience into narratives—is a universal and everyday human phenomenon. It has an anthropology, as it has a criticism and a history. This narrating in history-making is itself lived experience, not something apart from lived experience. In all its varied expressions narrating is, in Roy Wagner's word, an impersonation—the clustering of signifying actions into recognisable roles, such as bard, novelist, prophet, historian . . . This narrating is itself lived experience: in Aristotle's word, mythopoetic, the emplotment that engages an audience in its interpretation. This narrating is itself lived experience: In John Dewey's word, 'an' experience, pulled out of the stream of consciousness and given dramatic form. This narrating is itself lived experience: in Greg Dening's words, metonymic of the present, metaphoric of the past; it presents the past with the double meaning of the word 'presents'. Narrating both makes a now of the past and delivers the past in some dramatic display.

'Theory' and 'theatre' come to us out of the same Greek origin—*thea*, sight, viewing; *theoros*, spectator. Theory—a mind-set for viewing; theatre—a space-set for spectatoring; theatrical—a convention-set for mimesis. 'The theater', wrote Roland Barthes, 'is precisely the practice which calculates the place of things, as they are observed. If I set the spectacle here, the spectator will see this; if I put it elsewhere, he will not, and I can avail myself of this masking effect and play on the illusions it provides. The stage is the line which stands across the path of the optical pencil, tracing at once the point at which it is brought to a stop and, as it were, the threshold of its ramifications. Thus is found, against music (against text)—representation. Representation is not defined directly by imitation: even if one gets rid of the 'real', of the '*vraisemblable*', of the 'copy', there will be representation for so long as the subject (author, reader, spectator, or voyeur) casts his gaze toward a horizon on which he cuts out the base of a triangle, his eye (or his mind) forming the apex'.

The 'theatricality of history-making' involves the notion of viewing in a space so closed around with convention that the audience and actors enter into the conspiracy of their own illusions. The paradox is that self-awareness, performance consciousness, does not disturb the realisms of their understanding.

Leaves of a commonplace book . . .

This Poet is that Poet's plagiary
And he a third's, till they end all in Homer
And Homer filch't all from an Aegyptian Preestesse.
The World's a Theater of theft.

Thomas Tomkis, 1615

For myself, I prefer to utilize [rather than comment on] the writers I like. The only valid tribute to thought such as Nietzsche's is precisely to use it, to deform it, to make it groan and protest. And if a commentator says I am unfaithful to Nietzsche, that is of absolutely no interest.

Michel Foucault, 1975

The best grounds for choosing one perspective on history rather than another are ultimately aesthetic or moral rather than epistemological.

Hayden White, 1973

The development of civilisations is essentially a progression of metaphors.

E. L. Doctorow, 1977

The importance of innovative extension cannot be overstressed. Meaning is ultimately involved in every conscious cultural act, and cannot justifiably be detached from the events and actions through which it is constituted, or from the modes of its production. Eventless meanings are as inconceivable in a cultural context as meaningless events. The creation of meaning shares the rhythm of man's active and productive life; it neither forms nor presupposes a 'closed system' because, like the life of a society, it is 'open-ended' and ongoing. Human actions are additive, serial and cumulative; each individual act standing in a particular relationship to the life of the individual or the group, and it also 'adds' something in a literal or figurative sense, to these continuities and to the situation itself. Thus every act, however habitual or repetitive, extends the culture of the actor in a certain sense.

Roy Wagner, 1972

Life is no uniform uninterrupted march or flow. It is a thing of histories, each with its own plot, its own inception and movement towards its close, each having its own particular movement.

John Dewey, 1934

[Human solidarity] is to be achieved not by inquiry but by imagination, the imaginative ability to see strange people as fellow sufferers . . . This process of coming to see other human beings as 'one of us' rather than as 'them' is a matter of detailed description of what unfamiliar people are like and of redescription of what we ourselves are like. This is a task not for theory but for genres such as ethnography, the journalist's report, the comic book, the docudrama, and, especially, the novel. Fiction like that of Dickens, Olive Schreiner, or Richard Wright gives us details about kinds of suffering being endured by people to whom we had previously not attended. Fiction like that of Chodeleros de Laclos, Henry James, or Nabokov gives us the details about what sorts of cruelty we ourselves are capable of, and thereby lets us redescribe ourselves. That is why the novel, the movie, and the TV program have gradually, but steadily, replaced the sermon and the treatise as the principle vehicles of moral change and progress.

Richard Rorty, 1989

To paraphrase Abbie Hoffman, there is a manner in which one may legitimately say that the role of political theorist is to shout theater in a crowded fire.

Tracey B. Strong, 1978

An Ethnographic Present of an Ethnographic Moment

I make an ethnographic present out of a very ethnographic moment, the years between 1767 when Samuel Wallis 'discovered' Tahiti and 1797 when European hegemony established a first institutional presence in the central Pacific in a mission station. These years were towards the end of the period in which European *philosophes* exhilaratingly and self-consciously knew themselves to be 'enlightened'. Identifying with those who, as Immanuel Kant described them, 'dared to know', belonged to the naming process of discourse. We know the comfort it brings. The 'Enlightenment' of one century is 'structuralism', 'neo-marxism', 'post-modernism' of another. Recognition of keywords, a sense of the meta-phoric nature of styles of thought, a feeling that what one has just read is what one was about to say, knowing the truth in the caricatures of oppositional stands made by one's associates, knowing on the other hand how untrue the stereotypifications are of oneself—all the stuff by which paradigms and epistemes are made and seen—had given for nearly a hundred years a tribal sense to the lovers of criticism, the 'enlightened'. They had been to the top of the mountain with Petrarch and opened Augustine's Confessions with him there. 'Men went forth to behold the high mountains and the mighty surge of the sea, and the broad stretches of the rivers and the inexhaustible ocean, and the paths of the stars and so doing lose themselves in wonderment'. 'A new thought seized me', Petrarch had written, 'transporting me from space into time' (Gebser 1984: 13–14). To have discovered that everything in nature, everything in human beings was set in time, that the abstractions of law, science and the market, even God himself, were in time was indeed enlightening. It made for a season of observing.

Those years of the late eighteenth century were years in which England itself was thought to be eminently observable. Anglophilia was strong among the 'enlightened', mostly because the English were deemed to have managed time so well, so expediently and so stylishly, in government, in law, in political economy, in religion, in moral philosophy. Joseph Addison had helped make it so as 'The Spectator' in *The Spectator*. 'I live

107

in the World rather as a Spectator of Mankind, than as one of the Species'. 'I have acted all the Parts of my life as a Looker-On' (Marshall 1986: 9). Irony was the enlightened's trope, the spectator's worldliness. Irony requires a perspective, a line of vision that the looker-on has but that the participant does not. Of course, this can often be merely a matter of physical angles of vision in which one can be enlightened by seeing something from a different angle. But perspective is more composed than that. Perspective is the persuasion that vision is geometric and that our representations are the more real by that. The tricks of seeing the parts of the world 'as if' from the point of the pyramid of one's mind's eye are many. They were largely elaborated in the Enlightenment.

The exhilaration at seeing the world from new perspectives was manifold. From a balloon, in a microscope, through a telescope, by the precision of a perfect callibrating machine, the world looked different and inspired description. Above all the world looked different from a ship. 'Navigation' was a subject in every school, even the most landlocked, as the measurability of the heavens made the earth measurable as well. But 'navigation' was really the metaphor of the age as the world was encompassed. Our ethnographic present of 1767 to 1797 was supremely a moment of voyaging. *Voyage into Substance*, Barbara Stafford (1984) has called it, to indicate the eyes of Europe's ships probing eclectically into anything new—into icebergs, waterspouts, Banksia trees, cannibals, *hula* dances . . . In many ways it was the actual voyaging more than the discovered substances that excited. It was the experiencing of otherness rather than otherness itself. That was its theatre. The market for vicarious voyaging was immense. The mountain of texts describing that experiencing of otherness grew high. Paintings, engravings, journals, government reports, inside stories, pantomimes, ballets, poems—the ethnographic output was vast. And every single text of it had the reflective character of every ethnographic experience. It mirrored self in the vision of the other. It mirrored all those hegemonies that suborn self in suborning the other.

This season for observing, 1767 to 1797, was a short and intensive period in which the Pacific was *theatrum mundi*. It was a period in which the nations of Europe and the Americas saw themselves acting out their scientific, humanistic selves. Government-sponsored expeditions from England, France and Spain followed one another, self-righteously conscious of their obligations to observe, describe and publish, to be humane and to contribute to the civilising process of natives out of their superior arts and greater material wealth. It was a time of intensive theatre of the civilised to the native, but of even more intense theatre of the civilised to one another. The civilised jostled to see what the Pacific said to them of their relations of dominance. They vied in testing the extensions of their sovereignty and the effectiveness of their presence—through territorial possessions, protected lines of communication, exemplary empire. They shouted to natives, in that loud and slow way we use to communicate with those that do not share our language, the meaning of flags and cannons and property and trade, and lessons of civilised behaviour. But they were always conscious that this theatre was a play within a play. It was about world systems of power, about reifications of empire, about encompassing the globe, and hegemony. We historians for decades have poured scorn on the metaphor of the 'expansion' of Europe (Wesseling 1978: 1–16). Yet the theatre of the Pacific was about making that unreal metaphor real at home and abroad.

Theatricality is deep in every cultural action. Even if our sign worlds seem unconsciously performed, in hindsight, in our vernacular history-making, we will catch our performance consciousness and know how we manage the signs, make distinctions in the level of their meanings. That theatricality, always present, is intense when the moment being experienced is full of ambivalences. The 'encounters in place' of natives and strangers in the Pacific, 1767 to 1797, were full of such charades that were directed at producing effects in others. Government, law, property, justice, empire, civilisation and God were represented by the strangers in gesture, stylised action, and all the props of flags and weapons. The natives had their theatre too. The intruding strangers were mimicked or mocked or explained away. The ambivalences of the occasion were danced or sung or told in story or painted or carved. My thesis for this ethnographic present of an ethnographic moment is that I must present its theatre and its theatricality if I would represent what actually happened. Not what really happened. I do no care so much about what really happened. About what actually happened, I do.

ANTI-THEATRE

The phrase 'theatricality of history-making' is likely to sound threatening. Jonas Barish in his study *The Anti-Theatrical Prejudice* (1981) begins by remarking how some words, such as musical, symphonic, lyric, sculptural, poetic, epic, have a eulogistic quality, while others have overtones of hostility—theatrical, operatic, melodramatic, stagey. They are 'cheer' and 'boo' words, in an older theory of linguistic development. So 'putting on an act', 'playing up to', 'putting on a performance', 'making a spectacle of oneself', 'playing to the gallery' are nuanced towards insincerity and the emptiness of signs. The theatre is threatening. It always has been.

So the notion that history-making is theatrical is threatening, too. History-making, whether one understands it as an everyday vernacular activity and/or especially if one sees it as an élite and guilded activity is known to be a serious affair. Vernacular history has created too much pain and division to be clownish about it. Academic history has made too much a science of Apollonian sincerity to be playfully Dionysian about it. Conference room floors are likely to seethe at the suggestion that Clio might be subject to an anthropology of performance.

Let it be. I say with Richard Rorty '. . . the distinctions between absolutism and relativism, between rationality and irrationality, and between morality and expediency [and between past and present, representation and reality, ideographic and nomothetic, structure and form] are obsolete and clumsy tools—remnants of a vocabulary we should try to replace . . . So my strategy will be to try to make vocabulary in which these objections look back, thereby changing the subject, rather than granting the objector his choice of weapons and terrain by meeting his criticisms head-on' (Rorty 1989: 44).

The language of the theories of history-making have become so unrelated to the practice of history-making that maybe I should begin again by talking to myself. That way, at least, one practitioner will be heard.

SOLILOQUY ONE
On Soliloquy, Prologue and Authorial Presence

Authorial presence is disturbing. We are practised theatre critics of our everyday representations. So we know the ambivalences of our own presence. We are used to thick description of the meanings behind the appearance of things. We know how complicated and untrustworthy an 'I' is. We know when silence is golden and how mawkish speaking the unspeakable can be. And in any case, 'the history that showed things as they really were is the strongest narcotic of our century', wrote Walter Benjamin (1955: 217, 253). Absorption of representation in itself is a comfortable sort of theatre. Players looking out from the stage and incorporating the audience into the play or even making the audience the object of representation, blur the genres, leave an awkward feeling.

That is why Raymond Williams claims that soliloquies are something more than a stage device to reveal an inner mind or resolve internal conflicts. Soliloquies, he writes, are ontologically subversive. Audiences are taught to accept a conventionality that allows them to discover in dramatic form new and altered relationships, perceptions of self and others, complex alternatives of private and public thought (Agnew 1986: 112; Williams 1981: 141, 148).

Prologues, too, are ontologically subversive. Prologues are more than just beginnings. The prologue fills that marginal space between the conventionality of everyday living and the conventionalities of being in the theatre. The prologue mediates one and the other, educates the audience to its own role, blinkers the audience to its different way of thinking, prepares it for reflexivity and criticism, and most dangerously, liberates the audience's interpretive skills. By tradition, the deliverer of the prologue entered by a 'stage door' which was not part of the scenery but marked a special entry place of someone who for the moment was neither actor nor audience, but in-between, distinct by being a didact, dangerous by being an ironist, disturbing by being a relativist. On him or her there traditionally focused a deep anti-theatrical prejudice. The imagination he or she sparked was dialogic and by that the audience was enticed into the conspiracy of its own engagement in making realism. For those convinced by religion or politics or philosphy that realism was not of their own making, this representative of representing was a very dangerous clown (Hogan 1968: lxxiv; Knapp 1961: 204; Nicholl 1927: 10; Stallybrass and White 1986: 84).

There are those, of course, who protest that the 'I-witness' of the author is the ultimate blind of both historical and ethnographical writing, that 'being there' is the ultimate 'reality effect' (Clifford 1983; Clifford and Marcus 1986). But authorial presence is not necessarily a call on unquestionable authority. Authorial presence can be an invitation to an audience or readership to experience its own performance consciousness.

ANTI-THEATRE AGAIN

There are some famous exponents of the 'anti-theatrical prejudice'. Plato, of course. Socrates. The Puritans. 'Instructions that are given to the minde must be simple without mingle mangle of fish and flesh, good and bad', wrote Stephen Gosson, Oxford playwright, become Puritan anti-theatrical (Barish 1981: 89). William Prynne wrote *Historiomastix* as a nightmare vision of a world out of control because the stage displayed the possibility that men were not outwardly what they were inwardly. Inventiveness of culture was a rather scary thought to men like the Puritans who were their own witness to the eternal, but internal, character of their chosen nature. Their certainties required some fix between external sign and inward godly reality. Prynne's list of the sorts of behaviour that made that fix ambivalent was long: 'effeminate mixt dancing, dicing, stage-plays, lascivious pictures, wanton fashions, face painting, health drinking, love locks, periwigs, women's curling, pouldring and cutting their hair, bone-fires, New Years giftes, May games, amorous pastorals, lascivious effeminate musicke, excessive laughter, luxurious disorderly Christmas keeping, mummeries', he wrote, 'are all wicked unchristian pantomimes' (Barish 1981: 83). It would be a mistake to think that this is just a sort of wowserism. It is the theatricality of living that is being condemned. It is the possibility of there being some distance between external signs and inward realities that is most threatening. Playfulness is a scandal. True believers live in—and the powerful would like to live in—an *ex opere operato* world where all signs effect what they signify in the signifying, and everybody is sincere. So mimesis that somehow clones the world is acceptable. It changes nothing. Being playful in the slightest way suggests that things might be otherwise.

In the United States anti-theatrical prejudice came early. In 1778 Congress condemned all theatrical representation together with gambling and horse racing. And the prejudice stayed late. It gives us pause to think that an actor was denied Christian burial in New York as late as 1878. But the Church, even so sacramental a church as Rome, always feared actors. They made a profession of insincerity. Their mediation of signs bred uncertainties. Priests in their rituals cannot afford to be seen as actors. Nor can scientists. Churches and science come together on that. Their representations cannot be seen to be mediated in anyway by circumstance, by authorial presence, by passion, by culture.

John Witherspoon of Princeton inverted the usual Puritan argument that the stage was evil because it was a fraud on reality, by arguing that the stage was evil because it could be too true. 'Better for the world', he wrote, 'that several ancient facts and characters which now stand upon record, had been buried in oblivion' (Barish 1981: 83). That there are things better left unsaid is another anti-theatrical tenet.

Of course, the great anti-theatrical man of the eighteenth century, and the one who draws me back from the Pacific to the stage in London, by ways too devious to describe here, was Jean Jacques Rousseau. For Rousseau, it was the theatricality of civilisation that made it objectionable. 'Social man', that is civilised man, he wrote, 'is always outside himself, only knows how to live in the opinion of others; and it is, so to speak, entirely from their judgement that he draws the sense of his entire existence' (Barish 1981: 257). Savages, on the other hand, lived within themselves: they acted to no one. Artificiality was both the essence and the evil of civilisation for Rousseau. Simplicity, immediacy—the character and virtue of the savage. The theatre was artificial twice over and therefore doubly evil. The only proper representation for Rousseau was open-air celebratory pastorals, where he thought spontaneity was uninhibited either by the physical space of the theatre or the social space of behavioural rules. Rousseau, by his polarity of oppositions in the artifical civilised and the natural savage put time into the distinction. The natural was how we used to be before theatricality made us what we are. This hankering after a golden past and suspicion of modernity is another facet of an anti-theatrical prejudice. To those who see either the Now or some Golden Moment as a still-life, the notion of the invention of culture is anathema. But modernity is of the essence of culture. Living cultures are always representing the otherness of the now and making sense of it. Where else in the world than among those who Franz Fanon identified as *The Wretched of the Earth* (1963) is so much poetry being made, so many stories being told, so many being histories written, so many paintings being painted? Such theatre is never just repetitive. It is always inventive. It is always liberating.

SOLILOQUY TWO
On Producing Effects

'Effects' is a word of the theatre and representation. We meet it nowadays in such phrases as 'effects microphone', 'special effects', the one catching and controlling the noise of crowds, the crunch of bodies, the crack of bat on ball, to give a sense of presence and immediacy; the other exploiting the blinkered view of camera or stage to create the illusions of realism. There is more than a two-hundred-year history to its changing use in criticism as thinkers from Denis Diderot to Richard Wagner puzzled with the problem of how the manipulation of signs could be conventional and real at the same time. But the problem is not just an aesthetic one. Everywhere—where a missionary friar whispers over bread and wine that they are body and blood, where an observer provides an 'illustration' for an ethnography, where a voyaging captain makes an example by a bombardment—

everywhere where there are signs made, there is the possibility and the likelihood that the sign-maker and the sign-seer will have a manipulative strategy to effect in someone else some meaning. Every narrator has to produce effects as well. But in an age in which 'reality effects' suffuse historical paradigms, the judgement that 'he/she writes well' can be the ultimate put-down. The turgid command respect for seeming to be scholarly. Being 'only an ordinary historian' is a coy boast. Ever since the 'enlightened' discovered perspective, being the spectator has allowed one to bumble words for the sake of appearing to be honest. Plain-speaking is seen to be untheatrical, even if it is theatre of another sort. Indeed, being literary when one is meant to be something else is seen as somewhat feminine. Hegemony, for preferences, is dull and male.

Renato Rosaldo (1984, 1986) has often urged us to reflect on the fullness of living that historians ordinarily miss—and ethnographers only sometimes catch. In particular he has reflected on the paradox that elements of the highest human import in living are unlikely to have cultural elaboration, unlikely to be in a 'forest of symbols'. Catch the words of some narrator telling the story of some hunt, for example, and they are found to be bland, trite and without apparent depth. (We only have to remember how nearly unintelligible the transcripts of the 'Nixon Tapes' were to know how silence, presence, gesture and tone filled the Oval Office.) Framed in a significant landscape, and when the biographies of teller and listener are bound together in rich understanding of telegraphic forms, the words catch and narrate the 'force' of human emotions. The 'force' is there in living and needs to be represented. We should add 'force', Rosaldo says, to those other words of our analytic expectancies—thick description, multivocality, polysemy, richness and texture.

The 'force' is there to be represented in our history-making, I would argue. But more than that, to produce effects in our narration, our history-making itself must have 'force'. I wish I could now describe how the 'force' can be made to be present in our writing. I offer a few thoughts instead. They are made on the presumption that comes from Nietzsche in his reflection on the Birth of Tragedy. The effects one produces in one's history-making should be powerful enough to outlast the experience of reading our histories and in some way change our audience.

Style, suggested Peter Gay (1975), is not the dress of thought, but part of its essence. It is a happy thought, but not nearly liberating enough. Style itself can be binding and blinding. We have to add what Roland Barthes said (and excuse his genderisation): 'The writer—and in this respect he stands alone, apart from, and in opposition to all speakers and mere practitioners of writing—is he who refuses to let the obligations of his language speak for him, who knows and is acutely conscious of the deficiencies of his idiom, and who imagines, untopically, a total language in which nothing is obligatory' (in Gossman 1978: 37). And something more, this time Stanley Fish: 'The meaning of an utterance is its experience—all of it' (in Strong 1978: 247). Rosaldo's Ilongot hunters' stories stand bland and trivial when we transcribe them. We cannot experience them as utterances.

But we for our part begin our history-making on an empty piece of paper. Our utterance is an inscription. To produce our effects, to make our utterance an experience we have to discover ways to make the silences present. The silences must be there, not as emptiness, but, in Paul Valéry's words (1970), 'the active presence of absent things'.

The effect most worth producing for a writer, it seems to me, is a creative reader. We have to stir the exegete, make the critic, join them to a conversation. What tricks do we have for that? Aphorisms? Riddles? Perspectives of Incongruity? Irony? Metaphor? All of those. Our readers need to be rid of their fear of flying. They will not easily do that if they catch ours. We need to perform our texts. We need to perform in our texts.

THEATRE: ENIGMA VARIATIONS

Spaces privileged for performance are common to all cultures. They need not be bounded by material signs or be architectural. Conventional gestures, attentive postures, crowd silence will do. A Tahitian *heiva* or dance ground where natives mocked the grotesqueries of the intruding strangers, a scaffold (a word significantly borrowed from the stage) where a victim was sacrificed to the abstractions of the law, were spaces where actors and spectators entered conventionalities of what Victor Turner has called 'the subjunctive', the 'as if it were'. It happens in law courts, on altars, in market-places, in books. It happens most of all in theatres.

The indicative and the subjunctive are the Yin and Yang of our problem, passive/active, potency/act, existence/essence, feminine/masculine. The indicative mood, grammarians and dictionaries tell us, is 'the mood of a verb which states a relation of objective fact between the subject and the predicate'. It is a very modernist mood, Yang in character. The subjunctive mood of the verb 'that denotes an action or state as conceived' is a touch postmodernist, Yin. The enigma of the theatre, indeed of living, is that the one does not exist without the other. Wherever there is an 'is', there is an 'as if it were'. We make poles of them at the risk of fantasising.

David Garrick, the great eighteenth-century English actor who transformed the English stage, was the enemy of formalism. He hated the reduction of characterisations to formulaic narratives, such as 'tragic struts, elaborate gestures, chanting declamation'. 'He realised the fiction', one critic said (Dibdin n. d.: v. 328). Not the fantasy, the fiction. He realised the fiction. It would make a nice epitaph for any historian. 'He/she realised the fiction.' He/she had a way of telling stories by which the readers could see the plot in them, and then the stories themselves emplotted the readers' lives. Put a footnote on the gravestone, if you like: '"realise" (OED) to give reality to, to understand, or grasp clearly or to have actual experience of'. There is no historical fact which is the real and representation which is the unreal. They are one and the same thing.

There was something else said of Garrick which might interest an historian. 'His business', the critic said, 'was not to methodize words, but to express passions'. 'Not to methodize words.' Aren't historians always working the irony in the fact that words themselves have histories, across time, across space? There is not a word that does not hold some surprise. Historians work the surprises and the *double entendres*. To methodise words and the narrative that shapes them is like staining a living cell to see its structures. All you discover are the structures of a dead cell.

And something more that the great man himself said. (I squeeze him for all the reflective history-making that is in him.) 'The greatest strokes of genius have been unknown to the actor himself till the warmth of the scene has sprung the mine, as it were, as much to his own surprise as that of the audience' (Burnim 1964: 1030). In the end it is audience and actor that make the performance, as it is reader (or listener or viewer) and narrator (or writer or artist) that together make the history.

Garrick was not being less conventional by being more realistic. That is another enigma. The realisms of his representations became in time as unreal as those he rebelled against. Fashions and the theatre itself changed. Style and modernity belong to the realism of history-making as well. There was a dialectic between audiences and actors, between the environment of the theatre and the performances that ensured that the liminality of the theatre, the subjunctive space, lay somewhere between replication and representation. The technology of lighting, the size of the theatre, the machinery of the stage, the consistency of the costumes, outside politics, all affected the ways in which conventionalities of gesture and voice conditioned the interpretive possibilities.

The theatre was and is 'an' experience. Victor Turner has shown what surprises there are in that word 'experience'; how it has a twofold quality of the riskiness, fear and experimentation there is in 'living through' something, plus the reflectiveness that makes sense of it. The subtleties by which this experience in the theatre catches or discounts the hermeneutic relationship between the signs given and the things signified are great. These interpretive skills cannot be divorced from the texts and the plots within the texts of the performances. They are, if anything, blunted by the spectacular, by plotless display. That is why the theatre of power preoccupies itself with the spectacular, in which seeing drowns out interpreting. However, given half a chance to see that it is a fiction that is being realised, even in the spectacular, an audience will know what is real. I think one of the most difficult tasks an historian has to do—to perform! why was I reluctant to say it?—is to represent what is actually being displayed and audienced in all the theatres of living, but especially in the theatres of power.

SOLILOQUY THREE

On the Past in Present Participles

Participles brought out the grundy in Henry Watson Fowler, grammarian, iconoclast, curmudgeon. UNATTACHED PARTICIPLES were 'as insidious as they were notorious'. FUSED PARTICIPLES were close to 'German ponderousness' and were 'ignorant vulgarisms'. 'Every just man who will abstain from fused participles . . . retards the progress of corruption.' SENTRY PARTICIPLES—editors must discipline the newspaper writers of inch-long paragraphs lest they encourage 'the survival of the unfittest'. 'Tender grammatical consciences', he wrote in a slightly more accommodating tone, 'are apt to vex themselves, sometimes with reason, sometimes without, over the correctness of the -ing form of the verb' (Fowler 1965: 438, 284).

Participles participate in the nature of two language forms, the noun or adjective and the verb. They soften the essentialising quality of nouns with the being and acting quality of the verb: not life, but living, not gender, but gendering; not culture, but culturing; not science, but sciencing; not change, but changing. The way we represent the world is hindsighted, past participled, stilled like frames on a film. The way we experience the world is processual, unfinished. We see the real; we experience the actual. We sense the power in every definition. We cringe at the ugliness of such words as 'reification', but we know the energy with which we materialise the static images of our social world. 'All reification is a process of forgetting', wrote Herbert Marcuse. 'Art fights reification by making the petrified world speak, sing, perhaps dance' (in Taussig 1980: 154).

Perhaps another word for the present participle would be practice or praxis. Listen to Pierre Bourdieu describe this tension between the outsider's description and the insider's experience. He writes of anthropology. He could have written of history. He could have written of common sense. 'The anthropologist's particular relation to the object of his study contains the makings of a theoretical distinction

119

inasmuch as his situation as the observer, excluded from the real play of social activities by the fact that he has no place (except by choice or by way of a game) in the system observed and has no need to make a place for himself there, inclines him to a hermeneutical representation of practices, leading him to reduce all social relations to communicative relations and, more precisely, to decoding operations . . . Linguistic research takes different directions according to whether it deals with the researcher's mother tongue or with a foreign language . . . [There is a] tendency to intellectualism implied in observing language from the standpoint of the listening subject rather than that of the speaking subject . . . Exaltation of the virtues of distance secured by externality simply transmutes into an epistemological choice the anthropologist's objective situation, that of the 'impartial spectator', as Husserl puts it, condemned to see all practice as a spectacle . . . It is significant that 'culture' is sometimes described as a map; it is the analogy which occurs to an outsider who has to find his way around in a foreign landscape and who compensates for his lack of practical mastery, the prerogative of the native, by the use of a model of all possible routes. The gulf between this potential, abstract space, devoid of landmarks or any privileged centre—like genealogies, in which the ego is as unreal as the starting point in a Cartesian space—and the practical space of journeys actually made, or rather of a journey actually being made, can be seen from the difficulty we have in recognizing familiar routes on a map or town plan until we are able to bring together the axes of the field of potentialities and the "system of axes linked unalterably to our bodies, and carried about with us wherever we go", as Poincare puts it, which structures practical space into right and left, up and down, in front and behind' (Bourdieu 1977).

The present participle in history and ethnography returns the privileged space to those who are experiencing what is actually happening. That those who are thus experiencing process in the practice of it are also experiencing distance within themselves and are being subjected by many powers to emplot their living in a distanced, mapped way is no argument to exclude one or the other polarity of human experiences from our representations. It is surely more an invitation to discover mimetic forms for the dialectic of these apparently contradictory elements of living. The paradoxes of living will not escape paradoxical transformations. The theatricality of history-making will always demand that the many voices of every cultural moment be heard. It will discover that the interpretive genius of the audience can cope with these paradoxes and multivalencies.

THE PARADOX OF ACTING

'The Paradox of Acting' is also the paradox of living. 'Performance consciousness' or authorial presence does not destroy the realism of our everyday sign-making and representations. Such self-distancing in the making of signs is part of our realism. The phrase 'The Paradox of Acting' is the title of an essay which Denis Diderot began to write in 1769 (1958). Diderot admired David Garrick greatly, and having watched him perform and read his pamphlet on acting, enunciated the paradox. Diderot's Paradox was that the more great actors appeared to be overwhelmed by the emotion of their role, the cooler they were and the more in command of themselves. 'It is extreme sensibility that makes actors mediocre. It is middling sensibility which makes a multitude of bad actors. And it is the lack of sensibility which qualifies actors to be sublime' (Diderot, in Wilson 1972: 621). Many actors since have been offended by the word 'sensibility', reading it as if it meant 'sensitivity', and that Diderot was denying their human ability to share emotions with others. But for Diderot 'sensibility' meant such absorption in representation that there was no consciousness of signs. 'I require of [the actor] a cold and tranquil spectator. Great poets, great actors and perhaps all the great copyists of nature in whatever art, beings gifted with free imagination, with broad judgement, with exquisite tact, with a sure touch of taste . . . are too engaged in observing, recognizing or imitating, to be vitally affected witnesses. All the actors talents consist not in feeling, as you imagine, but in rendering so scrupulously the external signs of feeling, that you are taken in.' 'Reflect a little as to what, in the

121

language of the theatre is being true. Is it showing things as they are in nature? Certainly not. Were it so, the true would be commonplace. What is the truth for stage purposes? It is the conforming of action, diction, face, voice, movement and gesture to an ideal type, invented by the poet and frequently enhanced by the player.' 'If there is anyone sure to give and present this sublimity, it is the man who can feel it with his passion and genius and reproduce it with complete self-possession' (Diderot, in Cole and Chinoy 1949: 163–6).

Passion and discipline, natural and artificial, immediate meanings mediated by cultivated signs—Diderot discovered his paradox in the necessity of combining these oppositions to make the complete representation. It is the same paradox that pursues historians when they themselves represent the past. It is the same paradox inherent in the past actions that are being represented. We separate the parts of the paradox and centre representation on any one of them with risk. Our history will hold no truth. The past that we historicise will make no sense. Polarise our representations into these dialectically dependent bits: they will only reflect our falsifications.

So the ultimate taunt of the absolutist to the relativist: 'Are you certain that you are a relativist?' is nothing but a sad joke. On the other hand, the inventions of the semiotician of more and more words to isolate less and less are just as sad. A curse on both their houses. The theatricality of history-making is to narrate the paradoxes of the past out of the paradoxes of the present in such a way that our readers will see the paradoxes in themselves.

SOLILOQUY FOUR
On Going Native

'Going Native', the impossible dream of anthropology, has held, of late, some fascination for the historian and the literary critic. True, one will hear the occasional sigh: 'I am growing so tired of the Other', or, 'I myself have never met the Other, only others'. True, also, the Other of this latter-day fascination has more to do with reflections of the

Same that are seen in the Other. The Other is 'Mirror for Man', we can safely say, given the gendered images of power to be found in reflections of the 'discovered' and colonised Other (De Certeau 1989). Of course, the Other is nearer home than the South Seas or the New World. The grotesque is recognisable as a trope of reflexivity now that we have read Michail Bakhtin's history of laughter (1984). The Other, whether this is the monkey at the fair, or the cannibal savage on display, or the educated worker, or the chauvinist-appearing woman, is reduced to a frightening or comic spectacle set against the antithetical normality of the spectator, as Peter Stallybrass and Allon White have noted. The theatre of the grotesque, these two writers suggest, is not so much in the display of total strangeness, as in the awkward mimicry of the truly civilised by these strangers. The Other is the Same, only worse, and inept, ugly or evil. The laughter in the theatre of the grotesque is the laughter of relief at discovering that the Other is not Other after all (Stallybrass and White 1986: 41).

That is why 'going native' has always been such a scandalous act. In the Pacific, the beachcomber who escaped regulated ship-life, the missionary who made some distinction in the accidents and essentials of belief, the colonial administrator who accepted native political and social status as something more than make-believe, even the occasional explorer who wondered what he had 'discovered' and whether his 'discovery' was truly to the good of the native were a scandal to the civilised and became objects of prurient interest.

In the view of those at the centre of empires, of course, distance made everybody a little 'native'. The changed accent and vocabulary, the social awkwardnesses, the unstylishness of dress and behaviour marginalised the colonials as somewhat strange, as having given deference to something uncivilised. Colonials are always grotesque because they lie in the liminal space between being stylishily modern and nostalgically antique.

Recognition of such grotesquerie is laughable and empowering but not threatening in itself. 'Going native' stirs the blood a little more. 'Going native' always began—always begins—with some deference to the realism of another cultural system. It catches in that deference something of the consistency and interconnectedness of things. It was—and is—a lonely act, better done out of sight of the mocking gaze of co-culturalists. Even a touch of cultural relativism, like a dab of postmodernism, is counted dangerous. The world is suddenly filled with threatened people, the moment one subjunctively cuts the cultural tie. Cast one rope of a cultural tie and someone is sure to shout, 'The pier is sinking'.

Everyone who would represent the past must 'go native' in some way or be condemned always only to represent the present. Even the 'native' must 'go native' in finding a past. We might think we are privileged in some way towards a past by being black or white, male or female, poor or powerful, but that privilege is only towards all the others of our living present. The past to which we each 'go native' is a lot farther off and no one gets there but by giving a little. That is because there is no moment so civilised as the present moment. There is no temptation stronger than to make the past a grotesque and laughable mimicry of our civilised present. The past, that way, can be mocked and judged so easily and with such little cost.

'Going native' in the past is not easy. It takes something more than a little Collingwoodian Diltheyesque re-thinking of past events. And who can be Romantic ever again? Who will believe us when we say 'we are natives now'? Edward Said (1989) will hound us if we claim to be interlocutors between the victims and the lords of empire. Who will hound us if we claim to be interlocutors between the living and the dead? Few of us can find a voice which is neither white nor black, male nor female, young nor old. Few of us can deny the hegemonic mode in our translations of other linguistic forms into our own. 'Going native', for all the scandal it seems to cause, is actually a very difficult thing to do. That is why I used to take comfort from a headstone in the cemetery outside the Hawaiian Mission Archives—a place where I have done my all to 'go native' in the past. 'Sister Kate', the epitaph reads, 'She Did What She Could'.

The subjunctive mood should encourage us to do what we can. The theatre is the place to learn from possibilities. The past has reduced all its possibilities to one. History still contains them all.

Reflective History

'Reflective history' is not a term of notoriety among historians, as the terms 'Reflexive Sociology' and 'Reflexive Anthropology' are among sociologists and anthropologists. Historians are likely to call self-consciousness about history-making 'philosophy of history', 'historiography' or 'theory and method of history'. Reflexive Sociology and Reflexive Anthropology were born of these disciplines' discovery that they had a political past as well as a political present. Their reflexivity concerned the politics of their knowledge. To whose ends was it constructed? Whose interests did it serve? Reflexivity had aggressive disestablishing connotations as anthropology, especially, discovered its roots in imperialism, cultural hegemony and class structure. It is true that academic history in the decades of the 1960s and 1970s, when most disciplines lost their innocence, was not free of some of the cultural forces that demanded disestablishment. Gender and people's history, history from below were beginning to claim centre stage, and Vietnam and the civil rights movements raised radical voices about 'relevance'. But History had long discovered its own politics and, in a sense, was satisfied with them. The radical voices sounded gauche, 'unhistorical'. It was one thing to recognise the politics of all history-making, quite another to pursue self-consciously political ends in research, writing and teaching. History's engagement in its own reality effects was such that there were no philosophies capable of sustaining it in its own self-contradictions. The alternative was to appear to have no philosophy at all. Or to claim to have none, anyway (Chesneaux 1976: Lynd 1969).

E. P. Thompson's *cri de coeur*, *The Poverty of Theory* (1978), should not be seen as a familial squabble between curmudgeons and parvenus. Thompson was Everyhistorian protesting at being gobbled up by philosophers and theorists. The 'history' of any and every philosophy of

125

history has been barely recognisable to the practitioners of the craft. That 'history' of the philosophers of history has been all lateral pursuit of covering law, colligations and the like. Historians see few reflections of themselves in the mirrors of the philosophy of history. There is a half-suspicion that they see instead some White Rabbit disappearing through the looking glass.

Capitalise 'Reflective History', and historians are likely to cringe a little. Everybody likes to think that their history is reflective. Everybody knows that their history is somehow reflective of themselves and the conditions in which they write it. Everybody knows that the ultimate source of the questions they ask of the past is their reflective self. But 'Reflective History' seems to imply new commitments, conferences even, journals, new languages to learn. The past, even an hour of it, leaves mountains of texts. One lifetime would not be enough to read all that there is. Fires, earthquakes, wars, accidents are, in one sense, a blessed relief. There is less to read, more scope for interpretive genius. If 'Reflective History' means 'know thyself' in the present as well as in the past, the complaint is made, then we are likely to be lost in some vortex of pleonasms. Narcissus had it easy. Reflection only turned him into a flower. Reflection for us is likely to send us mad in a postmodern hall of funny mirrors.

Reflective history does not need to be 'Reflective History'. It need only be the heightened sense of experience in our utterances. It need only be a conscious effort to join the conversations around us. It need only be honest to the uncertainties of knowing. It need only be a sense that all narrations are *to* somebody as well as *of* something. It need only be an effort to regain the moral force of writing.

There are many reasons given why the academic discipline of history has lost its moral force. Some of its disciples will bemoan the superficialities of presentist culture and blame the insidious forces that have sapped the energies of the young and rendered them culturally illiterate. History, others will say, has been trivialised by the pluralisations of subjects and enervated by the evermore frequent succession of theories (Himmelfarb 1987). I think something to the contrary. Academic history has lost its moral force because it has been subverted by its own reality effects and has lost its sense of theatre. Academic history has come to believe that accuracy is truth and that to represent the past accurately somehow clones the past. There are very few academic historians who do not know what E. H. Carr meant when he wrote: 'the belief in a hard core of historical facts existing objectively and independently of the interpretations of the historians is a preposterous fallacy, but one which is very hard to eradicate' (Carr 1961: 12). But there are also very few academic historians who write history as if what he said were true. Reflective history ensures that the interpreting is discernible in the interpretation. In an age which has experienced Picasso, Stravinsky, Mickey Mouse and Dale Carnegie, a sense of the multivalency of things is an expected realism. In an age that has experienced horror beyond measure from the perversions of true believers, we are well educated to the interpretation of signs. A history that is seen to believe its own fictions is fraud and a bore. It loses moral force on both scores.

The brilliance of theatre is that it represents experience and offers us the conventionalities by which the representation can be interpreted. We do not enter a theatre as if it were a Time Machine in which past experience is repeated. Henry Kissinger said of the tape-recording Richard Nixon had made in his Oval Office for the sake of true history: 'That's not history. Eight years of tapes takes eight years to listen to'. No! Even the most accurate replication is not representation. The energy expended in replication squeezes out everything else. Ultimately such replication is the stultifying nostalgia of re-enactments and living museums. Experience represented in the theatre is dressed with the same particularities of everyday experience and has the larger-than-itself quality of everyday experience, but is transformed by being selected and shaped for interpretation. It does not replicate reality. It redresses reality. Theatricality in history-making will do the same.

Possessing Tahiti

HERE is a ceremony performed nowadays at Tahiti each year in the Bastille Day holidays. At the *marae* Arahu Rahu, reconstructed for tourists and 'folkloric' celebrations, the 'King' and 'Queen' of Tahiti are invested with a *maro ura,* a wrap or girdle of red feathers. It is a symbol, like a crown and sceptre, of their sovereignty for the time of the celebrations. Thousands are there to see the ceremony. The royal couple 'fly' on the shoulders of attendants, as the high chiefs of old 'flew', lest their sacred feet touch the ground. 'Priests' are there, decked out in fantasies and improvisations of what priests used to wear. Sacrificial offerings of food and cloth are made. All process to the sacred stones before the altar for the investment. It is a carnival of monarchy in republican days. It is not peculiar for that, of course. If clowns might be kings in the topsy-turvy world of carnival, then native citizens might well be kings in republics on holiday remembering the overthrow of stranger monarchies ten thousand miles away.

These ceremonies in Tahiti have the familiar quality that we sometimes stress in our weariness with the ritualistic. They seem meaningless empty actions, distanced from the realities of living, forms without structures. Ritual robes become fancy dress, symbols become decoration. It is a syncretism of a make-believe past and a fatuous present. We are familiar with it: Mickey Mouse as King of Disneyland, 'Dale Carnegie' as Sincere Man, the blank face of Homo *touristicus,* Advertising Man, Plastic Man. Life seems filled with its emptiness. Who can make sense of signs that do not signify, of symbols that crush with their weightlessness, of sacraments that leave no mark?

In a culture such as ours in which the student is likely to know our mythic nature in order to sell us soap and underwear, it is difficult not to be sceptical about the appearances of things. We see the manipulation and declare the manipulation to be the reality. One could imagine, for example, the organising committee of the Tahiti Bastille Day celebrations wanting a 'divertissement' in the 'folkloric' mode. To choreograph the ceremony they call on the cultural memory of 'experts' who, by all the complex modes of the transmission of historical consciousness, have their translations of 'how things used to be done'. One could not now describe the syncretism and translations, the extensions and changes in Tahitian cultural perceptions of the *maro ura,* of 'flying', of investitures and sacrifices. These signs and symbolic actions enjoy some continuity with past, they have some cultural presence, yet they establish different realities. They are 'Tahitian' in character, but present distinct expressions of what being 'Tahitian' might be. In a metaphor of the Pacific, the symbols of the past are 'cargo' to the present. The present possesses the relics of its past with all the inventions and conservation with which cultural artefacts out of time and out of place are received across a beach. How does one write history as if that were true?

THE POLITICS OF A FEATHER GIRDLE

For that, the *maro ura* is very pertinent. If young George III of England needed a crown to be king in 1760 and to sit on the Coronation Stone of Scotland and Ireland, then a 12-year-old Pomare of Tahiti needed the maro *ura* to be *ari'i nui,* chief, in 1791, and to stand on the robing stone of his *marae,* that sacred preserve of his titles. His *maro ura* was a feather wrap, five yards long and fifteen inches broad. The brilliant red head-feathers of the parakeet and the whitish-yellow feathers of the dove were sewn to a woven backing. The black feathers of the man-of-war bird bordered the wrap, top and bottom. The *maro ura* has come to be called the 'feather girdle' in the way archaic words get some establishment in the history of things. The girdle was always unfinished. The bone to sew it was left in the weave. The social moments of chieftaincy, sacrifices, wars and peace all found their register on the girdle with added feathers and folds. In the feathers was a history of sovereignty, more mnemonic than hieroglyphic, capable of being read by priests who had the custody of the past (Rose 1978; Oliver 1974: 763).

Tahitian politics turned around the feather girdle. There are uncertainties about the girdle. There were two of them; maybe Pomare's was a third; maybe there were more. The two we know from legend and myth were the *maro tea* and the *maro ura*, the yellow and the red girdle. Pomare's girdle we know from a number of descriptions of European visitors who saw it and from William Bligh who drew it. The descriptions are all agreed that Pomare's girdle was made of both yellow and red feathers. That Pomare's girdle might be a third sacred *maro* and in concept be syncretic of both *maro tea* and *maro ura* belongs to our later story. There were more syncretisms more immediately important. Its distinction from the traditional sacred *maro* of Tahitian polity did not put it outside the paradigm of Tahitian politics. That paradigm allowed a distinction between power and authority. Power was recognised to rise and fall independently of authority. The feather girdles were the currency of authority. They conferred title and rank which it was the consensus of powerful and weak alike to recognise (Oliver 1974: 1213–16, 1279).

If the feather girdles were the sacraments of authority—in that they signified authority and established it at the same time—it was because they were the sign of the god 'Oro. 'Oro, the god of sacrifice, had always been part of the Polynesian pantheon, but in the eighteenth century 'Oro had begun to play a special part in Tahitian politics. He had begun to emerge from his island of Raiatea, first to Porapora, then to Tahiti.

There was an element of mission or colony in 'Oro's expansion. His priests would establish a new sacred place with some stone transported from an original temple. These places sacred to 'Oro all shared a common name, Taputapuatea, 'Sacrifices from Abroad'. They were all close to the sea and stood opposite some passage through the reef to the open sea. The rituals at Taputapuatea always focused on canoes and their arrival with sacrificial victims. Tahitians, like all Polynesian peoples, had some preoccupation with the origins and voyages of their ancestors and with strangers who came from beyond the sky. In their legendary memory of Taputapuatea they told of grander days when the 'Friendly Alliance' of the islands would send processions of canoes in double file through the sacred passage to the beach of the temple. Each canoe would have on its prow the paired sacrifices of man and fish and they would beach the canoe at Taputapuatea on the rollers of the victims' bodies. They remembered the names of 'Oro's priests in phrases like 'Persistent Growth', 'Steady Growth', 'Extension of Power'. 'Oro himself was incarnated in a log or a club-like basket of sennit covered in feathers, more abstract in his representation than anthropomorphic. He himself was a voyager around their islands in an ark or feather basket coffer set on a canoe called 'Rainbow'. He had first come to the Tahitian islands on a rainbow that joined sky and land. As the *Maohi*, the native islanders of the whole Society Group, saw it, the great celebration of 'Oro at his birthplace of Opoa on Raiatea was a time of commitment to alliances that stretched beyond the bounds of their individual islands (Henry 1928: 157–77; Green 1968).

Under 'Oro's patronage functioned the only group in the islands who called on loyalties wider than tribal and local divisions. They were called *arioi*, a privileged group who travelled and played. 'Comedians' was an old missionary word for them that caught the topsy-turvy carnival that was structured in their role. They would play the clown to established authority: they overturned the rules of proper behaviour, and danced and played without responsibility. The masters of the different *arioi* lodges wore their own *maro ura* of red-tinted *tapa* cloth. They travelled with 'Oro in his canoe. 'Oro, present in his stick and feathered basket, would travel with his priests and his court of *arioi*. The grand sight of their largest canoes decked with streamers, beautiful with their every valued decoration and transporting 'Oro, belonged to the annual cycle of Tahitian experiences (Henry 1928: 120–7).

The Taputapuatea were places of sacrifice. They were also treasure houses of the sacred paraphernalia of 'Oro. The representations of 'Oro were kept there in special feathered containers, as were the sacred *maro* and the other accoutrements of priests and chiefs. Pomare kept his *maro* in a sacred spot to the south-east of Matavai. Pomare's *maro* had been brought there in 1791. It had come from other sacred places, firstly the *marae* Mahaiatea in the district of Papara and then *marae* Utu'aihamurau in the district of Paea. In the *maro's* voyages of twenty-five years is a whole history of Tahitian politics. In 1792 William Bligh saw Pomare's *maro* at Tarahoi near Matavai. When he saw it, he drew it, and in that drawing we have our only relic of it. (The London Missionary Society 'collected' one, but lost it.) Bligh also drew 'Oro's canoe, 'Rainbow', with its ark. Joined to the huge streamer of bark cloth that flew from the canoe's stern was a Union Jack (Green 1968; Bligh 1976 [1791]: April 26; Bligh n.d.; Tobin n.d.; 1791).

Bligh also commented that the Tahitians had sewn into the feather girdle a thatch of auburn hair belonging to Richard Skinner, one of the *Bounty* mutineers who had elected to stay at Tahiti when Christian went on to Pitcairn. Poor Bligh, he was always sensitive to his relations with the socially élite. He was mystified why somebody as insignificant as Skinner should be remembered in so sacred an object as the girdle: 'an ostentatious mark of their connection with the English and not of respect to the Person it belonged to', he remarked. Skinner was the ship's barber. He had astounded the Tahitians on the arrival of the *Bounty* by producing a barber's model head with its latest hair fashions from London. In Tahitian eyes, Skinner was somebody special. As barber, he had a special power to touch *tapu* places. And his own head was *tapu* red, as special as a feather. One could wave it to catch 'Oro's attention in prayer: one could sacrifice it to Pomare's sovereignty (Bligh 1976 [1791]: April 28; Mackaness 1960: 41).

Collected in this sacred place of 'Oro where Bligh saw the girdle was other cargo. There were the skulls of two *Bounty* mutineers. One of them, Coleman, had been raised to be chief at Taiarapu. The other skull was that of Thompson, Coleman's murderer, who had been killed in his turn. Pomare's family had conquered Taiarapu, won the skulls and, temporarily, sovereignty over all of Tahiti. At the *marae* at Tarahoi were also drums and carved statues of gods which the mutineers had brought back from Tubuai. There was also a portrait of Captain James Cook painted by John Webber. Like the *maro ura,* the portrait was an unfinished document. The Tahitians would take it to each ship that visited the island for the captain to sign a message on the back. The portrait was wrapped in red cloth and all made bare-shouldered deferences to it when it was uncovered. For years after Cook had given them the portrait and a huge box with lock and key to keep it in, the Pomares, father and son, took it with them on important expeditions, unveiled it on special ritual occasions, had it present whenever they offered formal hospitality to Stranger captains (Morrison 1935 [1785]: 85, 114–16).

Bligh saw something else in the *maro ura* besides Skinner's auburn hair. It was the most famous thing of all. He saw a British red pennant sewn into the body of the girdle, as a lappet or fold of its own. 'Red Buntin' he calls it on his drawing. It was the pennant that Samuel Wallis, captain of HMS *Dolphin*, had erected on a pole on 26 June 1767 when he took possession of Tahiti for King George III. The Tahitians had taken down the symbol of sovereignty and incorporated it into a symbol of sovereignty of their own (Rose 1978: 9–15).

Tarahoi was a Tahitian museum of their contact with the European Stranger. The hair, the skulls, Cook's portrait, the red bunting were cargo. They were Strangers' things remade to Tahitian meanings and kept, as in some archive, as documents of past experiences that were repeatedly read for their meaning in ritual actions that displayed them and preserved them.

Pomare's *maro ura* was a parable in feathers and red bunting of the translating process. Its expression was Tahitian, in the language of 'Oro, of sacrifice. Pomare was a boy of ten when the feather girdle was wrapped about him for the first time in 1791, a year before Bligh saw it. He took title at that moment to a status his father never had and could never reach. His father with all the others became bound to all the deferences owed Tahiti's most sacred person—his son. The father even lost his name and all the extravagant dignity the name was owed. The boy—Pomare II in our translation of who he was—in his investiture took the left eye of the sacrificial victims and made as if to eat it, read the signs in the cries of the sacred birds in the trees around. He listened (because the Strangers, the English, were now there) to a volley of muskets which the *Bounty* mutineers were invited to fire (a translation in itself in mimicry of the thunder of 'Oro that auspiciously would be heard in the ceremony).

At the end, after being raised to extraordinary heights of dignity, Pomare stood in the *marae*, and his people, who were all about or were in the trees like some incarnation of 'Oro's birds, turned their deferences around. What they did we do not altogether know. Those who saw it were always reluctant to describe the obscenities. What we think they did was to pour, or to make as if to pour, as Pomare had made as if to eat the eye of the sacrifice, their semen and excrement over him. They danced naked uninhibitedly around him. When it was over he was *ari'i nui*, 'king'. He was *ari'i nui,* because what he wore, his *maro ura,* took him back to 'Oro and the beginning of title, but what he wore as well, the red bunting, took him back to the beginning of a new time. This new time, the coming of the Stranger, was enclosed in the old time, the coming of 'Oro. The feather girdle was as much an invention of culture as an invention of the past (Green 1968: 79; Morrison 1935 [1785]: 114–16).

The next investiture in the Pomare kingly line occurred thirty three years later. Pomare III, Pomare II's only son, had been born with a missionary for a midwife. He was an infant of three years when he was crowned king of Tahiti. Missionaries were midwives to his kingly power as well. He came to his coronation in the royal chapel near Papeete under a canopy, behind a procession of girls strewing flowers. There were newly appointed judges of the realm and governors and magistrates to act as witnesses. The Protestant missionaries, more interested in sacraments of the Word than sacraments of sacrifice, nonetheless had an eye to ceremony. The Reverend Henry anointed him; the Reverend Nott crowned him; the Reverend Tyerman gave him a Bible and the Reverend Darling preached to him. They all shouted 'Long live the King' when it was finished and the day ended with a proclamation of amnesty and a coronation dinner (Montgomery 1831: 2/91–5; Malarde 1931).

A phial of oil, a code of laws, a Bible, a crown and a sceptre, these were the sacred things that made Pomare III king; they were the cargo that made him 'king'. 'Regents', 'governors', 'judges', 'church', 'people', these were the personifications of his 'kingdom' and the extensions of his sovereignty. From this distance they have the littered look of beached civilisation. One wonders what would turn their empty symbols into signs, what would make their metaphors into metonyms, what would make their rituals work. In these borrowed services of the civilising process, did they see themselves or did they see the Stranger?

MYTHICAL ENCOUNTERS

Captain Samuel Wallis of HMS *Dolphin* was in bed when he took possession of what he was pleased to call King George's Island in honour of His Britannic Majesty. Wallis and many of his men were sick—they thought deadly sick—of scurvy and its many complications. In the scurvy's painful lethargy, the island they stood off taunted them. Its sweet smells wafted to them and they knew it to be more beautiful than any island they had ever seen. For five days they had slowly moved along its northern shore, probing the reefs for an entry and an anchorage, looking for a beach where they might land without wetting their muskets. Their contact with the islanders had been good and bad. The islanders who had come to the ship were full of antics, made speeches at the sailors, threw plantain branches into the sea, made small gifts of food. But when the ship's cutter went closer to survey the bottom, the canoes crowded in threateningly. Already the 'Dolphins' had killed and wounded some islanders to show the force of the musket and to drive off the great double-hulled vessels that could easily overwhelm their cutter. In the wardroom the officers deliberated whether they should risk a landing or hurry on to Tinian, four thousand miles away, and let the Pacific do its worst to them in the shortest possible time (Wallis 1776: June 19, 1767ff.; Gore 1766: 2 June 1767ff.; Robertson 1948 [1766]: 138ff.; Hawkesworth 1773: 2/213ff.).

They really had no choice. Their bruised bodies, their suppurating gums, their swollen faces told them that. They had to stop their own rot with fresh food and get water in quantity before they went on. Matavai was their saving. The bay lay calm and deep behind the reef. A river curved behind the bend of the black sand beach.

'Port Royal' they called it, with half a dream for a British rather than Spanish Main that never was to be, but Matavai, its native name, in the end held the day. They had a scare as they ran aground on a reef inside the bay. Once off they were soon at anchor, undamaged except for a scrape on the *Dolphin's* new and experimental copper sheathing. Around them stretched a panorama engraved forever as paradise on the European mind. The 'Dolphins' saw the panorama more pragmatically. Their cannon could sweep it all, from off the port bow at what was to be later known as 'Point Venus', for the planet observed there, to 'Skirmish' or 'One Tree Hill' or Tahaara, two miles around on the starboard side.

At Matavai the score of the first meeting of European Stranger and Tahitian Native came to its counterpoint. The bits and pieces of contact became dramatised, staged for the understanding it gave them of one another. In the calm of the bay, the ship's people and the land's people could organise their confrontation and in that sense make it meaningful. Captain Wallis could have simply fed his men and watered his ship, and gone on. But he needed to 'make history' by 'taking possession' of the island he had 'discovered'. For that, proprieties needed some play. The Tahitians, to believe their later legendary memory, saw their prophecies of being visited by canoes without outriggers fulfilled, but they also began to collect themselves in Matavai for a more dramatic reception that made more mythical sense to them (Driessen 1982).

The 'Dolphins' prepared their ship with the suspicion that they might be attacked and the expectancy that if they were to get food and water they must discover a trade. Their preparations for fighting were well practised. They divided into four watches, loaded the great guns with shot and grape, armed every man with pistol and cutlass. They varied in their count of the canoes around them, but they were agreed these numbered between four and six hundred. Perhaps four thousand natives manned them. No doubt the 'Dolphins' were apprehensive, but they had also smarted a little under the captain's instructions to 'test the temper' of the natives in the days before. They had suffered the indignity of cuffs and rough treatment and uncomprehending exchanges and now were not averse to teaching the natives a lesson.

There was, as well an ambiguity in the situation. The 'Dolphins' had an etiquette for killing when they fought. They fought with rules, about prisoners and prizes, about surrender and the niceties of chivalry.

But on the edge of this battle, the Natives were other. Their otherness was nowhere so marked as in the wanton antics of the women who stood on the prows of most of the canoes. The women lifted their wraps and flaunted their nakedness. They made unmistakeable gestures and responded to ribaldry of the seamen as if sex had its own universal language of natural signs.

In the middle of this sea of sexuality, and in a canoe that everybody noted for its magnificence and for the 'awning' over the platforms that joined its double hull, was some sort of native director. The 'Dolphins' guessed he was one of the 'principal inhabitance'. He was wrapped in red-stained *tapa* cloth. He offered bunches of red and yellow feathers. It was he, someone said, who gave the signal with the wand in his hand. Thousands pulled pebbles from the ballast of their canoes and showered the *Dolphin* with painful accuracy. The *Dolphin* responded with awful effect. 'It would require Milton to describe', her master wrote. The canoes were smashed with round shot. When the natives rallied after the first shock and seemed to be returning, the three-pounders were loaded with seventy musket balls apiece and when the canoes were within three or four hundred yards they were sprayed, with 'considerable loss'. The great guns concentrated on the large canoe. It was the 'King of the Island', the 'Dolphins' thought. They admired the courage of those in the five or six canoes who stayed with the king even though he became the target of their firing. They will think us gods, some of the crew said, and others worried what revenge the natives might take if they came with firebrands. By nightfall the powder-smoke had gone and the officers discussed whether it was spices they now smelled on the warm heavy air. They would marvel later how little effect all this killing seemed to have on the natives. It seemed to justify their own carelessness. The *realpolitik* of discovery and possession meant the Native was not owed the ordinary etiquettes of war. The 'Dolphins' could think of nothing better to do in the aftermath of the slaughter than to 'act haughty' to the natives and teach them to trade more sensibly (Robertson 1948 [1766]: 154–8).

How the natives saw the Strangers is, by any standard of objective discourse, nothing more than informed guess. Yet to say that the meeting on the part of the natives was a co-ordinated and dramatised reception seems certain. That it was invented for the novelty of the conditions also seems certain. Their invention was suffused with their own old cosmological familiarities. It was not a 'natural' scene just because the Strangers saw it suffused with their own familiarities. The co-ordination of the natives' attack was not at the hands of the 'king of the island'. There was no 'king of the island', and later there was a strange silence about this incident of violence among those who had ambitions to be 'king of the island' when the European visits became more frequent.

It made no sense in the Tahitian way of things to see the 'king of the island' as a chief performing a political or territorial role, no matter how natural it seems that they should have been defensive against an invading 'other'. The 'other' of their wars and battles was always territorially specific—other alliances, other islands. The 'other' of this encounter was much more generic to their categories of identity. The women performing 'wanton tricks' in the canoes were a clue that something other than battle or ambush was in their minds. We know something of Tahitian war at sea. They had their etiquettes of killing too. They had their ceremonies of engagement and disengagement. In none of these were women performing 'wanton antics'. But in other circumstances, especially in the rituals of 'Oro, women's dancing was sacramental to the presence of the god. Like the tufts of red and yellow feathers, women caught the eye of the divine to focus it on prayer or an offering. Indeed, failing these, abuse of and aggression towards the gods were not unknown. Tahitian gods were not so distantly divine, even 'Oro, that they could not be tested and contested. There was no great contradiction seen in raising the attention of the gods by arousing their lust or making them angry (Oliver 1974: 1221–5, 93, 332ff.).

No doubt it is commonsensical on our part to read the hurled pebbles and signalled attack as ordinary ambush. A keen perception by the Tahitians of the lust in the seamen's eyes might have led to a strategy of subterfuge in staging the women's dancing. The Tahitians had no experience of cannon and were not necessarily convinced of the power of the musket. Native greed, Strangers' callousness, misread signs are thus the commonsensical history of the event. But they are not, and it is common sense that is the deceiver. Greed, callousness and misread signs have their play, but the 'king of the island' was likely to have been an *arioi* master of a lodge or a priest of 'Oro. His double canoe was no battleship. It was likely to have been 'Rainbow'. The awning he stood on was likely to have covered the ark of 'Oro's accoutrements, and who knows, the *maro ura*. What the Tahitians saw on the *Dolphin* was Tahitian gods, divine in the Tahitian way. Their agnosticism, their relativism was a long way off, long after the *Dolphin's* going, long after the supposedly humanising effect of the 'Dolphins' very ordinary behaviour. Tahitians were adept at seeing the divine in the human, whatever the contradictions. It is a Stranger's view, not a Native's, that there is a necessary contradiction between common-sense realism and mythical understanding. Missionaries would later be scandalised at idolaters' irreverences to their idols, as if reverential piety were a measure of belief. Cook, and later Bligh, was cynically convinced of the superficiality of Native beliefs because each had seen the Natives' distracted, formalistic behaviour in rituals. Natives as well as Strangers, ourselves as well as others, easily bridge apparent contradictions between myth and common sense. The insider knows that myth and common sense answer different questions.

What always embarasses the Stranger's effort to understand the Native is the Stranger's insistence that the Native perceptions should be literal, while the Stranger's own perceptions are allowed to be metaphoric. So the Tahitian Natives' supposed belief that the European Strangers were gods, 'from beyond the sky', is seen as a belief of literal equivalence between man and god, easily dispelled by the very ordinary behaviour of lusty, cantankerous seamen. Whereas the Strangers' more typical understanding of themselves is that they hold things in their varied meaning, so that there is for the Stranger no difficulty in taking 'he is a god' into any number of metaphors about perfection in physical beauty or intelligence or morality, without any necessary incarnational literalness. So that if one argues that the Native Tahitians received the *Dolphin* in a dramatic play that made sense to them out of their cosmology of 'Oro, there is a half expectancy that the illogicality or contradiction in the experience should have destroyed the literalness of their understanding. Their consequent make-believe in the face of contradiction is seen as either a sign of native simplicity, or as evidence that they were by this forced into a cultural agnosticism that was the seed of change.

History, myth, sacrament, ritual do not work that way. They all colligate the past and make understandings that bring order to the present. They do not prophesy what will happen or give a rubric for future behaviour. They make sense of what has happened by economising the wealth of possible causes of events down to principal determinants that really matter. This, from another perspective, is the issue that Marshall Sahlins addressed in *Historical Metaphors and Mythical Realities*. The Hawaiians had a mythic understanding of Cook as the god Lono. They did not, because of that, act out the narrative of their legends with predictable literalness. Non-mythic factors in the event—fear, anger, imprudence, pride—had their impact. But these factors, like all the other inconsistencies and contradictions and novelties surrounding the events did not matter beside the simplicities that came from a few recognisable clues. To suggest, as I do, that the Tahitian Natives put the arrival of the European Strangers into the context of their beliefs about 'Oro with all the resonances those beliefs had in politics, religion and society, is not to write the history of their contact. What 'actually happened' is inevitably reduced in the story of it to a finite mixture of infinite actions and meanings. What significantly happened for the Tahitian Natives was much simpler. The arrival of the *Dolphin* was the occasion of another 'Oro incarnation or materialisation and all the Tahitian associations of sovereignty and sacrifice, of colony and coming from 'beyond the sky', of alliance and title, were at work. It did not matter that the Tahitians were soon to discover that the 'Dolphins' were very much flesh and blood qualities of deified chiefs and the man-made quality of deified things. Their transformations of their past and present experience were about a much more real and immediate world beneath the appearances of things.

The *Dolphin* sailed into Matavai by what might always have been, but certainly by her entry became, a sacred passage off the *marae* Tarahoi. She was, by any measure the Tahitians had, a special ship, of the quality of 'Rainbow', even perhaps of the quality prophesied when news of similar vessels that had visited other islands reached Tahiti. She streamed with the magnificent decoration of white sail and bunting and flag. The Tahitians offered her, from the moment they saw her, 'Oro's token human sacrifice. The plantain branches they offered her, the inducement of naked dance and sexual gesture by which 'Oro's presence was attracted to his sacred *marae*, spoke the metaphors by which they grasped the novelty of her arrival. Slain pigs, the bunched red and yellow feathers, which no doubt meant that at some Taputapuatea a human sacrifice was lying, made the novelty familiar. If the tone and direction of myths of 'Oro collected later are any indication, the *Dolphin* came like the marvellous canoes of old from afar and Tahitian expectancy would be that she would make a landing, be the centre of sacrifice, be the occasion for re-instatement and investiture of the *ari'i rahi*, be the circumstance for alliance and treaty, and the establishment in them of some hegemony. The arrival at Matavai was true to the myth of how 'Oro would arrive to colonise a new place. It had happened at Taiarapu long ago and more recently at Ata-Huru. The novelties did not matter, nor even the contradictions. The Tahitians were entertained by its simple meaning.

Social Actions of a Symbolic Kind

The day after the violence was quiet. All day the Tahitians used 'a great deal of ceremony'. They stood in their canoes, peered hard at the *Dolphin,* made long speeches, held high their plantain branches. They clearly watched every move of the 'Dolphins' and if a sailor 'looked surly' or if there was any gesture that seemed hostile, the Tahitians held their branches high. In the end they threw their branches into the sea and came toward the *Dolphin.* Pointing to the shore and talking to the ship all the while, they threw a plantain branch on board. By this they had made a sacrifice and in their eyes made the situation manageable, for they then began to trade quite freely. The trade that afternoon was interrupted for a while when a seaman defrauded a Tahitian and the native made as if to strike the seaman and created a great fuss. The seaman, already bruised by the stones of the day before and no doubt remembering that he had tried to kill these same natives, was given a dozen lashes by Wallis. For him, it was a rueful token of the ambiguities of every meeting of Native and Stranger.

The 26 June was the day for possession, the first of many such days for Tahiti as it turned out. Wallis took possession of Tahiti in the name of George III with a pennant and a pole, a turned sod, a toast to the King's good health and three British cheers. Nine months later, Comte Louis Antoine de Bougainville buried an oak plank inscribed with the message that Tahiti belonged to the French. He left the names of all his men in a bottle. Then the Spaniards, when they came, set up a Holy Cross, processed to it with lighted candles, sang their litanies, said a mass, fired their muskets and their guns, wrote a solemn little convention to themselves. Elsewhere it was diffent and the same. Three crosses on Easter Island for Spaniards, cairns and inscriptions in New Zealand for the British, white flags in Tonga for the Dutch. Turning the sod, pennies in a bottle, throwing sand into the sea, loyal toasts, carvings on a tree, scratchings on a piece of paper, showing the colours, nailing copper and lead plates to a post, ancient ceremonies of 'turfe and twygge' the English called them: solemn acts 'to bring faith and testimony in public forms' was the Spanish phrase (Bougainville 1967 [1772]: 232–3, 238; Corney 1913 [1772]: 1/153–7, 257; Keller 1938).

Wallis, being in bed ill, sent Tobias Furneaux, his second lieutenant, to take possession of Tahiti. When Furneaux lined up eighteen able seamen, a sergeant with his twelve marines and three 'young gentlemen' or midshipmen on the black sand of Matavai bay, he was making ritual. He was making signs about authority and power, dominance and proper order; authority, power, dominance and proper order were established in the making of the signs of them. Presumably Captain Wallis could have shouted out from his sickbed, 'this island belongs to us' but that was not 'the right way of doing things'. That did not contain the double talk of straight lines, smart appearances, silence in the ranks, snapped orders, reverences to the flag. The ritual occasion is marked off from everyday actions by special languages, formal postures, the slow motion of meaningful gesture, the fancy dress of formal occasions, careful etiquette. There is always a 'priest' at ritual moments, someone who knows the established ways of doing things, someone who plans and marshalls the actions. Or there is a book of rubrics, a permanent record of the order of things. Of course in social actions of a symbolic kind it is always, in the phrase made famous about the thick description of them, 'wink upon wink upon wink'. The actions are a text in which the abstract realities are mythically read, certainly, but the participants are also observing many levels of meaning. A ritual about possession might be at the same time a ritual about the hierarchy of authority between seamen, midshipmen, sergeant and second lieutenant, or as in the case of the possession of Tahiti, it might have been telling the sailors about the wardroom divisions of their superiors. This was not the first time that the first lieutenant of the *Dolphin*, 'Mr Growl' they called him, was absent and the running of the ship and its occasions had fallen to the young and willing Toby Furneaux. Standing at attention, looking with a fixed gaze, feeling the ambience of sight and sound, even perhaps sensing the irony between their bedraggled condition and the solemnity of the symbols, they made ritual of never-ending amplification in its meaning (Wallis 1776: June 26, 1767; Robertson 1948 [1766]: 162).

Tobias Furneaux marshalled his guard on the beach. Behind him in the bay were three boats, Mr Molyneux in charge. Their musquetoons were trained on the small crowd of natives gathering on the far side of the stream. Behind the boats was the *Dolphin,* cannons trained on the same target. The guard set a pole and a pennant, or 'pendant' as was the navy's word. The pole was nothing grand or permanent, a spare spar, but tall enough to let the tapering colours stand free, and firm enough to hold them stiff in the breeze. The colours were red. James Cook saw them years later and simply called them 'British Colours' and, as we have seen, William Bligh sketched them and called them 'red buntin'. Whether red, then why red, might seem idle questions, but being curious about symbolic action is more complicated than idle. Furneaux would have asked his wardroom colleagues and then his captain which was correct, or he would have known that British colours were more appropriate than naval colours in acts of possession. And if accidents affected proprieties—say that they had none of the proper bunting to spare—its replacement would not have been made because only the 'indians would see'. Who saw it was themselves and the proprieties observed were a currency in their own relationship, about being responsible, about being a good officer. There is a comment from a later date about naval ceremonies that is relevant:

'Ceremony is to a marked degree the cement of discipline and upon discipline the service rests. Worth of ceremony rests mainly upon the fact that it binds us to the past while at the same time it lends an air of dignity and respect in all official relations'.

And the same author quotes Alfred T. Mahan on Admiral John Jervis, a man of these times, who had a strong belief in the value of forms and the habits of reverence:

'The very atmosphere he breathed was saturated with reverence. Outward reverence to the national flag, to salute the quarterdeck as the seat of authority were no vain show. Conventional good manners, rendering the due of each to each knit together the social fabric, maintain the regularity of common life, remove friction, suppressing jars and ministering constantly to the smooth and even working of the social machinery' (Lovette 1939: 4, 9).

There is a phrase we use when we see other people doing something memorable or beating some record or doing things for the first time. We say they are 'making history'. Contained within the phrase is a sense that what is remembered will change the environment in which others will act. They will have to respond in some way to the history that has been made. Samuel Wallis and Toby Furneaux were 'making history' in taking possession of Tahiti. They did not impose any system of ownership on Tahitian land. They did, however, leave an historical marker. They acted out events done with proprieties which they expected others to recognise. That memory of an act of possession was meant to change the relations of other sovereignties to this land now possessed. When James Cook came to Tahiti later and found that the Spaniards had written *Carolus Tertius Imperator* on their Holy Cross, he scratched it out and wrote *Georgius Tertius Rex* there instead. The Spaniards were furious for years. The Viceroy of Peru constantly tried to get another expedition together to scratch out Cook's inscription. It was not as if Wallis began British empire in the Pacific: he left no delegates, he built no forts. He simply 'made history' with the presumption that the

IMAGES

PLATE 1

On this hill in Hawai'i overlooking the bay of Kealakekua, where the *Resolution* and *Adventure* were at anchor, the Hawaiians possessed Captain James Cook in the ultimate way. They sacrificed him and mythologised him as Lono. They had killed him at the water's edge when he had made aggressive gestures towards their chief. Then they made history of him.

PLATE 2

Before this painting of the
Apotheosis (the divinisa-
tion) of Captain Cook,
eighteenth-century audi-
ences possessed the Hawaiians and other Pacific
islanders, also in an ultimate way. They mytholo-
gised them as objects of
their humane generosity
and scientific interest. Then
ingratitude to the civilised
was always an excuse to be
savage to the savages.

PLATE 3

PLATE 4

The Maohi possessed Strangers coming across their beach through the places of worship to 'Oro, Taputapuatea, 'Sacrifices from Abroad'.

The British took possession of Tahiti by violence in the first instance, gunning down what they saw as signs of resistance and unwelcome. Then they incorporated Tahiti into their theatre of empire. Purea became a laughable 'Queen', then a sorceress in a pantomime.

PLATE 5

David Porter believed that the Marquesans' 'republican spirit' was good enough reason to make them American. Here at Taiohae on Nukuhiva he established a fort and village which he called Madisonville before he went to fight the British. The *Essex* was a marvel of American ship-building, and Porter sailed her well until Captain Hillyer and history caught up with him.

PLATE 6

PLATE 7

PLATE 8

There never was a ship that evoked performances like the *Bounty*. William Bligh had many faces, but none has impinged on twentieth-century imagination as has Charles Laughton's impression of him. Fletcher Christian's face was caught by only one artist, but Errol Flynn and Marlon Brando give him two. Film, ballet, poetry and pantomime have given him many more.

PLATE 9

PLATE 10

The school, being on a hill, and being full of ideals, has many vistas—of the city, of religion, of sport, of sacrifice. It enfolds its memories in ritual. But history sometimes lives uncomfortably with vistas. Xavier's warriors had a very human look as they went to war. It was matched by very human stories of their sufferings.

Plate 11

This is the saddest beach in Oceania. July 1995 is the quatrocentenary of the beginnings of its sadness. Four hundred years ago a Spanish expedition, led by Alvaro de Mendana and piloted by Pedro de Quiros, 'discovered' and named the Marquesas Islands here in Vaitahu Bay on Tahuata. They called the island Santa Christiana and the bay, Madre de Dios. I still cannot tell, even after all these years of telling, the story of the terrible events which followed the Spanish 'discovery' without a catch in the throat. Any historian of cultural encounters in the Pacific should be immune to the wanton killings and mutilations that were the apparently inevitable consequences of these encounters. But somehow the extravagant thoughtlessness of the more than two hundred killings by the Spaniards is given 'composition of place' for me in a scene in which the Spanish soldiers raised three bodies on high stakes and then pierced the heart of the central figure with a lance. If there are re-enactments for the quatrocentenary, I wonder whether there will be re-enactment of this Golgothan scene.

Acknowledgements

Photographs of Hawai'i, Tahiti, Marquesas by Greg Dening; 'The Apotheosis of Captain Cook', Philippe Jacques de Loutherbourg and John Webber (Courtesy of the British Library); '*Dolphin* at Matavai', 'Purea Welcoming Wallis', John Hawkesworth, *An Account of Voyages Undertaken* . . . 1773 (Courtesy of the Baillieu Library, The University of Melbourne); 'The Prophet', 'Oberea the Enchantress', Philippe Jacques de Loutherbourg (Courtesy of the National Library of Australia); 'David Porter', 'Madisonville', David Porter, *Journal of a Cruise made to the Pacific Ocean*, 1822; '*Essex*' (Courtesy of the Peabody Museum, Salem); 'Capture of the *Essex*', *The Naval Monument*, 1816; William Bligh by John Webber (from a Private Collection), William Bligh by J. Smart (National Portrait Gallery, London), Charles Laughton, *MGM Campaign Book* 1935, Fletcher Christian by Robert Dodd (The Museum of Art, The University of Melbourne), Errol Flynn, Charles Chauvel, *In The Wake of the 'Bounty'*, 1933, Marlon Brando, *MGM Presents the Mutiny on the Bounty*, 1962; 'School at War', photographs by Douglas Kennedy (Courtesy of the Xavier College Archives).

PLATE 12

history he made would hold others to the efficacy of his symbolic acts (Beaglehole 1967 [1776]: 1372; Corney 1913 [1772]: 3/401).

This is the beginning of events in the Pacific that have virtually no concern with the Pacific at all, but with the ways France, Spain, England, the United States, Portugal, the Netherlands, Russia, Germany, Chile, Peru, Australia, New Zealand and Japan have tried to make the other see the symbolism of their history making. It might be a fancied insult to a British consul in Papeete, or a slight to a French missionary in Hawaii. It might be a claim that an American trader had 'discovered' an island first. It might be a diplomat's argument that an island on his Pacific map was strategically placed on the 'crossroads' between China and Cape Horn, Panama and Sydney. Empires would jostle one another to impose some hegemony for their historical markers. Maybe one might be skeptical that the appearances of things should be so determining of the reality of things, but recently Britain and Argentina were at war—more accurately, were fighting a 'non-war'—in the Falklands. The historical markers about which that non-war was fought and the past joined to the present were made in the very years Tahiti was possessed by the same English, French and Spaniards making the same rituals. Wallis 'made history' in his acts of possession. He performed formal acts of which there was made a formal institutional memory. The King of England proclaimed the memory when he sent Cook out to the Pacific to explore it further. The Stranger nations stored their memories of possession against one another and made sense of the past to rationalise their current divisions and statuses.

Wallis left a more concrete historical marker at Tahiti. He left his flag on its pole. By the time Furneaux had read his proclamations and hauled the pennant to its place, a crowd of four or five hundred Tahitians had gathered on the bank of the river that divided them from the beach. They each held a plantain branch, a forest of a crowd, a crowd of sacrifices. If a flag might stand for something else—for nation, for legitimate power—if gestures around a flag might stir moods and sentiments of loyalty and pride, then so might a plantain branch. Cook remarked three years later how ever present was the symbol of the plantain, and how effective. It was a sign of peace, of deference, of sacrifice.

Ta'ata meia roa, 'man long plantain' it was called, when a branch was offered to a god or to a chief as substitute for a human offering. Pulled from its natural environment where it abounded in rich variety, the plantain branch could calm an angry man, placate a god, legitimate a chief, given the conditions in which the sign could be read. As a flag could stir a manly bosom given martial music, a solemn tread and a supportive crowd, so a plantain branch might raise reverential awe, given the smell of rotting sacrifices, the shade of sacred trees, the beat and tone of a temple drum, the call of sacred birds, and the deferences of bared torsos and averted faces. It was the ambience of ritual action that made an environment in which the symbols worked. This was not easily experienced by Strangers. Instead of being entertained—held between the ordinary movements of social experience in a space to read the meanings of actions—the Strangers were the observers, catching the symbols but not the signs, translating the conventionalities of the Other's signals but not their meaning. To the Strangers the forest of sacrifices looked like a Palm Sunday procession and was depicted as such in Hawkesworth's publication of Wallis' voyage (Hawkesworth 1773: 1/243).

The Tahitians had their own layers of meanings, their own 'wink upon wink upon wink' to discern in the Strangers' ceremonies on the spit of land between sea and river. The Native Tahitians were intrigued for more than twenty-five years at the symbols of the Strangers' flags and their ceremonies about them. During Cook's stay at Tahiti as well as Bligh's, bored as the Tahitians became with the exotic behaviour of Strangers, they would collect nonetheless for their evening parades and their ceremonies about the flag. Even the *Bounty* mutineers erected their flagpole and on Sundays would have large crowds to see them haul their flag. Before such fundamentalisms of authority Tahitians never ceased to have an anthropological wonder. On the occasion of the *Dolphin's* arrival in 1767, whatever else the Tahitians saw they interpreted it as a moment in which sacrifices were owed and they came with their forest of plantain branches to make them (Morrison 1935 [1785]: 81).

When the 'Dolphins' left the beach and returned to the ship, they saw the crowd of natives approach the flag tentatively. With many gestures of deference, the islanders laid plantains at its foot and an offering of pigs. They were startled at the movements of the flag in the breeze. An old man came nearly all the way to the *Dolphin* in a canoe and made a formal speech. The sailors did not know its meaning, but it seemed to concern the flag. He threw a plantain branch into the sea and made an offering of pigs to the people on the ship as he had done to the flag, as if he had struck an agreement. With others he took the flag down and carried it away. That night the 'Dolphins' saw many large fires along the shore and on the sides of the hill (Robertson 1948: 161).

Next morning early, a crowd of several thousand processed along the coast. In the midst of them a young man held the flag aloft on a pole. They seemed to be making for a cluster of canoes near the *marae* Tarahoi. The 'Dolphins', worried that it augured a repetition of the day before, broke up the crowd with a few cannon shots, then harrassed them with grape, and destroyed the canoes. When the remnants of the crowd collected at Tahaara, 'Skirmish Hill', the 'Dolphins' fired their cannon again, so that the crowd could see the balls bouncing across the landscape, ploughing through the trees. The cutter was sent in to the canoes and the crew finished with axes what the cannon had not done.

Perhaps the 'Dolphins' were correct in surmising that the flag was being taken to the canoes. We cannot know. It was unlikely that there was to be another attack however. Right-handed processions, like those of *makahiki,* described by Sahlins for Hawaii, were rituals for acknowledging sovereignty. Later, other British flags acquired by the Pomares were carried at the head of these processions. In all probability the Tahitians were making for some canoe, some other Rainbow of 'Oro. We know they were soon to take the flag to the other side of the island, to the district of Papara, to a *marae* called Mahaiatea then being built or about to be built by the chief of the Landward Teva, Amo, and his wife, Purea. Amo and Purea were about to make an invention. Amo's name meant 'Wink'. They were indeed about to put 'wink upon wink upon wink'.

Making Englishmen's Fantasies Work

Purea, or 'Oberea' as a much wider English public began to know her, was about to enter the stage of history as the 'Queen of Tahiti'. She was not queen, of course, but a royal personage was needed to make the Englishmen's fantasies work. How they invented her and she invented them belongs to the story of how Native and Stranger became symbiotic to one another, how they possessed one another. Indeed one has to say, even if the complications become confusing, the inventing of Purea did not end with the eighteenth century. Inventing Purea has been part of a long historical process and is illustrative not merely of the ways Native and Stranger become environmental to one another but also of the ways the past becomes environmental to the present (Oliver 1974: 1200).

Purea entered the stage modestly enough. Two weeks after the rituals of possession, George Robertson, the master of the *Dolphin,* saw a small fleet of ten or twelve double canoes, all wearing streaming pennants of red, white, blue and yellow, land near the *marae* of Tarahoi. Then Mr Pickersgill 'on a walk in the country' ten days after that came upon a great house, the 'palace' as it came to be called. There he was entertained by the queen, and she in turn was fed hand to mouth by her 'ladies in waiting'. On 20 or perhaps 11 July—there is some conflict in the records—Purea came on board the *Dolphin.* The captain treated her royally and there began a series of pseudo-social occasions in which Wallis and his officers displayed their civilised ways and enjoyed the gaffes that showed the satire in savage queens. They laughed at her simplicities in handling telescopes and cutlery and mirrors, but they were divided in their opinion at her extravagant sorrow at their departure as to whether it was a subterfuge to ambush them again, whether it was the childishness of natives, or whether it was they who were something special. On the whole they seemed to like their relations with this queen-but-not-a-queen: in them they had control over their own marginality (Wallis 1776: July 13, 1767; Robertson 1948 [1766]: 203–6).

In the way of things, the day-to-day relations of Purea with the officers of the *Dolphin* were less important than the history of them. That history was to compress Purea into one invention of two ethnographic encounters. No sooner had Wallis returned to England than Cook was sent out to Tahiti to check on Wallis' supposed sighting of the Great South Land and to measure the Transit of Venus across the sun for the Royal Society. The young Joseph Banks went with him. Cook and Banks found the politics of Tahiti changed. More correctly, they found they had to change their suppositions about the politics of Tahiti. Purea and Amo had been defeated in their plan to establish their son Teri-i-reree as the most highly titled and the most politically significant figure on Tahiti. The seaward Teva had erupted from Taiarupu, massacred many of the people of Papara and destroyed any hopes Purea and Amo had of making Mahaiatea the ritual centre of the island, the treasure house of the *maro ura*, and specifically of the *maro ura* with Wallis' pennant sewn into it. That *maro ura* had gone now to Utu'aihamurau at Pa'ea (Oliver 1974: 1213; Rose 1978: 9).

Purea was no longer 'queen'. The politics of the island, in so much as it concerned the Strangers, was in the hands of Tu and his line, the chiefs of Pare-Arue, near Matavai. These real events hardly made any difference to the history of them. Purea was about to be presented as queen to the public of England in the recounting of them. In that way Tahiti was about to be possessed in another way.

Cook returned to England in July 1771 and within five months was on his way to the Pacific on his second voyage, too briefly at home to publish an account of his first discoveries. Joseph Banks was in a huff at not being allowed to dominate another Grand Tour of the Pacific, and in any case was involved in the harum-scarum of his social-scientific life. The task of presenting the Pacific discoveries of Byron, Wallis, Cartaret and Cook was given to Dr John Hawkesworth by the Admiralty. Hawkesworth was a savant, more of a moralist than a geographer. The Admiralty contracted him, but the publishers, William Strahan and Thomas Cadell, made sure his *Voyages* would be entertainment by giving him £6000 for the copyright, the largest payment in England for the whole of the century. Hawkesworth did not live to enjoy the money. Within months of publishing his volumes he had died, killed by the anxieties which the jealousies, scandals and criticism of his work had raised. Possessing the Other is always filtered by the more immediate concerns of the familiar.

Dr Hawkesworth was a reflective man, very conscious of what he was about when he was translating other men's ethnographic moments. Was it *his* book? Who was the 'I' of the author that joined the navigators', different experiences? What did it mean to join not one but dozens of logs and journals together? What was the real experience—the dull data of sailing or the moral issues of the encounter? He had a sense that if his book was about Pacific discoveries it was also a vehicle for something else. That something else, his sense of the universal significance of totally particular events, is what got him into trouble. His critics were loud. The sailors, who he purported to represent, said he was not like them at all. Dr Samuel Johnson, always cantankerous about natives and foreign places, thought that for Hawkesworth there were better things to write about and for Banks better things to do. Horace Walpole got into a fluster. John Wesley disapproved. All sorts of people did not read the *Voyages* for the reputation that the critics gave it. It was an 'attack against religion and an outrage against decency', and £6000 was just too much to pay for what many believed they themselves could do better.

The extravagance of the critics' rage concerned almost everything about Hawkesworth's book, but they reserved a special sense of scandal that a moralist, who had been given a Doctor of Letters for his uplifting thought, should have displayed the gross sexuality of the Tahitians and the randiness of Mr Banks. There was horror, as well, that Dr Hawkesworth should have denied what everybody knew to be a 'particular Providence' in the saving of Cook's *Endeavour* after its shipwreck on the Australian coast. A 'Christian' who hounded Hawkesworth in the press for months said it all:

'Our women may find in Dr Hawkesworth's Book stronger Excitements to vicious indulgences than the most intriguing French Novel could present to their imaginations—and while our Mariners no longer look up to the Almighty for Deliverance from Shipwreck—or feel Gratitude rise in their Breasts on being saved from impending Evils—our Libertines may throw aside the *Women of Pleasure*, and gratify their impure minds with the Perusal of infinitely more lascivious Recitals than are to be found in that scandalous Performance!' (Abbott 1982: 161).

Actually, Dr Hawkesworth was a disturber, an entertainer, on two counts. His exposition of native sexual customs was history, a story of what happened, not a fantasy. To tell it he had to affect a neutrality which, in his critics' eyes, he did not have by his telling it. His sus-

pension of judgement was seen as a judgement. He disturbed and entertained in his relativist stance. Hawkesworth had remarked that he did not
think it was by a particular divine intervention that the *Endeavour* was
saved when the wind dropped as she ran aground on a reef off the New
Holland coast. It was no more especially providential, he said, than the sun
rising every morning. It was his comment on an old and unfinished debate
about the efficacy of prayer and the problem of evil. But it was transformed from a theologian's squabble into a confrontation about myth
by the dramaturgy of his contentious publication. The fever of excitement
about Pacific discoveries, the fever of excitement about a book that was
£6000, the fever of excitement about the gossip concerning famous people,
all transformed private opinion that did not matter into a public declaration
of faith on which civilisation was seen to turn. People who would never
have read Hawkesworth berated him for undermining the confidence
of the masses who prayed for a helping intervention by a loving God.

Without wanting to over-dramatise matters for the sake of a small
point, let me say that within a European culture on the edge of a revolution in its own myths about the relationship of the supernatural and the
natural, Hawkesworth's view on a 'particular providence' became an
occasion in which many, in being forced to look at the Other, were
entertained by ambiguities they discovered in themselves. 'Entertained',
you will have noticed, I have begun to use with special stress. I refer to
those social moments in which by many signs and actions we establish a
setting in which we abstract or display the meaning of what we do.

Purea appeared in Hawkesworth's *An Account of the Voyages . . . by
Commodore Bryon, Captain Wallis, Captain Cartaret, and Captain Cook*
in an engraving entitled 'A representation of the surrender of the island
of Otaheite to Captain Wallis by the supposed Queen Oberea'. She was
depicted as presenting a plantain branch as if it were a palm branch of
peace. Behind her came a procession of her people, bowing and defer-
ential to Wallis who held his musket like a sceptre and was supported
by his guard who looked like a troop of Hessian mercenaries. A large
crowd of Tahitians looked on, out of a pavilion-like grass hut. It was, of
course, a 'representation' of a 'surrender' that never took place, with gestures that could never have been made. In that it was both as abstract and

as concrete as Toby Furneaux's rituals of possession on the beach. In being history of something that never happened, it abstracted a truth whose accuracy did not matter: 'Tahiti belongs to us'. But Purea became famous in England most of all, because she had a tattooed bum, because she orchestrated a public copulation, because she watched while a young girl danced naked before Banks, and because, while she slept with Banks, he had his clothes stolen. She entered the English imagination not as the Other but as a setting for an argument about morality and corruption. To know her was to know and laugh at the real Mr Banks (Hawkesworth 1773: 1/243).

The British possessed Tahiti by compressing the complexities of their ethnographic moment into a few experiences made memorable because they displayed Tahiti as a mirror for themselves. Beginning with Hawkesworth's account, descriptions of Tahitian ways and the Tahitian environment began to accumulate in books, magazines and newspapers, in notes and programmes for museum collections, in caches of letters and journals, in the memories of myriad conversations with those who had been there. There is no measure of their impact other than guess. There is no way of knowing if the infinite variety of experience was drawn together in any one image of Tahiti. Let me argue, however, that there was such a compression of this varied experience, a reduction to simplicities. These simplicities emerged not so much out of philosophical systems concerning soft primitivism or out of a romantic mood, as out of dramatic ironies in which the Strangers were entertained by themselves.

To judge from the constant guffaws, one of the principal dramatic ironies turned on Queen Oberea's 'pinked bum'. Maybe there has been a British cultural preoccupation with the lower anatomy over the centuries, but at the end of the eighteenth century there was clearly something very delicious in seeing the appearance of native courtly dignity shattered by the revelation of a 'tattowed breech'. Hawkesworth's account was followed by the publication of an extra-ordinary series of poetic and satirical letters. They were purported to be written by many people—by a 'Professor of the Otaheite Language in Dublin and of all the languages of the undiscovered islands of the South Seas', by a 'Second Professor of the Otaheite and every other unknown language'. 'Oberea' herself supposedly wrote two to her lovers, one to Banks, one to Wallis. Omai, as her plenipotentiary, supposedly wrote to her and then to the 'Right Honourable the Earl of **, Late *******—Lord of the *******'. 'An officer at Otaheite' wrote to 'Lady Gr**v*n*r' a 'poetical epistle (Moral and Philosophical)', and a 'Lady of Quality' wrote to Omai. The 'Injured Harriet', Banks' jilted fiancée wrote to the 'presumptuous Indian' and 'savage usurper' 'Oberea'. The publications jabbed and jibed at Banks, stuck like a butterfly on his own collection board by the pin of his own naivety. They caught others as well, Lord Sandwich and his various ladies, 'the English arioi' of Pall Mall, venal bishops and ambitious bishops' wives, Methodist preachers with their 'bagpipical drawl' preaching messages 'dangerous to society'. And always there was the 'luscious' Hawkesworth who 'scenes obscene his pencil painted best'. These poems and letters cannibalised one another in their diversion: they came back again and again to the same incidents on the voyage. They made simplicities by repetition. They were redolent with classical and literary allusion: Dido and the Aeneid as representative of real high culture mocked the spurious charm of savages. They played the ironies every way— of English courtly cultivation seen through innocent primitive eyes, of raw savages seen by exquisite sophistication. 'Here painted faces bloom on every strum/ In Otahiete we tattoo the bum'. 'Vain Oberea will in vain beseech/And to the bawdy winds betray her painted breech' (Roderick 1972; Court of Apollo 1774; English Alphabet 1786; Epistle from Mr Banks n.d.; Epistle from Oberea 1775; Historic Epistle 1774; Injured Islanders 1779; Letter from Omai 1780a, 1780b; Mimosa 1779; Omiah's Farewell 1776; Poetical Epistle 1775; Second Letter n.d.; Seventeen Hundred 1777).

Banks' botanical interests were the subject of every conceivable *double entendre* as critics explored the metaphorical field around his *plant*. 'Oberea' was a 'hapless fair one' for losing both her crown and her lover Banks. But she was also a 'hotty-tooty queen' for her easy morals. Nothing gave an edge to their satire more than three sexual incidents in which Banks and Oberea played a part. One concerned a small Tahitian girl apparently marshalled by 'Oberea' and observed by Cook. The third was the stealing of Banks' vest and pistol while he slept on 'Oberea's' canoe. There was a fourth whose context would take us too far afield. It was the subject of forbearing humour rather than satire. No doubt this was because promiscuity of the lower classes was less figurative than dissipation among the upper. This was the incident of the nails and the 'old trade' of Tahitian women's sexual favours for the new currency of spikes and iron. There was a natural inflation as the women found there were bigger and longer nails. In these circumstances a *nail* was also a *plant*.

> With nails we Traffic for the blooming maid
> And the ships planks supply the dangerous trade
> At last the fair ones see with strange surprise
> Some nails produced of more than common size
> The happy females with this treasure grac'd.
> Display their triumphs and our coins debased.
> In vain we sue, the Nymphs comply no more.
> 'Give us large nails', reaches from the shore.
>
> (Poetical Epistle 1775)

Maybe there was a fifth interest that showed how the meeting of the Other was translated into more self-centred concerns and were made memorable because of that. This was the furious debate as to who introduced the 'venereals' to Tahiti, Wallis or Bougainville? These British poems were sure that 'pining Venus mourns the gift of France' or were confident that when 'a Frenchman gave, a Briton heal'd the wound' with Harray's patent venereal medicine. Beyond the poems, whose attention to venereal disease was slight, there were louder and more official protests of British innocence. The matter was quickly transformed into an issue of national honour and international diplomacy, the continued memory or history of which affected 'Tahiti–Europe' relations for decades.

'Timorodee' became a word of some common usage at the end of the eighteenth century (J. C. Beaglehole suggests 'timorodee' was Cook's hearing of the Tahitian *te ai maro iti,* pseudo-copulation, but Oliver, measuring his certainties more precisely, is non-committal). It was taken to mean lascivious dancing of the sort that was performed for Banks by a young girl who ceremoniously, by his account, 'displayed her naked beauties' in making a present to him of the clothes that clothed her.

While, as she turns her painted bum to view,
With fronts unblushing, in the public shew,
They search each crevice with a curious eye,
To find Exotics—where they never lie.
O Shame! Were we, great George, thy gallant crew,
And had we—damn it—nothing else to do,
But turn thy great design to filthy farce
And search for wonders or an Indian's a . . .?
But then to print our tale!
O, curse the thought.

(Epistle from Mr Banks n.d.)

The public copulation of a young man and a girl of ten or twelve years at the gate of Fort Venus under the direction of 'Oberea' was commented on by Cook. In his interpretation it was done 'more from custom than lewdness'. But Cook's niceties of judgement did not stop the howls of derision at such incipient cultural relativism. With barbarism so blatant, the soft savage was a mockery, and the lesson to be learned was that there were no lessons to be learned. The image of the young Banks crying 'thief' in the middle of the night for the loss of his silver-frogged waistcoat and pistol while he lay naked beside his 'old friend Oberea' on her double-canoe was a gift beyond price for the satirist.

Didst thou not, crafty, subtle, sunburnt strum
Steal the silk breeches from his tawny bum?
Calls't thouself a Queen? and thus couldst use
And rob thy Swain of breeches and his shoes?

(Court of Apollo 1774)

It was a scene out of pantomime—I use the analogy advisedly for reasons that will become apparent. It was the farce of savage kingdoms, the malapropism of scientific gentlemen. 'Great Alexander conquered boys and belles', wrote the 'Injured Harriet', 'Mine sailed the world around for cockle-shells'. What Wallis, Cook and Banks saw and what Hawkesworth described were not 'exotics' at all. Banks' romantic effort, Cook's more puzzled attempt, Hawkesworth's tentative tries at discovering the Tahitians in their Otherness were denounced as insufferable license. The Tahitian were not Other at all: they were the same only worse. Even the most tenuous cultural relativism in understanding the Tahitians as they were threatened the common-sense realism. In the *realpolitik* of a joke all the world is the same. Strangers possess Natives in a laugh.

'A School for the History of Men'

Purea had another sort of incarnation. She appeared as 'Oberea the Sorcerer' in a pantomime at Covent Garden, December 1785. The pantomime was called 'Omai, or a Trip around the World' and proved to be entertainment in all the senses of the word that we have used. While pantomime at the end of the eighteenth century had not settled into all its conventionalities and still waited for the skills of such actors as Joseph Grimaldi to fix the prominence of such characters as Clown, nonetheless its rubrics set its formal structure. It was always a tale of a virtuous young love thwarted by authority or rivalry, the whole transformed magically into a romping charade of Harlequin, his lover Columbine, his rival Pantaloon and Clown through successive scenes till all was resolved in a splendorous finale. The timeless inevitability of the harlequinade was a setting for a vaudeville of topicality in which events and personages and environments were made comically present. The ritualistic taken-for-granted formalities of the pantomime made the relevancies more dramatic. There was no story, no masque in the topicalities, only scenes, the more real for the unreality of the magic and the make-believe. 'Omai', wrote the critic in *Rambler's Magazine*, was a 'school for the history of Man'. And the *Times* which reviewed nearly every performance said:

'The stage never exhibited such a combination of superb and various scenery—enchanting music and sheer fun. The scenes, characters and dresses being, except a few, novel and foreign to this country, contribute much to heighten the delight, for what can be more delightful than an enchanting fascination that monopolizes the mind to the scene before the eye, and leads the imagination from country to country, from the frigid to the torrid zone, shewing as in a mirror, prospects of different climates, with all the productions of nature in the animal and vegetable worlds, and all the efforts of man to attain nourishment, convenience and luxury, by the world of arts. It is a spectacle worthy of the contemplation of every rational being, from infant to the aged philosopher. A spectacle that holds forth the wisdom and dispositions of Providence in the strongest view'.

The pantomime was a 'beautiful illustration of Cook's voyages'. It was a translation in entertainment of an ethnographic moment (Joppien 1979; Allen 1962, 1965, 1966; Huse 1936; Mayer 1969; *European Magazine* Dec. 1785; *New London Magazine* Dec. 1785; *London Chronicle* Dec. 1785; *Universal Daily Register (London Times)* Dec. 1785).

The genius of this translation was Philippe Jacques de Loutherbourg and with him the Irish playwright, John O'Keeffe, and the musical composer, William Sheild. They were joined by the painter of Cook's third voyage, John Webber. It was the genius of them all to make their translations seem real. Loutherbourg was the great technological innovator of the eighteenth-century stage. In 'Omai', his brilliance was on full display. It caught up the simplicities of being Other in an exhibition of civilised technology. He even recreated the latest technological advance — the flying balloon, invented only two years before—to help in the mad chase of Omai around the world. All evening long the audiences knew they were seeing history as it happened because in the madcap farce they applauded and gasped at realities, both experienced and imagined, masterfully represented.

John O'Keeffe, the playwright, did not have to write a script—pantomimes were sung and mimed—but in his lyrics he verbalised the British mood of satisfaction at its humanism towards savage peoples. He also made a patter mixed with Tahitian words, solemnly referenced for their meaning in the printed programme. In his memories of the pantomime in later years, he singled out the realism of the actor Wewitzer, who played a Tahitian prophet and made his obeisance to Cook in *ex tempore* gobbledy-gook carefully 'translated' in the programme. The 'as if' was just as good as the real (O'Keeffe 1826: 2/115).

There was much praise for the composer, William Sheild. He caught the 'vernacular airs of Otaheite' in his music, imitating conches and mimicking wild beasts 'to make the performance as characteristic as possible'. Sheild was fresh from composing the 'Marriage of Figaro' and the critics revelled in his beautiful music. It was a real translation, 'as much as science can approach barbarity', they said.

John Webber lent the greatest authenticity of all. He could paint what he had seen: he was the expert adviser on landscapes and sacred places, on weapons and native crafts. He drew the costumes for the procession of Pacific nations that heroicised Cook in the final scene when a giant painting of his apotheosis descended on the stage. Webber, poor because of the embargo on exhibition and publication about Cook's third voyage before the official account was published, could make a few pounds painting scenes and giving dramatic focus to the dozen painters who worked for three months to put the sets together. Sir Joshua Reynolds, who had painted the real Omai, sat in the orchestra seats at the pantomime to get the best possible view. He pronounced the painting of the scenery very real indeed, though he had not got much closer to the South Seas than his own studio.

The relics surviving from the pantomime are few—reviews and descriptions in a dozen newspapers and magazines, the published lyrics of John O'Keeffe and a narrative programme, two maquettes or scene-models in a museum and a private collection, sketches of the costumes by Loutherbourg and Webber, Loutherbourg's pencil sketch of the apotheosis of Captain Cook and a painting of a painting of the same, and the original engravings of Cook's voyages that were the provenance of the scenes. The characters in the pantomime are, like the Tahitian words in O'Keeffe's songs, names snatched from the common records of the European encounter with the Tahitians. There was Omai, the living curiosity who had come to England and returned to Tahiti with Cook. But he had been transformed into the son of 'King' Otoo and made heir to the Tahitian throne. There was Oedidee, known by successive visitors to Tahiti, but now transformed into the rival of Omai and the protege of Oberea. Oberea (Purea) was now a menacing sorceress bent on raising Oedidee to the throne of Tahiti. She tried to foil the marriage of Londina to Omai. Yes, Londina, the daughter of Britannia, was promised by her mother to Omai to join the two kingdoms of Britain and Tahiti. Omai's rival to Londina's hand was the Spaniard, Don Struttolando, and it was the Don's pursuit of the lovers that set up the helter-skelter trip around the world: to Kamchatka, to the 'Ice Islands'—Arctic or Antarctic does not matter—to the Friendly Islands, to the Sandwich Islands, to Tahiti.

In Tahiti, the denouement took place. Omai was rescued from Oberea's evil spirit. Her famous palace was burnt down. Omai was installed as king. Then to Matavai, 'the Great Bay of Otaheite', came a procession of all the peoples of the Pacific islands which Captain Cook discovered or visited: Tahitians, New Zealanders, Tannans, Marquesans, Tongans, Hawaiians, Easter Islanders; and Tehutzki Tartars, Kamchatkars, Eskimos, Indians of Nootka, Oonalaski and Prince William Sound. The people of the procession, identified in the pantomime programme, were 'dressed characteristically' according to Webber's advice and Loutherbourg's design. They acclaimed Omai as King. A Mad Prophet stepped forward—it was Wewitzer's great moment—and congratulated Omai for paddling to the 'Country of the mighty George whose great sword in the hand of Elliott, keeps the Strong Rock from the Rich King of Lima, even in his own land' (the Mad Prophet, at least, knew the significance of Don Struttolando and the politics of Gibraltar!). 'Know all that Omai is the master of fifty red feathers, master of four hundred fat hogs; he can command a thousand fighting men and twenty strong handed women to thump him to sleep!' An English captain steps forward and gives a sword to Omai.

Captain: 'Accept from mighty George our Sovereign Lord
                In sign of British love, this British sword'.
Oberea: Oh joy! Away my useless spells and magic charms
                A British sword is proof against the world in arms.
Captain: Ally of Joy! Owhyee's (Footnote: The island where Captain
                Cook was killed) fatal shore
                Brave Cook, your great Orono (Footnote: A Demigod or
                hero and distinguished title with which the natives
                honoured Captain Cook) is no more.

Indians: Mourn, Owhyee's fatal shore
           For Cook, our great Orono, is no more!

At that moment the huge painting of 'The Apotheosis of Captain Cook' began to descend onto the stage. Cook, looking a little anxious it has to be admitted, was in the clouds over Kealakekua Bay where he had been killed and was being crowned by Britannia and Fame. The voices of the peoples welled into a great chorus:

> Ye chiefs of the ocean your laurels throw by
> Or cypress entwine with a wreath.
> To prove your humanity, heave a soft sigh
> And a tear now let fall for his death!
> Yet the Genius of Britain forbids us to grieve
> Since Cook ever honour'd immortal shall live.
>
> The hero of Macedon ran o'er the world
> Yet nothing but death could he give
> 'Twas George's command and the sail was unfurl'd
> and Cook taught mankind how to live.
>
> He came and he saw, not to conquer but to save
> The Cesar of Britain was he:
> Who scorn'd the conditions of making a slave
> While Britons themselves are so free
> Now the Genius of Britain forbids us to grieve
> Since Cook ever honour'd immortal shall live.
>
> (O'Keeffe 1785)

It was a very satisfying moment. O'Keeffe thought it the high moment of his lyrics. The critics felt a little cheated that, after an evening of extravagant spectacle, the apotheosis of Cook was represented rather blandly in painting. After all, they said, a deification was something special and deserved a little drama of its own. But it was enough for most. George III came to see the pantomime many times. It was performed fifty-six times in all.

It is a folly at such a distance and with such sparse evidence to say what was happening, what social realities were being established by these dramaturgies. Let me say what occurs to me. I think that, in the ambience of entertainment, mood and meaning were reduced to simplicities. In 'Omai' the absurdities and make-believe of the pantomime were blown away by the reality of the truth of the last scene. With music and chorussed voices and staged solemnity to set the soul aquiver, the humanism of Civilisation was set beside the quaintness of the Other. In that humanism was known the benignity of power, the good intentions of the end that will justify the means. It was (as it always is) the realisms of empire that properly bound Native and Stranger together. On the other hand, the Natives were more quaint than threateningly different. There was the quiet put-down of the Mad Prophet of the new 'King' Omai's power in fifty red feathers, four hundred pigs and twenty thumping women. But the unreal quaintness of kings-who-are-not-really-kings was set in an entertainment in which the audience were convinced they were watching a science of reality. 'Omai' was Loutherbourg's *eiduphusikon vérité* (if I might have a quiet joke with those who know of Loutherbourg's invention of the *eiduphusikon,* a sort of magic lantern). His talent was to make illusions realistic. The whole night long the audience saw the mildly make-believe and ahistorical persons, Omai, Oberea, Otoo, Oedidee, clothed in the realisms of their environment—their houses, their ornamentation, their language. And the realisms of this unfamiliar environment were made the more certain by the realisms of more familiar environment: of Kensington, of Margate, of Plymouth. That is why the audience could come away certain that they had been at a 'school for the history of man' when in the history of men and women the pantomime was an extravagant hocus-pocus.

Meeting Purea

The inventions of Purea and, in her, of her culture did not end with her dying or even with the dying of contemporary interest in her. I tell Purea's story as if the events of the past are disconnected with the present, as if our meeting with Purea was somehow direct. We know that is not so, of course, but we are adept in seeing the past 'as if' it were unmediated by its relics. Like physicists who see through the material qualities of the world around them to its nuclear structure, like botanists who see the classification of a tree, not the poetry of it, we too, by tone and tense and supportive agreement make 'as if' we are in touch with the past. The ambiguities are too many, the lateral pursuits too frequent, the operational judgements too complex for us to be anything but pragmatic. It is the present with which we are in touch. The past is mediated to us by all the inventions that have happened in-between.

You, the reader are mediated by me, the writer. One could suppose that you have heard of Purea at this moment for the very first time. More likely because of the conditions that make you aware of your desire to read this volume, you will have heard of Purea before. You will know that what I write belongs to a discourse that has already engaged the attention of highly respected Polynesian scholars, such as John C. Beaglehole, Colin Newbury, Neil Gunson, Douglas Oliver, Roger Green, Roger Rose. You would know the problematic that has been shaped by their discourse: whether the hegemony of political power that was eventually established in Tahiti evolved out of Tahitian potentialities or whether it was effected by the European arrival, or whether some combination of evolutionary and external forces prompted change. Those scholars ask whether the Pomare dynasty's victory at the cost of Purea's family's defeat came from political violence or from manipulation of accepted legitimating symbols. You will know that my own or anybody's entry into that discourse would be by way of both removing and increasing the ambiguities. I justify my right to tell the story of possessions by submitting my statements to the test of accuracy, by having read all the extant sources, by warning about their contradictions, by elaborating on the grades of my sense of certainty, by argument and extension of argument. I could not tell the number of times I have 'met' Purea: in undergraduate essays I correct now, in researches for something else in all the books that I have read. There is not a sentence that I write of her that could not take a page or a chapter to balance its probabilities, to make explicit the meandering trail by which I come to it. And you, the reader, are in any case a figment of my imagination. I write for you, making decision on decision about what I select, what I leave out, wondering what you would know, what would tease you to read more. It cannot be that I write just for Douglas Oliver or Neil Gunson or Colin Newbury or Roger Green or Roger Rose, although they will know my licences. It cannot be that I write to make my readers equally expert as them or me about Purea. I write to have my inventions join my readers'. Poor impossible-to-reach Purea is not the mutual goal of our knowledge but the vehicle for our joined understanding. Her exemplarity is surely our shared invention.

Purea and the whole context of her life comes to us through a chain of inventions and possessions by an infinite number of Strangers and by Purea's own Native descendants who in time became Strangers to her as well. The inventions of the Strangers came by way of their own historical reconstruction and out of many references, direct and indirect, made by later seamen and missionaries. Mostly these were a jigsaw of references to Tahitian men and women connected to Purea by marriage and descent. Much of it was in the way of reflections by the likes of Cook, Forster and Bligh, correcting the misinterpretations of one another. Its history, like all history's inventions, were made by what has been called colligation, the drawing together of the bits and pieces of many pasts, of many discoveries (Oliver 1974; Beaglehole 1976; Gunson 1963; Newbury 1967a, 1967b, 1980; Rose 1978; Green 1968).

Among the many little inventions of Purea, however, there has been one large one. It came a hundred years after her death, and it came from an unexpected pen, that of Henry Adams, American historian. Wounded by his wife's suicide, inspired by Robert Louis Stevenson's wanderings in the Pacific, Adams arrived in Tahiti in 1891. There he was more bored than enchanted, but in his last days as he looked for a ship to get away he met with an old woman of nearly seventy years, Arii Taimai. He met her, as it chanced, at the ceremonial opening of a bridge. The bridge had been built with the stones of the dismantled *marae* Mahaiatea, the sacred place which Amo and Purea had built for their son in 1767–8 in the days of their high ambitions. The old woman was pleasantly garru-lous, full of the legends her father had taught her. Arii Taimai was of the Teva clan. Her great-grandfather had been Amo's brother. She had, in her own name, title to more than thirty Tahitian *marae*. She had also been adopted by the widow of Pomare II, had spent nearly the whole of her life suspended in the web of rhetoric about dominance and legitimacy of Tahitian lines and titles.

For days on end in 1891 Arii Taimai talked to Henry Adams through the interpreter, her daughter Marau. Adams had to leave before he made sense of it all, but Marau forwarded further notes to him in Washington when he returned in 1892. Tati Salmon, son of Arii Tamai, visited Adams in Washington later in the same year. Adams returned the hospitality he had received in Tahiti and used Salmon as informant. Adams, back among his books, soon absorbed the accumulated history of Tahiti through the journals of Wallis, Cook, Bougainville and Bligh, as well as the publications of the London Missionary Society. With the extravagance of the wealthy and the fastidious, he had a few copies of his researches privately printed in 1893. Then, feeling he had discovered his own American cultural commercialism in Tahitian idealism, he abandoned his mundane researches and went looking for his medieval spiritual roots in Europe. In 1908 he edited a version of the *Memoirs of Arii Taimai*. In it he maintained the fiction that it was Arii Taimai's pen that had written the memoirs. It is no great exercise of higher criticism to balance the heaviness and lightness of Adams' hand as he made an English text out of Tahitian memories interpreted to him in French by Arii Taimai's daughter. Every element of the *Memoirs* is a translation. None is so much a translation as Adams' projection of a Teva understanding of the past won from the experience of the waxing and waning fortunes of Purea who had lost, and of their enemies the Pomares who had lost and won and lost (Adams 1947, 1964; Gunson 1963).

Henry Adams, speaking in Arii Taimai's voice, wrote of Purea: 'If a family must be ruined by a woman, perhaps it may as well be ruined thoroughly and brilliantly by a woman who makes it famous'. As the Teva clan remembered her, Purea upset proprieties by demanding acknowledgement of her social superiority in symbolic ways. Her son, a boy of eight or nine in 1767, was the most highly titled person in Tahiti, the possessor of both the *maro ura* and *maro tea*. In their polity,

Tahitians had no difficulty in distinguishing the deference they owed to higher titles and the deference they owed to the politically dominant. Deference to high titles they paid at the sacred places of these titles, at the Taputapuatea in the case of titles that were owed sacrifice. Deference to political dominance they showed in submissive ceremony to symbols of extended authority. Submission ceremonies surrounded the acknowledgement of some sign of dominance as it was processed around the island. Political power was expressed not so much by the person and the presence of the *ari'i* as by the extension of his person in his symbols and by his messengers. It was acknowledged by gift and sacrifice. Purea's downfall occurred over her effort to equate the titled dominance of her son with the political dominance of herself and Amo. As the Teva told it, it was an affair of women. Purea, in building the *marae* Mahaiatea, imposed a *rahui,* a prohibition of food and behaviour that was the right of *ari'i rahi* alone to impose. To obey it was to acknowledge superiority. Two women, a sister and a brother's wife to Purea, challenged the *rahui* by paying formal visits to Purea. These formal visits demanded hospitality and therefore the lifting of the *rahui* between equals. The rift that followed Purea's refusal to acknowledge the womens' equality and raise the *rahui* was said to be the cause of battle and then of the defeat of Purea that followed (Adams 1947: 44).

Different sources put the matter differently. After the investiture of Teri-i-reree at Mahaiatea, Amo and Purea were said to have demanded the ceremonial submission that came with the procession of symbols around the island. Submission by the Seaward Teva was refused and in the battles that followed, Amo and Purea were defeated and the m*aro ura* of Teri-i-reree moved to a new (but older) sacred place in Ahuru. This attempt by Amo and Purea to establish political hegemony over the whole island of Tahiti followed the Tahitian possession of the Wallis flag and its incorporation into a *maro ura*. The sources say quite explicitly that it was not the British jack that was paraded around the island but some other symbol. The most knowledgeable of modern historians of ancient Tahiti, Douglas Oliver, says that he favours the view that the British flag was incorporated in an already existing *maro ura*. It is, let there be no doubt, a question of guess and probability. Let me invent another sort of past out of what I see as a different set of likelihoods (Oliver 1974: 1221–35).

The *maro* with the British colours was a new symbol. Descriptions of those who saw it say it was made of both red and yellow feathers, not just the red of the *maro ura* or the yellow-white of the *maro tea*. There is a logic in the combined colours that says that this *maro* had the qualities of all the others. The drawing Bligh made of it showed the bunting to be at one end. It seems finished. The rounded tassels that were essential to the sacred wrap were attached to the bunting. If the bunting had been added to an existing *maro,* one would expect twenty years of sacrifices (from 1767 to 1788) to have enclosed the bunting with lappets of feathers. Let us say that the British flag, possessed by the Tahitians in the context of their 'Oro beliefs and seen by them as a symbol of political dominance and sovereignty after their violent disaster, was taken by the people of Amo and Purea to Papara. There it was constructed into a *maro ura* (the term is used generically by the Tahitians as well as specifically) that symbolised a different sort of title to a different sort of sovereignty.

Their translation was certainly some extension of the potentialities of their own symbol system. It was neither a totally new nor a totally old way of doing things. This new *maro ura* was in itself a history of the first Native encounter with the Stranger. It was a document, a text to be read by those with immediate knowledge of its meaning. It gave institutional continuity with all the structures and roles of its preservation and its ritual re-presentation. Perhaps Amo and Purea had already begun to build their new *marae* Mahaiatea before the *Dolphin* had arrived. Perhaps the new *maro* demanded a special place. Certainly Mahaiatea was grander and more ambitious than any other sacred site on Tahiti and could have been something new for something new. The procession around the island demanded submission to a new sort of authority. That the Wallis flag itself was not processed is of little significance. They had only one flag. When they possessed more than one flag they did process with it, as they did at Pomare II's investiture. When they had several flags they attached them as well to their most sacred vessels, such as Rainbow, 'Oro's canoe. It makes sense to see the British possessing Tahiti in their flag and their violence, and Purea inventing an interpretive document of those events and making it symbolic of the hegemony she claimed.

Possessing Tahiti was a complicated affair. Indeed, who possessed whom? Native and Stranger each possessed the other in their interpretations of the other. They possessed one another in an ethnographic moment that was transcribed into text and symbol. They each archived that text and symbol in their respective cultural institutions. They each made cargo of the things they collected from one another, put their cargo in their respective museums, remade the things they collected into new cultural artefacts. They entertained themselves with their histories of their encounter. Because each reading of the text, each display of the symbol, each entertainment in the histories, each viewing of the cargo enlarged the original encounter, made a process of it, each possession of the other became a self-possession as well. Possessing the other, like possessing the past, is always full of delusions.

HOLLYWOOD MAKES HISTORY

PROLOGUE TO A TRANSCRIBED ILLUSTRATED LECTURE

I was honoured to have been invited to give the keynote address to the VIth Australian History and Film Conference in November 1993. My writing of *Mr Bligh's Bad Language, Passion, Power and Theatre on the Bounty* (Cambridge University Press 1993) had been wonderfully completed for me by my access to the Metro Goldwyn Mayer archives and to the massive collection of scripts in the New York State Film censor's files in the New York State Archives, Albany, N.Y. The 'Press Books' and 'Campaign Books' in the MGM archives especially helped me 'read' the *Bounty* films. And the scripts in the censor's files displayed the artfulness of the films in ways in which sitting in a darkened theatre never could.

Films as cultural artefacts have a disembodied feel. Their function is to be seen, but writing the history of seeing is difficult. A film in its can is not like a book on its shelf or a manuscript in an archive. A film requires theatre of some sort to be seen. Fast-forwarding, rewinding and replay are different experiences from rippling through the pages or re-reading. At the end of the twentieth century we are all culturally postmodernist. To survive culturally we must be expert readers of texts for both what they say they mean and for what we know them really to mean. Reading and living have become very close. With a film it is different. Everything is subterfuge and camouflage. Living is out of camera and off set. We see films in crowds and argue with one another over what we have seen.

The difference between reading texts and seeing films is somewhat analogous to the difference in presenting a text of an address and the performance of it. The honour of addressing the conference was mine, although I thought that with so many film-makers and film experts it would be I who would learn more than I would teach. I thought, moreover, that I should make my lecture to such an audience a seeing as well as a hearing experience. So it was full of slide projections and video clips. Now that my keynote address is reduced to bare print and stripped of all its filler images, I must discover some postmodern way in which you can read all that you otherwise might have seen.

T HE mutiny is over. You missed it. Bligh is in the launch about to begin his extraordinary voyage of fifty-seven days and 10 000 km in an open boat. He is totally preoccupied in these first hours as to what caused his mutiny and he is highly suspicious even of his eighteen companions in the launch. How could it be that in a ship so cramped as the *Bounty* no one knew that there would be a mutiny? Even with the bottom of the launch in some bedlam with what personal possessions and supplies the mutineers had allowed them, Bligh calls for quill and paper, and one by one writes down the description of each of the men—pirates now for seizing His Majesty's ship—as well as mutineers. Fletcher Christian first of all.

Fletcher Christian. Aged 24 years—5 ft 9 in. High. Dark Swarthy Complexion
Complexion—Dark and Very Swarthy
Hair—Blackish or very dark brown
Make—Strong
Marks—Star tatowed on his left breast and tatowed on the backside—His knees stands a little out and may be called a little bow legged. He is subject to violent perspiration and particularly in His hands so that he soils any thing he handles.

It is the first invention of Fletcher Christian that we have—socially disturbing in his clammy-handed presence. Hyperhydrosis, a dermatologist tells me his condition was; a breakdown in the sweat regulation mechanisms, likely to be genetic, likely to be triggered and augmented by emotional disturbance. But Bligh only knows he 'soils everything he handles'.

Bligh's last sight of Christian is of him standing on the flag box on the stern of the *Bounty*. And he thinks he hears him shout 'Huzzah for Otaheite'. But Bligh is the only one who heard him make this shout. And we have to think that Bligh wanted to hear it. The cause of the mutiny he knew within himself was not anything that he had said or done. The cause of the mutiny was the decadent lecherous days at Tahiti.

SHAPING THE IMAGES OF THE MUTINY

The most famous picture of the Mutiny of the *Bounty* is Robert Dodd's aquatint and engraving, 'Lieutenant Bligh Leaving the *Bounty*', printed just three months after Bligh's return from his famous launch voyage. Christian is standing on the flag box at the stern of the *Bounty*, the mutineers around him, all in stances of aggression and insult. Breadfruit trees can be seen behind them. Bligh, in shirtsleeves—or probably in breeches over his nightgown—he had stood bare-arsed in his nightgown at the beginning of his mutiny—with his eighteen companions in the launch, trailing behind the *Bounty*. In these same three months after his return, Bligh had had a book of his adventures published. There was already a staged version of the mutiny at the Theatre Royal. Ralph Wewitzer, a Jewish jeweller become comedian-actor was the first 'Captain Bligh'. William Bourke, a keen dancer of the double hornpipe, it was reported, was the first 'Fletcher Christian'. The theatre of the *Bounty* began very early in painting, play, book and poem.

We don't have a picture of Christian, other than a blow-up of the watercolour by Robert Dodd. We might not notice, but every contemporary who saw this painting would have noticed. Christian is wearing a hat. He is not some primitive hero of an anti-cancer campaign. The hat was a more threatening emblem. This is 1790. During these months the fourteen newspapers of London were filled with the revolutionary happenings in France. The King of France is on his way to prison and in the end to execution. In a world turned upside down, the *sans culottes* in France were the symbol of radical politics. In England, the symbol of radical working-class politics was the hat. Rioters, arsonists, rabble rousers, pamphleteers were made to wear hats in any representation of them. Dodd in the painting of Christian was giving a clear sign that the mutiny on the *Bounty* was bigger than itself. The navy was seen to be England's only defence against the Revolution across the Channel. There was no way in which this unpolitical mutiny on an unimportant ship at the ends of the earth would go unpunished. The navy would waste another fifty lives and lose another ship in dragging back whomever it could catch of the mutineers to hang. Fletcher Christian, had he ever seen it, would have trembled a little at this portrait of him in a hat.

We have no lack of portraits of William Bligh. He was a friend of painters and engravers. And they caught him at different significant moments in his life. There is an oil painting of him by John Webber, done on the eve of his sailing as Master to Captain Cook's *Resolution* on Cook's fateful last voyage. Bligh was happier about this voyage with Cook before it happened than after. After it he was full of hatred for nearly everybody on the *Resolution* because he thought they had not recognised his contribution to its discoveries and because there were dark, but untrue, rumours about his role in Cook's killing by Hawaiian natives.

There is another watercolour of Bligh that deserves attention. It was done by John Smart to commemorate Bligh's brave actions at the Battle of Camperdown, where Nelson singled him out for praise. It was painted sixteen years after the mutiny on the *Bounty*. He looks a young forty-seven years old. He has, to us who have his image mythologised into our historical consciousness, a look of unexpected serenity, slightly teasing.

Maybe we find his looks unexpected, because for most of the twentieth century, the face of Bligh has really been Charles Laughton's. If there is a 'Captain Bligh' myth of our twentieth century, it comes more than anything from the performances of Charles Laughton in the 1935 Metro Goldwyn Mayer film *Mutiny on the Bounty*. We have lost the immediate impact of Laughton now, of course, as he is condemned to the nostalgia section of our video shops and to the midnight hours on our televisions. But his cliché of Captain Bligh as a sadistic, even pathologically violent man, who flogged his men mercilessly, masted them, gagged them, keelhauled them, tortured them in irons, has remained a cultural memory with us. Indeed critics have been prone to argue that the *Mutiny on the Bounty* films that followed the Laughton/Gable film were unhistorical for omitting what the 1935 film invented. I don't propose to argue the historical accuracy of these films back and forth. They each could not do what they set out to do without being historically inaccurate. Rather I want to savour the theatre of their different performances and out of their raw differences reflect on the role of images in their own narrative construction,and how they affect the mythological structures of our society and shaped politically correct attitudes.

It is rare enough that there should be five major films on one historical event: the 1916 Raymond Longford silent film, Charles Chauvel's 1932 *In the Wake of the Bounty* in which Errol Flynn made his screen debut as Fletcher Christian, the 1935 Laughton/Gable MGM version, the 1962 Marlon Brando/Trevor Howard and the 1984 Mel Gibson/Anthony Hopkins version. That each should be different won't surprise us. Nor will it surprise us that each reflects and shapes the different cultural perceptions of their times: of a world war for Raymond Longford, or world depression for Charles Chauvel and Frank Lloyd, or international turmoil in a decolonising world for Carol Reed and Lewis Milestone, or of the psychological ambivalences of our more modern moments for Roger Donaldson.

Time forces me to be ruthlessly selective, and give you virtually nothing about the Longford and Chauvel films. We have only a few stills from Longford's *Mutiny on the Bounty*. He shot the film in Rotorua, New Zealand, and Norfolk Island. He made more play on the paradox of Bligh's reputed brutality towards his sailors and his tenderness as a father to his family than any of the other film-makers. Bligh and his wife Elizabeth lost their twin sons a day after their birth and one of his three daughters was handicapped. Many of Bligh's troubles came from his constant preoccupation with money to care for his family.

Chauvel's docudrama, *In the Wake of the Bounty*, was half narrative of the mutiny told by the blind Irish fiddler, Michael Byrne, whom

Bligh had taken aboard the *Bounty* to make the crew dance, and therefore be well exercised to counter the scurvy. The other half of the film was a documentary of Chauvel's visit to Pitcairn Island. *In the Wake of the Bounty* got virtually no showing. Its premiere was delayed by Australian censorship of bare Tahitian breasts and a sensitivity of the descendants of the First Fleet in Sydney to portrayals of flogging. Then MGM bought *In the Wake of the Bounty* to clear the way for the Laughton/Gable film. They made it into short travelogues and cuts for the preview of their own film. Of course, *In the Wake of the Bounty* is famous in film history for being the vehicle for Errol Flynn's screen debut. His photogenic, if somewhat pasty, portrayal of Fletcher Christian was no great thespian triumph, but he himself said 'I was without the least idea of what I was doing, except I was supposed to be an actor'. He was relieved to find that film actors only had to learn the lines for the day's shooting. Not that he had many lines in *In the Wake of the Bounty*! And he was not a little bemused that he 'had touched on something the world called an art form, and it affected me deeply'. Later in life, and through the alcoholic haze that misted it, he remembered that his family possessed a sword of Fletcher Christian, and that his mother was related to Edward Young, the mutineer who had come from the West Indies, and whom Bligh had described as having a 'dark and rather bad look' with terrible teeth.

I have to believe that there are advantages of physically seeing the three later Mutiny on the *Bounty* films rawly side by side. Seeing them like that outweighs the advantages of long discourse about them. As an historian and anthropologist I have to confess that I have had difficulties interpreting films as texts of the past. How does one discover the meanings audiences take away from them? How does one measure their influence? How does one describe them as cultural artefacts of their times? Let me propose one humble discovery that I have made. It is this. As historians we have an interest in understanding how films both reflect and shape our cultural myths. To come to that understanding, we cannot afford to think of a film as simply a projection on a screen, or as an artefact in the cans of our archives. As mythmaker, the film has to be seen as a total event—in its production, in its marketing, in its performance, in its viewing and criticism, and in the cultural milieu in which it is theatre. My reading of these Mutiny on the *Bounty* films is that each defines a certain hegemony or political correctness which audiences come to understand in complex ways and by means sometimes totally external to the film itself. Audiences come out of the theatre reinforced in hegemonic values. There is plenty of evidence in these Mutiny on the *Bounty* films to show how an old hegemony is being enforced against new understandings. If the old hegemony is more presumptive, it is the more powerful for that.

Films about a mutiny have a problem. In whose voice is the story told? To whom and to what is the commitment of the presenter? On what side lies political correctness—the order to be sustained by the institution, or the injustice experienced by the individual? When Irving Thalberg, the creative genius of Metro Goldwyn Mayer, in the early 1930s in the turmoil years of his relationship with the studio suggested to Louis Mayer that MGM do a film on the mutiny on the *Bounty*, Mayer was very reluctant. He did not want to be responsible for a film in which mutineers would be the heroes. Louis Mayer was a Russian-born Jew, one of several eastern European Jews, who, as Neal Gabler has written, invented Hollywood (Gabler 1988). Carl Laemmle who founded Universal Pictures was another. Adolph Zukor of Paramount Pictures, Benjamin Warner of Warner Brothers, William Fox of Fox Brothers, Henry Cohn of Columbia yet others. They had all come out of utter destitution in eastern Europe. They had all grabbed their entrepreneurial moment on the east coast of the United States, first leasing vaudeville cinemas, then gaining distribution rights. Then each came to realise that it was in production that fortunes were to be made. They had moved westward to Hollywood for year-round film production and to escape the expense of generating klaxon lights for filming when coal in a world at war was so costly and scarce. To a man they worshipped the opportunities the Land of the Free and the Home of the Brave had given them.

Louis Mayer, more than any of them. Metro Goldwyn Mayer made movie after movie idealising a particular image of American women, beatifying and beautifying mothers, putting onto film what Norman Rockwell was putting onto the covers of the *Saturday Evening Post*.

Revolution, or mutiny, or even social change was not something Mayer was going to bless in any way. So Irving Thalberg had to find other heroes for his film than mutineers. It was the British navy. The navy was to be bigger than them all. Thalberg had experienced the anti-Semitism of Nazi Germany firsthand, and had come home to experience in Hollywood itself the leftist movement among screen writers being led by Upton Sinclair. For him the middle ground between Fascism and Communism was a stable institution that could sustain good order and bend to the legitimate demands of those who served in it. So he makes Bligh so horrendous that mutiny against him would be understandable if not excusable. Christian will have to be a tragic hero, unrewarded except by his sense of honour. The real hero of shining goodness, who never raises a hand against Bligh but has to suffer anyway because of his commitments to the ideals of a true navy is an entirely invented character, 'Roger Byam', played by Franchot Tone. The film will end with *Rule Britannia* playing and the Union Jack flying and the warm feeling that the navy can see true virtue and respond to it. Fade Out. It won't matter that men are flogged in the navy for fifty years after the *Bounty*, or that the whole fleet mutinies just ten years afterwards and thirty-six are hanged. The theatre of the film is that submission to legitimate authority even at the cost of personal sacrifice is always the proper thing to do.

It has to be said that Clark Gable was as reluctant to be Fletcher Christian as Louis Mayer was to film the mutiny on the *Bounty*. Gable had a number of reasons for being reluctant. One, because he had never been in a costume movie before and he believed that knee breeches and stockings would show off his bandy legs. Two, he would have to shave off his moustache. 'This moustache has been damn lucky to me', he said. Three, and most importantly—he was unsure how to play Christian against Bligh, how to be Good against transparently violent Evil without appearing feminine. His father always said he would become a sissy if he became an actor. This was his moment of truth. On the set there were several ugly scenes between Laughton and Gable. Laughton several times became physically ill at the intensity of his own acting. Gable couldn't cope. He felt the demeaning of him as Christian went beyond acting. He resolved his dilemma by playing the most American of all the Christians, with a sort of rascally swagger. He always shows his commitment to the proprieties of naval behaviour and honour, but always as well his personal distance and freedom within them.

WORDS IN LIEU OF IMAGES: 1935 MUTINY ON THE BOUNTY

1. Enter Clark Gable

No	Feet	Frames	Description	Reel 1
12			CS—Feet of Town Crier—the feet of Christian and Press Gang enter—CAMERA TRUCKS ahead as they walk forward—CAMERA PANS up to Christian walking forward—Press Gang following—	
	211	11	**Town Crier** o.s. Eight o'clock—all's well. Misty weather.	
13			CS—Sign reads: THE ROYAL GEORGE— CAMERA PANS down as Christian and Press Gang come forward to entrance—they stop— Christian gestures—CAMERA PANS Christian and Morrison to right to window—	
	227	11	they kneel by window—	
14			MLS—Int. Tavern—Muspratt and men seated about tables—Byrne in b.g. playing violin—	
	233	3	Woman serves Muspratt and man—	
15			MCS—Landlord—CAMERA PANS him to right to Ellison and Mary—he hands mug of ale to Ellison—CAMERA TRUCKS up on Ellison and Mary—he hands mug to Mary— she starts to drink—looks o.s.—reacts **Landlord** Here ye are, me lad.	
	247	3	**Ellison** Thank ye.	
16	249	3	MCS—Christian looking thru window—	

No	Feet	Frames	Description	Reel 1
17			CS—Ellison and Mary—she reacts—speaks— they rise	
	252	15	**Mary** The Press Gang! The Press . . .	
18			MCS—Christian looking thru window—he exits right—CAMERA PANS to right to door—Christian—Morrison and men enter— Christian looks o.s.—speaks—Morrison exits left f.g.—Christian and men come forward— CAMERA TRUCKS back—Christian speaks to Quintal—	
			Mary o.s. . . . Gang	
			Ellison o.s. The Press Gang!	
			Muspratt o.s. Let's get out of here! (ad libs from others)	
			Christian In the King's Name! Well, we got all the fish we need in one net. Line them up, Bosun.	
	383	9	**Quintal** I'm no seaman, sir. I'm a tailor.	

Gable makes the most cheerful, humane press-gang officer ever, but that does not really matter as there was no press-gang at all for the Bounty. *None of her crew were pressed. It is interesting that American film-makers could never cast an American as 'Captain Bligh'. Wallace Beery was briefly considered instead of Laughton, but was rejected for being too 'American'. Ellison—the sailor with the wife Mary, about to be revealed as pregnant, was really only fifteen years old at the time, unmarried. In the real story, Ellison would be one of only three to hang for the mutiny. He had '25 October, 1788' tattooed on his arm. It was the date they all saw Tahiti for the first time. Pathetic enough, but not enough pathos to develop Christian's (Gable's) kindness and concern and Bligh's (Laughton's) inhumanity. The film-makers had to throw in a baby and a young mother to counterpoint the cruelty of it all.*

2. Enter Laughton

No	Feet	Frames	Description	Reel 1
			Maggs Silence! The Captain's coming aboard.	
	131	4	**Smith** Oh . . . oh . . . dear.	
4			LS—On Deck-shooting over group of people crowded in lower f.g.	
	135	3	(ad libs and cheering)	
5			MLS—Over side of ship—Boat bringing Captain Bligh to ship—Sailors also in boat—	
	140	7	(Sound of whistle)	
6	144	0	LS—Group of people and sailors on deck of ship—	
7			MLS—Captain Bligh climbing gangway and arrives on deck as CAMERA PANS	
	150	15	SLIGHTLY—	
8			LS—Bligh arriving on deck and salutes officers—Sir Joseph follows him—Bligh looks at sailors	
	158	3	and group of visitors on deck—	
9			MCS—Bligh speaks to Christian who in turn gives out command—CAMERA PANS LEFT—Bligh gives order to Fryer—	
			Bligh Mr Christian, clear the decks of this rabble.	
			Christian Very good, sir. Clear deck! Everybody ashore! Clear deck!	
			Bligh Mr Fryer, we sail at six bells.	
	174	2	**Fryer** Sail at six bells, sir.	
10			MS—Christian ordering group off the deck—Man protests and Christian takes him by seat and throws him overboard	
			Man We've got our rights here.	
			Christian Off ship, Joe. Off ship!	
			Man I'm not going until the ship sails.	
	185	12	**Voice** Hey, you can't do that!	

No	*Feet*	*Frames*	*Description*	*Reel 1*
11			CS—Sir Joseph and Bligh stand in f.g. talking—Christian speaks o.s. **Bligh** Hmmm, a flogging through the fleet. We're included. Quite a compliment to the Bounty, Sir Joseph.	

Bligh's boat, then the boat with the flogging victim (who will be discovered to be dead, but whom Bligh will flog anyway!) is rowed among five old sailing vessels that was the 'fleet'. The filming was done on Catalina Island off the California coast. The filming of this scene ended in a violent quarrel between Laughton and Gable. Gable thought he was being treated like an extra by Laughton. The twentieth-century myth of the sadistic 'Captain Bligh' begins here. There was no 'flogging around the fleet' with the Bounty, *and Bligh in real life was one of the least physically violent of British captains to come into the Pacific. Hollywood has always easily mythologised pathological evil, but not so easily narrated evil when it is banal.*

3. Enter Franchot Tone

No	*Feet*	*Frames*	*Description*	*Reel 1*
2			MCS—Int. Court-Martial Chamber—Cabin of the Duke—Two guards escorting Byam in from b.g. CAMERA PANS RIGHT AND TRUCKS FORWARD on Midshipman's dirk on the desk—	
	24	2	**Officer** o.s. Prisoner and escorts, halt! Left turn!	
3			CS—Byam looks down f.g. Lord Hood speaks o.s. then Byam looks up and speaks— **Lord Hood** o.s. Have you anything to say before the sentence of this Court is passed upon you?	
	42	6	**Byam** My Lord, much as I desire to live, I'm not afraid to die.	
4	44	15	CS—Bligh sitting in Court looking off f.g.	

No	Feet	Frames	Description	Reel 1
5			MCU—Byam looks f.g. and speaks—then looks left—	
	61	12	**Byam** Since I first sailed on the Bounty, over four years ago, I've known how men can be made to suffer worse things than death. Cruelty, beyond duty, beyond necessity.	
6			MS—Byam looks f.g. and speaks to Bligh seated in the left f.g. Guards and others in b.g.	
	80	6	**Byam** Captain Bligh, you've told your story of mutiny on the Bounty, how men plotted against you. Seized your ship, cast you adrift in an open boat. A great venture in science brought to nothing, two British ships lost.	
7			MCU—Byam looks to left and then to f.g. as he speaks—	
	92	12	**Byam** But there's another story, Captain Bligh, of ten coconuts and two cheeses. The story of a man who . . .	
8			CS—Bligh looks f.g. listening to Byam o.s.	
	101	13	**Byam** o.s. . . . robbed his seamen, cursed them, flogged them, not to punish but to break their spirit.	

Franchot Tone, playing the invented character of Roger Byam, is about to give one of those famous 'Cut it! Can it!' performances. His speech allows Thalberg and Mayer an 'out' in filming a mutiny. The film's critics would feel that something else was going on. One of them remarked that more time was given to Gable's 'gams' and Tone's 'manly stems' than to Marlene Dietrich's attractive appendages, and they thought they knew why (wink, wink). Bligh, of course, was not at the court martial of the mutineers. He was out in Tahiti in the Providence *collecting the breadfruit he had failed to collect in the* Bounty. *Thalberg's fantasies succumb to bathos in this scene when the cameras pan to a kindly old man, supposedly Christian's father. He was long dead at the time.*

Many contemporaries to the mutiny on the *Bounty* believed that if there was a gentleman on the *Bounty* it was Fletcher Christian, not William Bligh. By any social register there was much truth in that. The Christians belonged directly to the line of the Deemsters of the Isle of Man. The immediate family of Fletcher Christian had fallen on hard times, and he had been forced by that not to go to university, where his brothers had been, but to sea. There were three bishops in the broader family, a Lord Chief Justice—Edward Hall, who had defended Warren Hastings—a High Sheriff, two Members of Parliament. His brother Edward was Professor of Law at Cambridge, 'a sixpenny professor' Bligh called him. Both Fletcher and Edward had been to school with William Wordsworth. Wordsworth's friendship with Samuel Coleridge meant that Coleridge's poem, 'The Ancient Mariner' was really a mystery play about Christian as the Everyman who commits some heinous crime against society and must wear the consequences like an albatross around his neck. Lord Byron's hatred of both Wordsworth and Coleridge meant that his poem, 'The Island', counted by most critics as his worst, invented a melancholic guilt-ridden Christian who in the end takes his own life and is no Everyman at all, except insofar as most of us have a little criminal in us. But, now I am into the poems and pantomimes and ballets and aqua-ballets about Christian.

After the mutiny, and after the court martial of those mutineers dragged back from Tahiti, and after the execution of the three unfortunates who bore the brunt of the navy's wrath, Edward Christian wrote a pamphlet about his brother Fletcher. There was no defending Fletcher, of course. Mutiny by law could have no reason—not in the captain's cruelty, not in any injustice done to or abuse of the sailors. But Edward could suggest there was another history to the *Bounty* than that heard at the trial. He and a number of gentlemen interviewed those who had escaped in the launch with Bligh. These gentlemen had some prominence in the great reform movement of anti-slavery. Suddenly, if one could not identify with Christian, one could identify with an anti-Bligh movement. Suddenly, if you were part of the great reform movement of anti-slavery, you knew that the *Bounty* with its plan to transport a cheap subsistence food, breadfruit, to the West Indies plantations was a tool of enslavement. Suddenly the Christians had strong allies. Missionaries who had been chaplains to the mutineers in their trial and who would go to Tahiti armed with the linguistic and cultural information given them by the mutineers, chaplains to the king's own children and to the court at Windsor, MPs and bishops in the Christian family network— the alliances were formidable, and if Fletcher Christian could not be a hero, then Bligh could be a devil. Invention by inversion if you like.

Marlon Brando did not want the play Christian either. He did not want to clone Gable's performance. He did not like the script Eric Ambler had made of the Charles Nordhoff and Norman Hall trilogy on the *Bounty*. In fact he did not want to make a movie of the mutiny at all. He wanted to make a movie of the murderous post-mutiny settlement at Pitcairn. And he wanted to play the part of John Adams the last survivor of the *Bounty*. Adams had outlasted the mayhem of racial murders that had killed Fletcher Christian in the first four years of the settlement. When the killings were done, Adams had discovered God and had remade the island into a paradigm of innocent belief and sweet charity. Brando wanted to make a movie of all that, because, he said, there was 'more philosophy' in it. Six million dollars persuaded him otherwise. Brando liked to read himself into his parts. The 'Campaign Books' for the 1962 film claimed he had read a million words on the *Bounty*. Among those million words he had picked up the fact that Christian was a gentleman. His imagination took off from there. A gentleman meant one thing for him: a wealthy, dillettante eighteenth-century fop. From that moment his story takes on an inexorable logic of its own. To make it halfway believable that such a creature would find honour in revolt against legitimate authority, invention is added on invention, until in the end the whole mutiny is reinvented. Trevor Howard, as Bligh, kicks a ladle of water out of Brando's hand as he offers it to a dying demented seaman against Bligh's orders. Brando strikes Bligh, as any gentleman would, and takes the ship.

Brando on set in both Tahiti and Hollywood was totally out of control. He drove off Carol Reed, the first director, then Lewis Milestone, and he was left responsible for the final scenes. Brando 'methodises' it by lying on 200 pounds of ice so that he could get the shiver of death. But his shivering makes him forget his lines. They write them on the forehead of Maimiti his Tahitian lover, as she bends over him in farewell.

WORDS IN LIEU OF IMAGES: THE 1962 MUTINY ON THE BOUNTY

1. Enter Brando

No	Feet	Frames	Description	Reel 1
10B			MCS o.s.—Bligh enters right, followed by Fryer—they react to coach approaching— **Bligh** What's this? A Royal visit? **Fryer** Uh—that's Mr Christian's carriage, Sir.	
	176	8	**Bligh** Is it now?!	
11B			MLS—Fletcher Christian alights from coach—Camera shooting from ship's deck —	
12B	182	6	MCS—Bligh and Fryer watching o.s. left— **Bligh** So, I've had a career fop palmed onto me as a First Mate. **Fryer** You haven't met him yet, Sir? **Bligh** Mmmm—he was assigned only yesterday. Moorechild was my choice. He was taken ill with some malady or other.	
13B	199	13	MLS—Christian and women—Shooting through ropes as they ascend gangway—CAMERA PANS up to right —laughter heard	
14B	204	11	MCS—Birkett, Williams, Byrne, McCoy react to f.g.—Williams hands cement block to Byrne—crewman puts block down o.s., as he exits—re-enters—	
15B	209	7	MLS—Christian and two women board ship—crewman enters right f.g.—Mack glimpsed in b.g.—others about—	

No	Feet	Frames	Description	Reel 1
16B	214	6	MCS Birkett, Williams, Byrne, McCoy and crewman—they react to f.g.—formers pass block to b.g.	
	223	0	**McCoy** Aye, nothin' compares with a woman washed all over, smellin' like a Frenchman.	
17B			MLS—Christian and two women—latters wait, as former walks foward b.g.—crewmen about—	
18B	230	4	CS—Bligh and Fryer watching o.s.—former steps forward—turns to b.g., as Christian enters left, removing his hat, and introducing himself—Christian shakes hands with Fryer—Fryer starts to left—	

Christian Fletcher Christian, Leftenant [sic]—comes aboard to join, sir.

Bligh Leftenant Christian—you are a naval leftenant, I presume?

Christian Uh—yes. Please forgive my appearance, Sir. I was staying with friends in the country, when my orders reached me. So I came directly.

Once it was decided that Christian was a 'gentleman' and that Bligh was not, there seemed to be no going back and Brando will 'ham' it up for two more hours. So they are forced into all sorts of lateral inventions, for example, that Bligh did not know Christian, when in fact Christian had sailed with Bligh to the West Indies three times and was with him by special arrangement on this voyage; or that Brando's preposterous costume as a dilettante would be explained by the fact that he had a day's notice to go on a two-year voyage to the South Seas! These and many other lateral pursuits played havoc with the script which went through four screen writers after Eric Ambler and would cost $327 000. Brando, later trying to defend the total collapse of discipline on the sets, said that at times he had to remember eleven different scripts. Many of the most awful scenes, however, seemed to have been 'methodised' into existence.

2. The Moments before a Mutiny of a Gentleman

No	Feet	Frames	Description	Reel 1
2B			MS—Christian comes forward with water—CAMERA PANS up as he pours it into Williams' mouth, as Byrne holds his head back—Bligh comes forward, kicking the ladle from Christian's hand—Christian slaps Bligh back—Mills and Birkett at right—Fryer and others in b.g.—	
	19	9	**Christian** You . . .	
3B			MS—Christian—Camera shooting past Bligh, as he sits up in right f.g.—crew in b.g.—	
	29	7	**Christian** . . . bloody bastard! You'll not put your foot on me again!.	
4B			MCU—Bligh smiles, then laughs—	
	36	4	**Bligh** Thank . . .	
5B			CS—Christian	
			Bligh o.s. . . . you. Thank you. I've been puzzling for a means to take the strut out of you . . .	
6B			MCU—Bligh starts to rise—	
	49	3	**Bligh** . . . you posturing snob.	
7B			MCS—CAMERA PANS Bligh up—he turns, glancing at Fryer and others in b.g.—	
			Bligh Now, you've solved that for me, haven't you? You have witnessed Mr. . . .	
8B	59	2	MCS—Christian—crew in b.g.	
			Bligh o.s. . . . Christian's act of violence toward a superior officer. He will be placed in confinement until a . . .	
9B	67	9	MCS—Bligh—CAMERA TRUCKS back as he comes forward, entering Christian in left f.g.—Birkett and Mills entered at right—Fryer and others in b.g.—	

No	Feet	Frames	Description	Reel 1
			Bligh . . . court martial can be convened. In Jamaica, I expect. And will your fashionable friends be there to see your execution, I . . .	

The actual mutiny took place at 6 a.m., 28 April 1789, with Bligh being dragged out of his cabin in his nightgown. Christian and his 4 a.m. to 8 a.m. watch were the culprits. Christian had spent the night till 4 a.m. in suicidal depression, making himself a raft to jump overboard, till someone, we don't know who, persuaded him to take the ship. We have to think that the reason for this bizarre invention of the water ladle episode was that the film-makers could not cope in the end with a mutiny so full of ambivalences as the Bounty's.

3. The Shivers of Death

No	Feet	Frames	Description	Reel 1
7B	120	7	CU—Christian reacts—lifts his head slightly— **Christian** Uhh—Am I—am-m I—am I dying, Brown?	
8B			MCU—Brown and Young	
	127	14	**Brown** Yes, Mr Christian.	
9B			CU—Christian—	
	145	2	**Christian** What a useless way to die.	
10B			CU—Young—	
	168	5	**Young** It's not useless, Fletcher; I swear it. Maybe we'll get to London, or maybe not. But, the Blighs will lose. We'll tell our story somehow, to someone.	
11B	179	1	CU—Christian— **Young** o.s. It only needs one of us to survive.	
12B			CS—Mills—looks to b.g. then rises— CAMERA PANS up—he exits right as Maimiti runs forward, looking down to o.s. Christian	
13B	197	6	CU—Christian reacts—	

No	Feet	Frames	Description	Reel 1
14B	214	0	CS—Maimiti—CAMERA PANS down as she kneels—pours some medicine—	
15B			CU—Christian—	
	225	12	**Christian** Never mind that, Maimiti. We haven't much time.	
16B	230	8	CS—Maimiti—	
17B			CS—Christian—shivers—	
			Christian Please—please know that—I—I loved you—more than I knew.	
18B	258	12	MCU—Maimiti—	
			Christian o.s. And—if I'd only had had time to . . .	
19B			CU—Christian—dies—Maimiti sobs o.s.—	
	298	10	. . . to—	
20B			CS—Maimiti, her hands covering her face as she sobs—Camera shooting past Christian in f.g., as she embraces him—CAMERA PANS down—PANS her up, as she looks at him—CAMERA TRUCKS right past them to *Bounty* as it sinks—	
			Maimiti Oh, Fletcher—(in Tahitian)	
	394	15	**FADE OUT**	

This death scene with the burning Bounty *in the background was apparently incorporated so that Brando's Christian could appear to be a hopeless idealist destroyed by circumstances outside his control. Pitcairn in real life was a place of mayhem and murder. Of the fifteen males (six natives and nine mutineers) who made up the original settlement, only two died of natural causes. The rest murdered one another or suicided. And Christian survived the burning of the* Bounty *by four years.*

Bligh's suggestion that Tahiti was the cause of his mutiny and then his defence of his opinion by quoting a former shipmate of Christian as saying 'He was one of the most foolish young men I ever knew in regard to the sex', was, at the end of the eighteenth century, a license for much ribald imagination and invention. It prompted a considerable literature of the 'knowing' type and soft porn descriptions of Tahitian native life. To his contemporaries, there was not much doubt over Christian's heterosexual propensities. But at the end of the twentieth century that clarity has become blurred. In 1984, Robert Bolt went not to the Nordhoff and Hall trilogy which it is estimated twenty-three million people had read even before the Laughton/Gable film, but to Richard Hough's splendid history, *Captain Bligh and Mr Christian* (1972*).* As befits the psychological interests of our time, Hough went to a suggestion by Madge Darby, an amateur historian of NSW, that if we wanted to understand Bligh's and Christian's conflict, we should think of what a heterosexual splurge on Tahiti would have done to a homosexual love affair on the *Bounty* between Bligh and Christian. She had no evidence for her suggestion other than Christian had said 'I am in hell, Mr Bligh, I am in hell' in the middle of the mutiny, and had whispered some secret to Peter Heywood to take home to his family. Considering that at this time about three sailors a year were hanged for sodomy and hundreds more a year were flogged for the less lethal charge of 'uncleanness', it is not a matter that would have been passed over lightly by contemporaries. I have to say, however, that there is little that I have read through thirty years of engagement in the *Bounty* that suggests that it is likely that there was a homosexual relationship between Bligh and Christian, or that no one would have known about it, if there was one.

There was an intensity about Bligh's and Christian's relationship that might have been homoerotic rather than homosexual. Some of those who had sailed with Bligh and Christian before the *Bounty* remarked on Bligh's partiality to Christian and were at a loss to explain it. It is clear that on the *Bounty* relations deteriorated after an incident at the Cape of Good Hope, when Christian borrowed money from Bligh and Bligh was able to force an early repayment by selling the 'IOU' to his merchant relatives in England. Christian's impoverished family would have been saddled with the debt, which Christian had probably planned on redeeming after the *Bounty* voyage, when he had been paid.

I cannot say whether the homosexual slant on Hough's story made Mel Gibson reluctant to accept the role of Christian. But Gibson, like Clark and Brando was a reluctant Christian. When I asked the man who helped cast Gibson how Mad Max could have been persuaded to accept the role, I was told a story. They wanted Gibson, I was told, because he was halfway physically similar to the original Christian—shortish, 5'9", olive complexion, strong built. So they pursued him to a lunch at Claridge's in London. They put it to him that he visit the Christian family home of Moreland Close in the Lakes District of England. There in the lead guttering was supposedly an imprint of Fletcher's foot put there by him in about 1783. If Gibson's foot fitted, would he take the part? It did, and he did.

Words in Lieu of Images: The 1984 Mutiny on the Bounty

Robert Bolt's screen play for the 1984 Hopkins/Gibson Mutiny on the Bounty *is the most accomplished of them all. The opening credits with Vangelis' haunting music makes for a 'sound and light' experience that sets a mood of mystification. Bolt uses the court martial of Bligh for the loss of his ship as the baseline of his narrative structure. That court martial—not the court martial of the mutineers—was much more formalistic than Bolt suggests. The public reaction—and the Admiralty's—against Bligh was much later. In this early court martial he was much more the hero. Hopkins gives a splendid nuanced performance as Bligh. Gibson is stilted and subdued. The supposed homosexual tension between Bligh and Christian is displayed by innuendo rather than explicitly dramatised. That, among other things, makes the theatre of the 1984 version a class above the 1935 and 1962 versions.*

I have to leave you, if you are interested, to follow my fuller story of the films on the *Bounty* in another place, in *Mr Bligh's Bad Language*. I hope that I would persuade you there that if we would understand the ways in which films inform our cultural literacy about the past, then we must see the film as a whole event—in its production, in the dynamic relationship between the actors and the public, in the campaign of publicity, in the occasions of its viewing, in the process by which the specialist critics and the critics in the theatre foyer abstract its explicit meaning and its underlying meaning, in the osmosis of its symbol processing as the significant issues of one domain of life influence another.

I haven't told half the story, of course, of all the inventions of Christian in plays, pantomimes, ballets, aquaballets, poems, musicals, ballads. But let me end with an archaeological relic of his life. After the mutiny Christian's immediate place of refuge was an island called Tubuai, 1000 miles south-west of Tahiti. Denied women by the islanders, the mutineers massacred some hundred to get them. Christian had the mutineers build a fortified settlement. Fort George he called it. He had commanded a Fort St George in Madras for a short time. It was a hundred yards square, surrounded by a ditch eighteen feet wide, with earthen walls twenty feet high, a drawbridge, the *Bounty's* four pounder cannons and swivel guns on the walls. It was Robinson Crusoe stuff. Maybe a little Freudian too. His mother's home, Moreland Castle was a border fortification. The remnants of Fort George can still be traced today. In its middle, there is a living monument to the pain of all their lives, a breadfruit tree.

INVENTING OTHERS

I HAVE in hand the latest *Newsletter* of the Association of Social Anthropologists of Oceania. It contains a bibliography of reviews and comments on Derek Freeman's recent book, *Margaret Mead in Samoa* (1983). The bibliography shows that the public relations officers of the university presses did their work well. The orchestrated uproar over a boffin's book has been an academic publisher's dream. 'Samoan Scholar/ Wife Blast Mead' headlines the *Pacific Daily News* (Guam). 'Was Margaret Mead's Samoa a Myth?' asks the *Iowa City Press Citizen*. 'Professor Tilts at Half a Century of Anthropological Dogma' in *The Australian*. 'Let's Not Confuse Myths with Reality' urged the *Akron Beacon Journal* in February. In March it revised itself stating that 'Despite Errors, Margaret Mead's Was a Better Message'. 'Mead's First Husband Comes to Her Defence' featured *The New York Times*, but *Time* thought it out as 'Bursting the South Sea Bubble'. Headline writers amused themselves playing on titles: 'Coming of Age in Anthropology' (*The Economist*), 'Coming of a Sage to Samoa' (*Natural History*). Or they featured all the ways in which scientific knowledge makes news: 'Exposure', 'Debunking', 'Uproar', 'Controversy', 'Angry Storm'. Or they enjoyed the seeming contradiction between a Pacific island and the wild debate over its significance: 'Trouble in Paradise', 'Paradise Lost?'. Mostly, however, they reflected on the scandal of being disillusioned in long-held beliefs: 'Exposing the Samoan Love-myth', 'Was Samoan Sex Idyll a Myth?', 'Margaret Mead's Story: Fact or Fiction?', 'Unmaking a "goddess" of Science?'.

The reviews, of course, have been only a small part of the publishing event. The press barons in all their incarnations as television crews, radio talk-back celebrities and weekend magazine producers were also pleased to organise a guffaw at Samoan sexual practices. They could make money out of titillating and entertaining, and it cost little to be prurient about Samoan defloration ceremonies. With mock seriousness and purpose, uninformed reporters could ask whether Margaret Mead really was correct in claiming little Samoan girls slept around and did not feel guilty about it. A whirlwind visit to Samoa could fill three minutes of television tape with outraged denials from sixty year olds that they were ever like that and coy giggles from adolescents to suggest that maybe they now are. There is nothing so suitable for electronic fillers as reporters on a Pacific island asking questions that could never be asked at home and displaying the answers with self-deprecatory claims of being unscientific, but nonetheless—wink-wink, nudge-nudge. Add to that the joy of having experts dramatise polarities with slogans and having academics fall out over questions of popular myth, and one has what one might call a 'nine days wonder', except that the attention span of press barons is eight days shorter.

Derek Freeman's book has made many people angry. Some have seen it as an attack on all American anthropology, not just Margaret Mead. Some have been upset at what they see as the vindictiveness of leaving such a debunking—decades in the writing—until after Mead's death. Some have been convinced that whatever Freeman's protest at scientific disinterest the book is directed to what Marilyn Strathern called in her review in *The London Review of Books* ,'The Punishment of Margaret Mead'. Others have been angry at the silliness of a book taking delectation in its lonely self-declared fight against entrenched ignorance. First year anthropology students, after all, have cracked their knuckles over *Coming of Age in Samoa* (1928) for years. The privileged Mead in anthropology that Freeman fights is a thirty years phantom of his mind.

For all the *brouhaha* of its publication, however, Freeman's book is probably not hypocritical or cowardly or even very wrong, and 'rage', as he himself has said in response to splenetic reviews, 'is a wind that blows out the lamp of the mind'. I would rather have some conversation about issues the book raises than review it yet again. In that conversation I have a simple point to make and a question to ask. The simple point is that if one would write a history of ideas, one must have an idea of history. The question is, what happens when we invent others, like the 'Samoans', in our ethnographies of them?

Let me begin the conversation by reporting another. It is a famous, uncomfortable conversation the British social anthropologist, E. E. Evans-Pritchard, had in a tent in the Sudan in 1930.

E-P:	Who are you?
Cuol:	A Man.
E-P:	What is your name?
Cuol:	Do you want to know my name?
E-P:	Yes.
Cuol:	Do you want to know my name?
E-P:	Yes, you have come to visit me in my tent and I would like to know who you are.
Cuol:	All right. I am Cuol. What is your name?
E-P:	My name is Pritchard.
Cuol:	What is your father's name?
E-P:	My father's name is also Pritchard.
Cuol:	No, that cannot be true. You cannot have the same name as your father.
E-P:	It is the name of my lineage. What is the name of your lineage?
Cuol:	Do you want to know the name of my lineage?
E-P:	Yes.
Cuol:	What will you do with it if I tell you? Will you take it to your country?
E-P:	I don't want to do anything with it. I just want to know it since I am living at your camp.
Cuol:	Oh, well. We are Lou.
E-P:	I did not ask you the name of your tribe. I know that. I am asking you the name of your lineage.

193

Cuol: Why do you want to know the name of my lineage?

E-P: I don't want to know it.

Cuol: Then why do you ask me for it? Give me some tobacco.

(Evans-Pritchard 1940: 12–13)

'E-P' laughed away the awkwardness of it all in his introduction to *Nuer* with a joke about 'nuerosis'. It was a disarming reflection on the marginality of being the professional stranger. Out of that awkward, frustrating condition came a brilliantly crafted artefact, *Nuer*. *Nuer* was not the Nuer. Out of bleak observation, tortuous talk and then the more comfortable reflections in libraries and seminars, came a portrait of the Nuer's different perception of time and space. *Nuer* was a fiction, something made, measured for its perfection by the economy of its words, the precision in its focus, the beauty in its writing. *Nuer* was an ethnographic experience become a book. It became a book on a shelf, renewed, remade by being read and being lectured on, being understood again and again for its ever-changing relation to an ever-changing discourse of anthropology.

As it happened, 'E-P' was the student of Bronislaw Malinowski, who before him had written his brilliant ethnography *Argonauts of the Western Pacific* (1922). If it was the skill of the student 'E-P' to invent the Nuer in their notions of time and space, it was the talent of the master, Malinowski, to unveil the whole of Trobriand Island culture in the part of one of its institutions, the *kula*. And the master Malinowski made his fame by showing—for British anthropology—that the future was not in meeting savages in libraries but in confronting them 'as they really were' in the field. Legends are legion of how succeeding generations of young anthropologists then went to the field minimally prepared to confront the Other 'as they really were'. Masters in anthropology, in advising their students what to do, have always been tongue-tied to such simplicities as 'take plenty of pencils'. But always the reflective ethos with which the anthropologist sustained the confrontation was cultural relativism. Understanding the Other required some suspension of judgement about what one saw and described. And yet anthropology has

194

been prepared with all the other sciences to parade the crafted product of research as if it were the immediate consequence of a crafted research experience. It was with some shock and scandal, then, that the anthropological world read Malinowski's intimate field diary published in 1966, twenty-four years after his death. His tortured self-doubts and self-hate, the brutal honesty about the trivialities of his interrupted love-life mingled with the daily battle against his lethargy belied the smooth equanimity of his ethnographic descriptions. There were no charming disavowals of objectivity, just his raw feelings. It was ethnography 'as it really was'.

'Sunday 12.23. Day set aside for writing Christmas letters. In the morning diarrhea. Then straight back to the tent. Read Stevenson a little. Under the mosquito net wrote the easiest and the most trivial letters—Dim Dim, Bruno, etc.—At about 12 watched making of Saipwana in the village. Then came back, slept, wrote more letters. Very tired, I lay down and dozed, woke up still tired but stronger. Crab with cucumbers. Then a short rest. The niggers were noisy—everybody idle because it was Sunday. I wrote to P. and H., began a letter to E.R.M., planned a letter to N.S.—At about 6, on the lagoon. Marvellously translucent evening. Children sail in a boat and sing. I am full of yearnings and think about Melbourne. Some worries about E.R.M.—when I realize what threatens her I am drenched in cold sweat. I think how much she has suffered, waiting for news of C.E.M. At moments I lose sight of her. Sensually she has not succeeded in subjugating me. I rowed as far as Kaytuvi, returned by moonlight; lost in reverie, clouds, water. General aversion for niggers, for the monotony—feel imprisoned. (Prospect of) tomorrow's walk to Billy and visit to Gusaweta not too pleasant. In the evening kayaku and linguistic terms—all around, singing (obscene song from Okaykods). Fell asleep quickly around 10'. (Malinowski 1967).

Let me call these experiences of Evans-Pritchard and Malinowski the ethnographic moment, the space between cultures filled by interpretation, occasions of metaphorical understanding and translation. The first product of the ethnographic moment is interpretation, an understanding of what is new and unexperienced in the light of what is old and experienced. Anthropology, of course, has long been preoccupied with the ethnographic moment. With its importance, first of all: the richness of observation in the field beggared the poverty of experience in the library. Then its epistemology: what happened in the translation of culture? what did it mean to seek understanding by entering the mind of the native and producing a model entirely foreign to it? Now, in its current crisis, there is anthropology's guilty discovery· that the description of other peoples' lives done in the context of cultural dominance over them can be as much politics as science. Because anthropology is affected (with all the other social sciences) by a wider concern for a hermeneutic of systematised knowledge, there is a sensitivity now to the ways in which the product of the ethnographic moment is a cultural thing. The ethnographic moment produces an interpretation. It might be, and usually is, an interpretation in words: it might be an illustration or a photograph; it might be a souvenir, private loot for a study wall, public loot for a museum. Whatever it is, the interpretation is a transformation of the Other into something whose form and continuity is determined by factors independent of the Other. The interpretation is not the Other. It is an invention that will have a cultural life of its own.

Margaret Mead's *Coming of Age in Samoa* must join *Argonauts of the Western Pacific* and *Nuer* as one of the three great anthropological books of the twentieth century. All three share a simplicity and directness that made the cultures they each invented a vehicle of understanding, both of the self of western society and the Other of human nature. By whatever trope great literature or great drama or great history is made, by the same trope these three ethnographies reflected and directed the cultures from which they came. All three are wrong, of course, if 'wrong' is the correct word to use of them. They are all now unacceptable in method and conception. What they did remarkably is established as normal because they did it remarkably. They have been revised over and over again, but they are benchmarks where all the revisions begin, and the revisions, make sense or gain notoriety because they are revisions of *them*. Ironically, too, their perfection and their craftsmanship stand against them and help us to see their feet of clay. Hindsight helps us to scoff at Evans-Pritchard, thinking that he could present the Nuer without mentioning the fact that the Italians were in their environment, bombing them to terror. Malinowski's revelations of his lusts and his hates scandalise those who think that to understand is to love, or who demand that somebody else's cultural relativism be political not methodological. Margaret Mead fuels her critics' arguments by presenting private revelations of her jejeune conception of what ethnographic fieldwork might entail. The critics punish them all for their not being what the critics are now because of them.

Margaret Mead was a student of Franz Boas, the larger-than-life founding father of American anthropology. In the 1920s Boas was embroiled in the nature/nurture debate. The growing racist doctrines of Europe were having their effects in the United States. Racist doctrines were supporting political studies for the exclusion of migrant groups and the separation of ethnic ghettoes. For Boas, the Other, the object of anthropology, was evidence enough of the ways in which human beings made themselves rather than were made by the materials of their bodies. Mead, with not much more than a few graduate review papers on Polynesian material culture behind her, proposed to go to the Pacific to test a theory of cultural determinism. Boas agreed only reluctantly, not because he had qualms about her project, but because he was concerned for her safety and her health. He insisted that she go to an island where ships called every three weeks and where she could get help if she needed it.

In Samoa, Mead was plagued not by dangers, but by the difficulties of being the observant stranger. On the margins of one's own and the others' culture everything is in caricature—smell, touch, sight, sound. Everything is a choice that has its negative consequences. Should she live in a Samoan home and lose the distance necessary for thought and reflection? Should she live in a naval officer's residence, get the distance, but make a boundary? Should she admit to her marriage when the Samoan presumption was that she could not be and should not be if she was there alone: she lost something in the hiding and the disclosing. Who would be her 'Samoans' when chiefs would not speak to her as a woman and women could not tell her all? Did one stay a lifetime to learn the language? Or was anthropology and the Other what one did and saw in nine months' fieldwork? Was it unscientific to know one's discomfort and inadequacy and within these limitations to do what one could? Or was being scientific being something one could never be?

Within the limits of living in, but not of, a culture on an island group acculturated by a hundred years of European contact, Mead selected twenty-five adolescent girls to interview about their own adolescence. It is clear that from the beginning she evoked her own cultural mythology or expectancy that puberty, a time of physical change, was also a time of tension, conflict and social adjustment. To put it another way, the myth of her own American twentieth-century culture was a natural determination about puberty. Puberty blues were natural, because that is what the body did. Her discovery among twenty-five adolescent girls of a sense of easiness, little conflict, no competitiveness, few restrictions over sexual play, made the dramatic point, with blinding clarity, that the disturbances of puberty are not natural. They are cultural, and if cultural, changeable by cultural means. On her return from fieldwork, under the influence of publishers, under pressure of public performances in lectures, she honed the polarities of American and Samoan adolescence. All her life she repeated her claim of good fortune in picking a feature of human existence and a culture in the Pacific that highlighted the constructive role of cultural institutions in making human nature. She might better have asked what it was that triggered so tremendous a response to her work. It was hardly the Samoans. It was the 'Samoans' as they reflected a truth Americans wanted to know of themselves or make of themselves. One could not count the ways in which the ethos of self-creativity was all-pervading in American culture. One could not count the ways in which Mead's *Coming of Age in Samoa* was brilliantly relevant. It was mythic. It was a parable about the Other that told an undeniable truth that we have the making of ourselves in our own hands. It was parable about social reform, about change, about optimism. Mead's 'Samoans' were no more Samoan than Shakespeare's Macbeth was a Scotsman. Samoans became 'Samoans', exemplars of a cultural truth that human beings made themselves. The product of

Mead's ethnographic moment was the means by which many millions of Americans entertained themselves with a truth about themselves. Accuracy did not matter: it rarely does when the truth is at stake.

For Freeman, the ultimate scandal of Mead's work was that her twenty-five adolescent girls were eccentric because they told Mead only what she wanted to hear. Freeman's informants, on the other hand and in his view, are really Samoan because they continually assure him about what Samoa really is; or they have written down, in commissions and reports, what Samoa really is. In an anthropological version of the hermeneutic circle, they know who they really are by knowing they are not what Mead says them to be. They are as entertained by Mead's 'Samoans' as the millions of Americans have been.

In describing the adolescent girls, Mead remarked on their qualities. They were egalitarian: they were co-operative rather than competitive. They showed little aggression, had little time for dogmatic religion, were not punished and never feared punishment, were reared benevolently and with the minimum of regulation. Freeman explores the contradictions he sees in this—not in the twenty-five adolescent girls but in something he calls Samoan Society. So his description of rank and the highly formalised status etiquette among the chiefs serves to contradict Mead's assertions that the girls in their Samoanness were little preoccupied with rank. His description of Samoan warfare and physical violence is meant to offset Mead's observation that there was little conflict in the nine months of her presence. He cites rape statistics for those nine months to mock her judgement that sexuality was easy and without guilt. He even quotes a virginity poll he and his wife took in 1961 to discover that seventy-three per cent of girls in some villages were virgins till the age of nineteen, to show that Samoans are very proper persons in sexual morality. I have to confess that if I wished to flog Margaret Mead for being wrong in her judgement that 'Samoans' were egalitarian, co-operative, peaceful and free, I would want to discover what possible meaning these terms could have when used of a culture. But being interested in history, if I, like Mead or Freeman, wanted to invent my Samoa, I would invent it in time. Their 'Samoa' is anything from before the European arrival until yesterday. But Freeman's timeless Samoa is worse than Mead's. He does not seem to have seen the dialectic in the making of cultures that comes from anthropology's invention of them.

Knowing the past, which we call history, and knowing the other, which we call anthropology, are the two great cultural metaphors by which we know ourselves and knowing ourselves constitute ourselves. I was among a group of American anthropologists when I first heard Freeman's book discussed. I was interested that their conversation was about their own public image. They saw the immediate consequence of a public awareness that Margaret Mead was wrong was that anthropology might lose its scientific aura. And with that, given the climate of American tertiary education and politics, anthropology would be further savaged by 'useful' disciplines that could claim to be scientific and certain. Being scientific in this sense is being able to propose a system of certain knowledge which, if learned, will train somebody to be comfortable in some occupation. Being ambiguous, being alert to the relativities of any knowledge, being able to gauge the uncertainties in certainty is treason to science. The anthropologists I speak of saw that in the positivist ethos that rules their culture, Freeman's book would do them harm and debating Freeman would only do greater harm by showing how wrong he himself has been. Freeman ends his book with a paean of praise for the scientific method. It is a sad song, really, optimistic that if only we shared his fetishes all our inventions would be real. There is not a whisper in it of the irony that is the soul of history and anthropology alike.

Returning to the Past
its own Present
HISTORY'S
EMPOWERING FORCE

NOT many have the words to describe the horrors of war. Edmund Blunden, poet and pacifist, did. He survived three years of trench life in Flanders from 1914 to1918, a miracle which he never did understand. His account of his experiences, *Undertones of War*, is a terrible book to read, not for its explicit bloody descriptions, but for the terrifying ordinariness of men in appalling circumstances. At one stage, he writes down his puzzlement at how he should make history of all this—dramatically? rhetorically? mythically? simply?

'Do I loiter too long among little things? Each circumstance of the British experience that is still with me has ceased for me to be big or little, and so appeals to me more even than the highest exaltation of pain . . . Was it nearer the soul of war to draw lines of coloured ink on vast maps at Montreuil or Whitehall, to hear of or to project colossal shocks in a sort of mathematical symbol, than to rub knees with some poor jaw-dropped resting sentry, under the dripping rubber sheet, balanced on the greasy fire-step, a fragment of some rural newspaper or Mr Bottomley's oracle beside him? Towards Hooge one brazen morning, running in a shower of shells along 'The Great Wall of China' (one dud shell struck within a rifle's length of us, and exploded somewhere else), Kenward and I saw a sentry crouching and peering one way and another like a birdboy in an October storm. He spoke, grinned and shivered; we passed; and duly the sentry was hit by a shell. So that in this vicinity a peculiar difficulty would exist for the artist to select the sight, faces, words, incidents, which characterised the time. The art is rather to collect them, in their original form of incoherence. I have not noticed any compelling similarity between a bomb used as an inkpot and a bomb in the hand of a corpse, or even between the look of a footballer after a goal all the way and that of a sergeant inspecting whale-oiled feet. There was a difference prevailing in all things. Let the smoke of the German breakfast fires, yes, and the savour of their coffee, rise in these pages, and be kindly mused upon in our neighbouring saps of retrogression. Let my curiosity have its little day, among the men of action and war-imagination' (Blunden 1989 [1928]: 123).

'Let my curiosity have its little day'. It seems a modest request, but actually it is a large one. He wants to be excused from the Big Picture, the abstraction. He wants to preserve the uncertainties, the inconsequences of the present moment—its ordinariness. Abstraction, he might have said with a later Herbert Marcuse, is a process of forgetting. To remember requires catching the present moment with all its might-have-beens.

Nothing can really be returned to the past. Not life to its dead. Not justice to its victimised. But we take something from the past with our hindsighted clarity. That which we take we can return. We disempower the people of the past when we rob them of their present moments. We dehumanise them, make them our puppets. We owe them more, it seems to me. We have to write history in the human condition and share their presents. We have to be as humble about the past as we are about the future.

Renato Rosaldo, an American anthropologist, once wrote a paper entitled 'Grief and a Headhunter's Rage: On the Cultural Force of Emotions' (1984). Renato and his wife Michelle had been graduate students with me at Harvard. They did their fieldwork among the Ilongot of Northern Luzon in the Philippines. The Ilongot had been head hunters. And when the Rosaldos asked the older men why they had cut off heads, they were told one-liners that they could never fathom. Rage, born of grief, they were told, made the Ilongot kill. In the act of severing and throwing away the heads, the Ilongot threw away the anger that possessed them from some bereavement of a child or in their family. These statements were impenetrable to the Rosaldos—not just because grief and rage should be so inordinately locked together, but because the words used to explain them seemed so shallow. Transcribed, the words seemed empty clichés that in no way conveyed the force of the Ilongot experience.

They were impenetrable to Renato, that is, until one day when Michelle was walking between two villages along a high mountain ridge. She slipped and fell to her death down a cliff. When Renato reached her body, he was convulsed with sorrow and the cold visceral helplessness at the finality of death. But he was also convulsed with rage. At Michelle—how could she abandon him? How could she have been so stupid as to fall? At himself—what should he have done to prevent it? At the unfairness of it. At the incompleteness and futility now of what they were doing. It was a long time before he could do or write anthropology. The writing of 'Grief and a Headhunter's Rage' was in some sense a catharsis, in that word of Aristotle's of the theatre, an enlightenment, an understanding of a drama. The catharsis came because Renato joined his own experience with an Ilongot one. He understood that if we would narrate the pain of others, there must be compassion, yes. He also suggested that to the familiar concepts we use to analyse narration—*thick description, multivocality, polysemy, richness, texture*—we should add another, *force*, the affective intensity which often lies hidden behind the clichéd or trivialised expression of emotion. I suppose for us as readers of texts of pain, silence and difference, the problem is how to recognise the intensity behind the clichés. And the problem for us as writers is how we foreground the intensity when language so easily hides it.

Richard Rorty has written that human solidarity is to be achieved not by inquiry but by imagination (Rorty 1989). When we talk of the politics of history, I think we are talking about history's empowering and disempowering force. Nicholas Hudson in his *Modern Australian Usage* (1993) says that 'empower means to give power without defining the nature or purpose of the power, though it is assumed to be political or social. This sense is not in the dictionaries, but it fills an apparent need and is readily understood, so it is likely to flourish'. Let it flourish, I say, although there will be a curl of the lips in some quarters. There always is at so-called 'trendy' words that catch a mood or a meaning. There is the politics already. Someone is sure to say: 'Don't threaten me with new words. You are trying to make me politically correct'. Yes, that is so. All words, old and new, are inducements to political correctness. Words are empowering things. Histories, being mostly in words, are empowering, too. Their most empowering force is the discovery they help us make of our humanity in both the past and the present. Strangely, it takes much imagination to do that.

SONGLINES AND SEAWAYS

A Reflection on the Occasion of the Rehanging of the Australian
and Pacific Collections in the National Gallery of Australia

*I have a vision of the Songlines stretching across the continents and ages;
that wherever men have trodden they have left a trail of song (of which we
may, now and then, catch an echo); and that these trails must reach back,
in time and space, to an isolated pocket in the African savanna, where the
First Man opening his mouth in defiance of the terrors that surrounded
him, shouted the opening stanza of the World Song, 'I am'.*

(Chatwin 1988: 282)

'SONGLINES' was Bruce Chatwin's understanding of how lives and
landscapes are intertwined in story. He suspected that forty thousand years were needed to make a Dreamtime in which the 'songlines'
so saturated the environment with narrative that every tree and rock
reflected an aboriginal spirit collectively and individually. In such an
intertwining it was difficult to know where human life and physical
nature began and ended, or whether the word forms of the narratives
were in the head or 'out there'. That united world of things and words
was not frozen still by time, but was always being enlarged by the pains
and joys of succeeding generations, even when the latest of these generations, maybe the two hundredth in one place, experienced catastro-
phic change, even when the outsiders to these songlines saw them as
fraud or rationalisations, or stories in the service of greed and politics.

Bruce Chatwin's early death denied him the opportunity to develop his understanding. Who am I to say what he really meant or to take him further? Indeed, it would be truer to him to leave his understanding in the piecemeal stories with which he clothed it. Perhaps it would be better, too, if I simply told Songlines of my own and leave the question whether they are entangling or enlightening to the end when they have been heard.

That is what I will do. We have a space so immense that the miles and metres of our personal experience can scarcely encompass it, so aged in time that the minutes of our days and the years of our lives can make no sensible measure of it. We have called that space for about 150 years 'Oceania'. Like all imposed names, 'Oceania' has had its seasons of fashion. For many years it comfortably described the overarching primitivity of 'Melanesians', 'Polynesians', 'Micronesians' and Australian Aborigines who peopled its continent and islands. Then as modernity and history divided the area into competing nation states and economic centres, the name 'Oceania' seemed a little too invented, the sort of place Gulliver might have visited or Jules Verne explored. Now there are island peoples who see how much they lose by describing their world with the song-lines of economists, bankers and world politicians. They feel that invented though it might be, the name 'Oceania' represents the 'sea of islands' that it was their triumph to encompass. Their own songlines are so entwined with sea- and land-scapes of Oceania that they are not who they are without some encompassment of Oceania's immensity, and some representation of how the 'sea of islands' is made by the language of the stories and science and rituals they impose upon it (Epeli Hau'ofa 1994: 147).

This space then that we call Oceania holds within it land as old as Gondwana and a sea that stretches across a third of the globe's face and reaches down seventeen kilometres deep and up a thousand light years high. It has a billion years of past and a billion years of future till our sun-star dies. It came as near to an infinity of time that we can conceive before us and will remain an infinity after us. It rests on a huge plate whose movement rouses Pele's anger in Hawaii and destroys freeways in

Los Angeles. We have stood on the land at its edges for perhaps only 90 000 years. We have entered its sea for perhaps only 3000 years. Oceania enfolds our time as it encompasses our space. It seems an arrogance to claim that we encompass it with our songlines.

Oceans are not easily encompassed. They are voyaged. They are mapped. They are narrated in story and odyssey. They are imaged in song and painting. They are modelled in laboratories, on diplomatic tables. They are taken possession of by empires, blessed by priests and haunted by pirates. There will be no one songline for an ocean. Perhaps you will remember the images of Oceania that Rachel Carson gave us in her poetry/science of her *The Sea Around Us*. She imagined the molten liquid surface of a young earth rising into a huge wave through five hundred years of sun tides. This wave whipped off the earth's surface and became the earth's satellite, the moon. The scar left by this launching is now the Pacific Basin, she thought. As the earth cooled, the steaming clouds rained for centuries and the oceans were filled (Carson 1989: 20–1).

'When the moon was born, there was no ocean', she wrote. 'As soon as the earth's crust cooled enough, the rains began to fall. Never have there been such rains since that time. They fell continuously, day and night, days passing into months, into years, into years, into centuries. They poured into the waiting ocean basins, or, falling upon the continental masses, drained away to become the sea' (Carson 1989: 22).

Since Rachel Carson wrote that in 1950 human beings have encompassed the moon itself by landing on it. One would think that we would know by that where it came from. But we don't. One astrophysicist says that it will be a hundred years before we know how the moon came to be the earth's satellite. But the same mathematics—three thousand years old in the songlines of our understanding of the heavens—the same mathematics that got human beings to the moon tells us that for the moon to have been born out of the Pacific Basin the earth must have been whirling in a 2.6-hour day. When the moon came into the earth's orbit, the earth's day was five or six hours long—too slow by far for it to have been wrenched free from the earth's surface. It must have come some other way.

Instead of looking to the heavens for the origin of Oceania we now look to the depths, even to the Moho, that strange discontinuity beneath the earth's crust. The root ideas of a songline expand fast. Thirty years of sonar mapping and deep sea drilling now convince us that it is the continents themselves that have been the voyagers in an odyssey that has not yet finished. The immense landscape beneath the sea is now so profusely named that it needs two world bureaucracies to control the naming. Giving names in the Judaeo-Christian tradition has always seemed an act of creation, the complete encompassment. The oldest songline of the Judaeo-Christian tradition, the Book of Genesis, has Yahweh making sense of the disordered universe by dividing it into dualities—light/darkness, heavens/earth, sea/land—but leaving it to humans to encompass all its parts by naming them. A sixty-first millenium voyage of 20 000 leagues under the sea would take you past the likes of Musicians' Seamounts, from Strauss to Mendelssohn, past Beethoven Ridge and Mount Mozart. I suppose that this exuberance to give names in a no-name space is no more kitsch than a Spanish propensity to fill new spaces with with the calendar of saints' feasts, or James Cook's propensity to name the world after Admiralty patrons, or the French propensity to invoke classical sexuality. And no doubt the historians at the end of the sixty-first millenium, when they ask what songlines are imbedded in the landscape beneath the sea, will have to wonder what had more force in the naming process, the record library on the scientific drill ship, or the cultural literacy of the discoverers (Hamilton-Paterson 1992: 38).

I suppose, too, that it is an arrogance to use the pronoun 'we' to speak of our encompassing and our songlines. How do I who can count my generations on my fingers have a claim to be 'we' with those whose generations seem countless? The truth is, I think, that we who live in this present moment all stand equal in the generations that come before us and in the generations that will come after us. We are all the last jelling drops on the stalactites of time. We are all the means by which those that come after us will hang on to their past. 'White man got no dreaming', the Aboriginal elder said to Bill Stanner, trying to describe the differences in the categories of time and space that the different songlines of black and white made (Stanner 1979: 24). But that is not true. The white man's dreaming is just of another sort. It might seem that a white man's religious dream might turn around an historical event reckoned to be 1994 years ago. It might seem that a white man's dreaming has been congealed or frozen by defining dogma. 'All reification is a process of forgetting', Herbert Marcuse reminded us. 'Art fights reification by making the petrified world speak, sing, perhaps dance' (Taussig 1980: 154). But two thousand years dreaming about the event leaches the historical moment of most of its historical detail and puts the believer in touch with it in an ever renewing way. A songline of incarnation and redemption entwines an individual in time, in much the same way as a songline about a rainbow serpent entwines an individual in a mountain range or river gully. There never was a fundamentalism so rigid that it never exchanges the detail of belief for what is seen as the real meaning of the belief. It is the same for the fundamentalisms of science as it is for the fundamentalisms of religion and politics. Their songlines are always changing and always remaining the same.

My thesis is not so much that both white and black have a dreaming, as that all our songlines by which our dreamtimes are expressed are interlocked. Our interlocked songlines, white and black, intertwine our lives and landscapes, intertwine our pasts and presents. For good or evil, these past 400 years of cultural encounters in Oceania have so bound together black and white that now there is no black without white, no white without black. The songlines of this new bound together time are just begun. The memories of the encounter and the joining are fresh. But the memories of a dreaming, even in so short a time as 200 years, are not so much fresh for individuals and generations, as renewed, the same, but changed. The past can never be changed, but the memory of it in the present is always changing. Nothing that has been said and done, and heard and seen, in our cultural past can be unsaid and undone. If heard and seen, a memory is made of it. Nothing that is said can be unsaid. Not what Jesus Christ said, not what Buddha, not what Anintjola the Rain Man said, not Galileo, not Marx, not Freud, not Einstein; not Bennelong, not Truganini. And now as we discover all over Oceania that the 'fatal impact' of the Euro-American intrusion was fatal for hundreds of thousands of lives but not for deep cultural memories, we are beginning to understand how, if we listen, we can hear what was said 40 000 years ago by those who painted their songlines on cave walls from the northernmost point of the continent to the southernmost. Or buried their dead in their thousands, clearly in some hope of some kind of resurrection, which, of course, they now have thousands of years later because the memory of them stirs. The memory of them stirs because our songlines of life and death are interlocked by an understanding of how much of an achievement even the smallest act of human creativity is. A hand stencilled on the wall of Fraser Cave in southwest Tasmania is a signature of a presence there 20 000 years ago; in sight of Antarctic icebergs, as far south on the globe as human beings had ever reached, it is our heritage, our triumph, because we do not know how we could have done it.

That voyage south, made after a slow encompassment of the continent through 20 000 years, was matched by the encompassment of the vast ocean. Though the space of this ocean encompassment was much greater than that of the land, the time taken was much shorter, 2000 years. A thousand years before a European civilisation had the knowledge or the skill to sail on it, or even the imagination to dream that the ocean was there, there was not an island of the 10 000 islands of this sea that had not been inhabited or visited by this voyaging people.

The first Euro-Americans to enter Oceania, being sailors, were always teased by the fact that their most brilliant discoveries were really only re-discoveries. Cook, Bougainville, La Pérouse . . . we can read them in their journals wondering how it could have been. Two centuries of inquiry have not answered their questions, but for the sake of the songlines embedded in their story, let me say something of what history, anthropology, archaeology, genetics, linguistics, botany and computer science seem to tell us. Three thousand five hundred years ago, the ocean was empty of human habitation and most of the food resources that made human habitation possible, or at least congenial. By 1500 years ago, AD 500, in a period of 2000 years equal to the Christian era, the island peoples had reached out to their furthest eastern settlement, Easter Island we call it now, Rapanui in their imagination, and to the north in Hawaii (Sandwich Islands) and south to Aotorea (New Zealand). Soon after, or perhaps even before, they reached even further to the South American coastline and brought back the sweet potato, with its name *kumara*, and spread it abroad as the subsistence food of all Oceania. How this expansion eastward against the prevailing winds and currents, without vast loss of life, has been long known as the 'Polynesian Problem'.

For forty years now there has been a sense that the sort of knowledge and skill that allowed the Oceanians to encompass their world was of a special sort that could only be known by doing it, reading the stars without instruments, interpreting the winds and swells, recognising the signs of landfall, constructing the canoes that could survive weeks of of open-sea voyaging. So the years have been filled with practical experiments in which, using native knowledge only, voyages have been made between Hawaii and Tahiti, between Tahiti and New Zealand and across all the open seas that seemed such a barrier to travel in the Central Pacific. For me, at least, the most enlightening moment in this debate has been provided by Geoffrey Irwin, archaeologist and sailor, in his *Prehistoric Exploration and Colonisation of the Pacific* (1992). It is his sailor's sense that exploratory sailing is always best against adverse conditions. Why? Because sailors are always thinking of return. Upwind navigation means downwind return to an environment totally integrated into the navigator's knowledge system. It is the total mastery of local environment which gives a navigator confidence to go outside it and come back. So the encompassment of a whole ocean was really a progressive series of encompassments of local domains through 2000 years. Succeeding generations have had to map the heavens and the stars, to locate in time and space the rising of the stars and the angles of the sun, to read the sculpture in water that constant weather patterns and land masses made. And because these maps were mental, always archived in the mind and not in books and things, systems had to be found by which the knowledge was handed on from generation to generation, and not merely preserved but accummulated and enlarged. Songlines had to be made. Words, the most transient thing of our cultural experience, blown away on the breath on our lips, had to be given a *longue duree*, endurance beyond the minute, beyond a lifetime. All the systems by which orality rather than literacy preserved and expanded cultural knowledge had to come into use. As we map these progressive steps across Oceania we can see that there were regular resting spots of 500 to 600 years, or 20 to 25 generations, in which an island people collected itself and made itself confident in its mastery of its environment before reaching out to something new.

How they did that we cannot say. We have to assume that they early evolved what they had later: the knowledge of their navigators was so precious that it was passed on in secret and after long apprenticeship; their astronomy was woven into the rhythm of their lives so that the beginning and ending of their seasons was matched to the stars and their cosmology was sung and danced; their understanding of their domains was translated into deep metaphors that kept their knowing alive and always enlarging itself; the poetics of their orality would have obeyed the laws we have come to recognise in the oral literature of our own culture. It cannot be my ambition here to describe all the ways in which the exhaustive knowledge of a domain is sustained through generations, only to remind you of them. We have to think that every generation in the decades that belonged to it was restless to extend the boundaries of the experience that had been given it.

I think I can best stir your imagination to what I am saying by taking you to a specific place in Oceania at a specific time. The place is Tahiti, and a particular bay on its north-west point, Matavai. The time is at the end of the eighteenth century, more particularly 1769 Anno Domini in the songlines of a Christian Europe. If the *maohi* or people of Tahiti counted the years of their beginnings, which they did not, it would be about the year 2500 since their arrival on the island. More pertinently it was Year 2 of their encounter with the strangers who came in their ships. One of them was in the bay at this time, the *Endeavour,* with its captain, James Cook.

Matavai in the European representations of it was the gateway to the Islands of Paradise. By the accidents of how the winds blew and the reefs were set, it became the most important anchorage in the South Seas. Successive visitors imprinted its images on the European mind, so that the courts of Europe knew its politics, its scandals and its gossip, and reported it in poems and satire and pantomime, in papers to the Royal Society and other academies, and of course in the paintings of Sydney Parkinson, William Hodges and John Webber, and all the other artists who put what they saw onto canvas or paper in pencil, watercolour and oil. They did it even in wallpaper, dramatically in Jean Chavert's hanging, more mundanely for merchant walls in London, Boston and Philadelphia. Matavai was the site of a Euro-American ethnographic experience in which the otherness of the South Seas was transcribed into all sorts of understandings about the Europeans themselves and the world they were encompassing. Traditionally, from our distant observation of this eighteenth-century European ethnographic experience, we have seen it as a Romantic moment in which Europe comprehended the artificiality of its own civilisation before the simplicity of native lives. I think it would be wrong to see this particular Romantic representation of the encounter with the primitive as any more than the exotic experience of a few. The overriding experience of otherness in Tahiti did not undermine European self confidence at all. On the contrary, the overriding experience was that natives were laughably grotesque, not really different at all, just like us, only worse. Of course, this self confidence of the civilised was to be lifted a level or two into a sense of the humane generosity, the scientific disinterestedness, and overlying carefulness that came from mythologising this very man in Matavai, James Cook.

That low point of Matavai Bay, divided by a river, is now called Point Venus, and James Cook had erected a palisade which he called Fort Venus. Behind the palisade was a tent observatory. Cook was at Point Venus on 3 June 1769, to observe the transit of Venus. If the songlines of Oceania enclosed canoes and birds in an understanding of themselves, then the songlines of Europe enclosed stars and planets in a view of the universe that had been unfolding for three thousand years. Tim

Ferris has called it *The Coming of Age of the Milky Way* (1988). These were years towards the end of the period in which European *philosophes* exhilaratingly and self-consciously knew themselves to be 'enlightened'. They were those who had 'dared to know', as Immanuel Kant described them. For nearly a hundred years there had been a tribal sense among the lovers of criticism. They had been to the top of the mountain with Petrach and opened Augustine's *Confessions* with him there: 'Men went forth to behold the high mountains and the mighty surge of the sea, and the broad stretches of the rivers and the inexhaustible ocean, and the paths of the stars and so doing lose themselves in wonderment. A new thought seized me', Petrarch had written, 'transporting me from space into time' (Gebser 1984: 13–14). To have discovered that everything in nature, everything in human beings, was set in time, that the abstractions of law, science, and the market, even God himself, were, in time, was indeed enlightening. It made for a season of observing and measuring.

There was no more enthused observing and measuring than in the heavens and at the stars. 'Navigation' they had taken to calling this watch on the universe at night. Mathematics, surveying and especially navigation were the vocational subjects of education, even in the smallest village school. Navigation was not so much a way of teaching small boys to steer ships. Navigation was the medium of progressive and current science. It gave cultural focus to the science of angles, circles and time. Its problems opened up the principal mathematical issues of the day. More than that. Gilbert Wakefield, Isaac Newton's teacher, said how much more: 'What subject of human contemplation shall compare in grandeur with that which demonstrates the trajectories, the periods, the distances, the dimensions, the velocities and gravitations of the planetary system: states the tides . . . contemplates the invisible comet, wandering in his parabolic orb for successive centuries . . . ? Language sinks beneath the contemplation so exalted and so well calculated to inspire the most awful sentiment of the Great Artificer'. God was the greatest craftsman of them all.

I suppose that it was of comfort to northern sailors coming into a southern world that, as their principle guide the northern pole-star disappeared beyond the horizon, God the Craftsman had put a sign for them in southern skies. They saw this constellation of stars as a Southern Cross. Of course it is their songline that let them see this skewed shape as a cross. The peoples of the southern hemisphere—the Aborigines, the Africans, the South Americans, the Pacific islanders—saw it differently according to their own songlines—as fishing spears, wild turkeys, pigeons. Spirit Tree the Aranda called it. Souls were launched from the Spirit Tree into a new life. Eaglehawk, the Luritja called it in totem that bound them to their clans. But the Spaniards coming south saw a cross in it and an omen of how their Christian faith would fare in a new world.

That their Cross should be Southern belongs to our deepest presumptions. Crux never disappears from our skies. It circles our skies all our nights. Of course it was not always so. In the precession of our heavens as our globe slowly waves its circles, the Southern Cross goes north every 28 000 years. It should give us pause to realise that aboriginal songlines included an experience of a Southern Cross that wandered north and south through 60 000 years. But even the four hundred and then the two hundred years of our cultural experience of a Southern Cross are enough to trigger in us all sorts of signals—of notions of grace and redemption, of a god who intrudes on human history, of the knowledge of good and evil, of the dualism of body and soul, of life here and hereafter. And because like all songlines there is a seepage across all areas of life, so that even the most religious of symbols can become a most secular myth, we easily experience in the sign of the Southern Cross a sense of freedom, of sacrifice. We would be hard put to disentangle all these signals from those we experience looking at the rows of crosses in Flanders Fields, or at a flag in times of triumph or mourning. And because knowledge is never distant either from our deep emotions or our aesthetics, we have an appreciation of how our most ordinary of symbols are transformed by miracles of science and technology. There's a dreaming in that, I think. David Malin had a dreaming of the Southern Cross. He published it in *A View of the Universe* (1994). He says the stepped focus technique which allowed him to unravel the colours of the stars came to him by accident. But the progressive encompassing of the heavens is no accident. It has the expanding quality of all dreamings. The more they change, as the saying goes, the more they remain the same.

I am not so distant from my subject or my particular space and time as it might seem. James Cook would have comfortably worshipped at a shrine to God the Craftsman and he was in the Pacific to observe the heavens and to measure them. There is a direct line between the views of the Southern Cross of David Malin and what Cook came to see at Tahiti.

James Cook, I say, would have comfortably worshipped at a shrine to God the Craftsman. Cook, The Discoverer, was soon to be quite reflective in his journals on what it meant to be a 'discoverer' and would soon know that discovering was not so much 'of' distant lands as 'to' an expectant world. Discovering held its own ambivalences. In these first months of his career, what delighted him most was discovering exactly where he was. Fort Venus, he knew by many calculations, was 17° 29' 15" S in latitude and 149° 30' 38" W in longitude. It would have given him great satisfaction that his longitude was only out by twenty-four seconds, by modern satellite navigation. He had no chronometer on this first voyage. He discovered where he was by observation and calculation and by use of Nevil Maskelyne's brand new *Nautical Almanac.* Maskelyne was passionately devoted to the public nature of science. He put 90 000 observations of moon and stars into the hands of navigators in his *Almanac.* He went through twenty-five assistants, bending their heads over calculations weeks and months on end. He made transit observations accurate to one tenth of a second. He was not much for theory, but put into practice the accumulated knowledge of centuries. His observatory and the ships of discovery he serviced were full of the instrument treasures of the day. Jesse Ramsden, Thomas Earnshaw, John Arnold, John Dollund, James Kendall made them. It is difficult for us to taste the satisfaction these artisans felt, that their hands could make instruments calibrated to one four thousandth of an inch.

So when Cook set up his tent observatory, a Shelton pendulum clock, a Bird Quadrant and a Ramsden sextant would be the means of observing this transit of Venus. It is the way of things that I could tell you where every one of these artefacts is now, and whose hands they have passed through in two hundred years. I could tell you, too, the occasions when they have been brought out and displayed. And I believe these displays would not be random things, but would be attached to our cultural systems of science, politics and living.

This is what James Cook saw with those instruments—the transit of Venus across the face of the sun. He was to be disappointed that a penumbra—Venus' atmosphere—that he had not expected, blurred the moments of Venus' entry to and exit from the sun's circumference. It made his and his colleagues' measurements ambiguous by some seconds, which seemed fatal for his experiment. That experiment had to do with the size of the universe. At these very same moments there were other observers in Siberia, South Africa and Mexico doing the same. It was organised science on a global scale, in the sense that it was conducted by professionals, sponsored by scientific societies and supported by government funds. Hence it was imbued with the politics of knowledge of all such endeavours. It had the altruism of all the ideals of shared knowledge, the self-interest involved in men living and making fame by their engagement. In deserts, on mountains, in jungles, on Pacific islands, juggling with concerns for their own survival as well as for the stars, men were trying to observe the unobservable—the extent of the universe. What they observed was the ever more refined calibration of their instruments. But they had to socialise themselves to the 'as if' world of their measuring, immerse themselves in a special language, and come out knowing that they had seen unseeable distances. Edmond Halley had urged them from the grave to make the most of this rare opportunity of a century and more. Johannes Kepler had determined the relative distances between the planets. Edmond Halley had seen that if one knew the distance between two observing positions on the globe and observed the angle of the apex of the triangle made by these separate observations to an object in the heavens, then they could calculate the actual measurement of the triangle's sides, and know the solar parallax and thus the distance of the sun.

'Seeing', wrote William Herschel, the maker of the finest telescopes of the day, 'is in some respect an art which must be learnt. Telescopes have played me so many tricks that I have at last found them out in many of their humours and have made them confess to me what they would not have conceded, if I had not with such perseverance and patience countered them'. The seeing of the universe is an art that is deep in our songlines. We now see Venus as the computer's eyes of a spacecraft called Magellan saw it. And out of its lines and figures, we 'see' Venus' surface. We 'see' our place in one small galaxy in paintings and models that figures from our radio telescopes let us build.

Telescopic seeing, whether into the past or into the heavens, is likely to foster a certain delusion of apartness in the observer, a sense of separateness from nature, and in that a sense of 'objectivity'. It is microscopic seeing that destroys the notion of passive observation. 'On the microscopic level', Timothy Ferris has written in his *Coming of Age in the Milky Way* (1988: 289), 'every act of observation is disruptive . . . and the manner in which we choose to make the observation influences the results of the interaction'. 'Quantum physics', he goes on, 'obliges us to take seriously what has been a more purely philosophical consideration: that we do not see things in themselves, but only aspects of things. What we see is an electron path in a bubble chamber, not an electron, and what we see in the skies are not stars, any more than a recording of Caruso's voice is Caruso. By revealing that the observer plays a role in the observed, quantum physics did for physics what Darwin had done for the life sciences: it tore down walls, reuniting the world with the universe'.

By the time Cook had left Tahiti, he had learnt not just the difficulties of telescopic seeing but the intrusive nature of microscopic observation. At Tahiti he was confronted with much that was to him bizarre and abhorrent—human sacrifice, violent power, flagrant sexuality, sodomy, transvesticism. He suspected at the time that what he was seeing he did not understand. He was touched ever so slightly by a cultural relativism. He knew he was seeing difference. Whatever judgement he made was irrelevant. He noted his ambivalence in his journal. It was a dangerous moment for Cook. He would be castigated for observing such lewdness and not trying to change it. And in any case he had already observed that just 'being there' was changing native lives, not necessarily for the better.

I dare say it is well beyond my ability to describe the songlines of our culture that entwine our understanding, our values, our sacred beliefs, or ambitions with such a cosmorama of physical and cultural observations. I have to say, however, that I would begin where I began with James Cook and celebrate the richness of knowing exactly where we are. I would end with the caution that knowing exactly where we are is no guarantee that we know exactly where we are going. After all the most frivolous of associations and the most awful associations are made with the same name in Oceania, Bikini.

I will not patronise you by trying to join together all the images I have given you, of Gondwanaland, of *Nautical Almanacs*, of computer reconstructions of Venus, of Polynesian star charts and the rest. I came in part to the notion of bound-together songlines because I was invited to speak on the occasion of the rehanging of the Oceanian collection of the Australian National Gallery. I was invited to speak on that part of the collection that represented the cultural encounter between the intruding Euro-American Strangers and the Oceanian Natives. So I had to explain why the representation of the encounter through, say, a Jean Chavert wallpaper, or a painting by John Webber of Poetua might not be all that they seemed. Traditionally, from our distant observation of the eighteenth-century European ethnographic experience, we have seen it as a Romantic moment in which Europe understood the artificiality of its own civilisation before the simplicity of natives lives. I think it would be wrong to see this particular Romantic representaion of the encounter with the 'primitive' as any more than an exotic experience of a few. The overriding experience of otherness in Tahiti did not undermine European self-confidence at all. On the contrary, the overriding experience was that natives were laughably grotesque, not really different at all, just like us, only worse. If we pause a little before the sensuous Romantic portrait by John Webber of the young island woman Poetua, it is good to remember that it was painted during the four days that Poetua was held hostage while Cook demanded her father find some deserters from the *Resolution*. Of course, this self-confidence of the civilised was to be lifted a level or two into a sense of humane generosity, of scientific disinterestedness, and of overlying carefulness that came from mythologising James Cook.

Anthropology and history are uncomfortable disciplines. They undermine any confidence we might have in our own originality and uniqueness by underscoring the plagiarisms of our lives and living. But at the same time they demand some deference to the differences of the past and the other, even to a past so intimate to us that it seems always present, even to an other that because of the weakness of our vision seems only to mirror ourselves.

That space, that *limen*, in which the disciplines of anthropology and history demand us to be, in which everything is the same and different at the one time, in which even the ambition to be unpolitical is seen as politics, requires at times a special voice. It is the voice, Richard Rorty has suggested, not so much of inquiry as of imagination (Rorty 1989: xvi). Imagination, like poetry, is risky. It sometimes takes us where we do not want to go.

Some of the things we have to imagine are the deep narratives that engulf our cultural experience. Sometimes deep narratives are mistaken for the Unconscious, but the Unconscious is too much the creature of model-makers to be real. Deep narratives are not unconscious. Deep narratives are consciously present to us, but always in transformed ways. That is why it takes imagination to see them. That is why a better word to use of them is the imaginative one invented by Bruce Chatwin, 'Songlines'.

The beginnings of the encounters between the natives of Oceania and the Euro-American intruders, and the beginning of the intertwining of our songlines, were universally and inevitably violent. Men and women killed one another in uncountable numbers. There is no withdrawing from that. It is what happened. The memory and history of it will be with us forever. The memory perhaps will divide us forever, or until the history of the killings is transformed into a cultural understanding that the killings were not of 'them' and 'us' but that the killings by those bound together by their own obligations to one another. Who can tell when these memories will be so transformed? By our tercentenary? By another 60 000 years of dreamtime?

While the killings actually took place and after them, there always occurred what I have called the Ethnographic Moment. As both Native and Stranger tried to cope with each others' otherness, they tried to represent it—in dance or in play, in story and painting, in song or learned paper, in temples or in academies. Who could count the myriad ways in which this otherness was represented? And these representations were archived in some way in social memory—by rituals and mythical replay, on library shelves, by collections of all descriptions. This archiving of memory was not haphazard. It had system—social and cultural—and obeyed all the systems enclosed by what is social and cultural—systems of class and gender, systems of politics and economics, systems of psyche and symbol. As we sat there on the occasion of the re-hanging of the Gallery's representation of the cultural encounters of Oceania, could we have unravelled the systems at work in this re-representing it involved? As we sat at this second re-hanging, could we have said how many more there will be? How long will the National Gallery last? A hundred years? 40 000 years? We don't know how many re-hangings there will be, but we know that any one we experience now will inevitably be transient. We know that each new re-hanging will be in response to the one before it. Each hanging will be like a sentence in a conversation that we are having about ourselves and the memory of the time when Native and Stranger became so bound together that they have never since been able to represent one without the other. It is the essence of culture always to be modern. The present moment is always the latest sentence in a never ending discourse, the latest line of a songline whose beginnings we could not trace and whose ending we do not know.

The third millenium is upon us, or, rather, the sixty-first millenium of settlement of this continent by islanders from the north is upon us. Two hundred years of cultural encounters is not long in sixty-one thousand years. But two hundred years of war is long enough, long enough to ask when it will end. When in the sixty-first millenium of settlement in this country will a monument be erected to celebrate the end of the more than two hundred years war between black and white in Australia? Make no doubt. There will be such a monument. I shan't see it. Maybe not you. Maybe not your children's children. Maybe it will be a thousand-year war. But the end will happen and there will be a monument. And there will be a debate about that monument. Should it be 'useful'? Should it be something that will mend the consequences of this war—some social scheme, some educational programme to ensure it will never happen again? Or will it be not 'useful', but a sacrifice that the present must make for the pain that has been made—some part of the Land that will belong to nobody but only to the past and the Land itself: some sacred space, shaped to rouse a memory, bring tears, give strength to resolutions? The debates about that space will be endless. Will it be a vaginal slash in the earth? Or will it be stiff and erect? Will it be black or white? Whose names will be upon it? Will the names have that ordered look by which we manage the dead, or will they be randomly represented, as chaotic and senseless as the occasions of the killings? Will it be mirror-shiny so that we see our faces in the past? What sorts of rituals will subdue its artificialities? When will it move from mere symbol—something to which those who see it give purely notional assent—to become sign, that whose mere presence conveys its meaning?

When that monument to the 200- or 300- or 1000-year war is made, it will be because the songlines that bind together all those living in this land will say that the killings have not been so much of other as of self. On the presumption that the processes of creating such songlines has begun, we can at least explore their beginnings.

Anzac Day

THE Shrine, as it is called in this city of Melbourne, stands in gardens on a rise that dominates the wide boulevard leading directly into the heart of the city. It is the Shrine of Remembrance, the memorial to Australian servicemen lost in World War I. Harsh and heavy, like some pillbox standing in Flanders fields, it is all contradiction in architectural design, a ziggurat on top of a columned temple. The only memorial like it is said to be in Leipzig, the Germans' memorial for their dead.

Through the tiers of the ziggurat is carved a shaft. At the eleventh hour on the eleventh day of the eleventh month every year, the light of the sun beams through this shaft directly on the Unknown Soldier's tomb set low in the temple's floor. Or it used to, before daylight saving. It is all done with mirrors now.

That is one of the problems of erecting monuments to freeze some memory forever. Times change. The carefully orchestrated moment to end the war that was to end all wars—11 a.m. on 11 November—is blurred now in memory and importance. The city used to stop for two minutes of silence. Now life goes on. The Shrine itself had to be changed to accommodate the memory of the dead of World War II. Then even the genre of wars was blurred—were Korea, Malaysia, Vietnam really wars? And would their dead be remembered?

I remember being struck by the problems of setting the past in memory when I was writing the history of a school. The chapter on the school at war was important to me. I had spilt tears reading the letters of boys describing the horrors of their experience in Flanders' fields and at Gallipoli. I

225

had read the letters of their officers writing home to parents and school-masters, trying to make sense of senseless death. And I had seen all around on the school walls the honour boards of the dead and photographs of the brave. I had known from my own experience how on Anzac Day it was difficult to catch pain and sorrow, or even pride, as names were read from long lists. I had wanted to catch in my history something of the war's awfulness. One day I was scavenging in the basement of the school chapel, looking for sources for my history—what else do historians do? The basement was a sort of elephant's graveyard of past piety. Statues of the Sacred Heart gave truncated blessings. St Francis Xavier pointed a broken finger at a headless St Anthony. All the litter that was a meta-phor of one sort of religious experience displaced by another lay around me. I found a pile of honour boards too—of captains of cricket, of cham-pionships won. And among them was a small board with half a dozen names on it in gold. I recognised the names. They were the names of the boys of the school killed in the first days of the landing at Gallipoli. In the fervour of their pride, and in the certainty they had heroes to remember, they had begun to inscribe the names of the dead as they came to hand. To their horror, they realised the spaces they left for the names to come was a register of their pessimism or optimism. So they took them away, to wait till the war was over. Then the hundreds of names had an ordered, finished look.

That is the problem of history, of myths, of signs and symbols. They are all in time. They cannot be set in stone or in gold. If one would catch them, see them culturally at work, one must catch their changing, their inventions, their attachment to a fluent present. I think that one way to do this is by observing them, by writing an ethnography of their realities rather than a history of their rhetoric. I have taught ethnography to my students by asking them to observe the expressions of historical consciousness in the Anzac ceremonies. For ten years between 1971 and 1981 we would assiduously plan our observations, attend the meetings of various groups of returned soldiers as they orga-nised reunions and the social occasions of the day, made our assessments of the symbolic environment of the Shrine, attended the Dawn Service, followed our groups through the march, tried to see them through the eyes of the spectators, joined the reunions.

These were the post-Vietnam years and almost all my students had been born after World War II and had been too young to be confronted personally by the dilemmas that the Vietnam War posed. Indeed, they were a generation pretty much untouched by war. But I should say, too, that I belonged to a family and a generation that was also untouched by war. My father was born in 1900. He was too young to go to the 1914–18 battlefields. And, because he could find employment easily, could delay marriage and get economically settled before having a family. Born in 1931, I was sheltered from the depression and too young to go to war in 1939–45. Had I children, they too would have missed the wars in Korea and Vietnam. My family and I have been out of step with war experience.

There was a difference between the perceptions of my students about war and mine, however, even if we shared a non-experience. I was drawn to it like a moth to the flame, not nostalgically, I think, not wanting it, but wondering at its incomprehensibility, wondering what my response to it would have been if I had been challenged by it. My students were far less wondering. They needed to be persuaded that an ethnography of the experience and rituals of Anzac would be interesting. They laughed at the rhetoric of the day, believed it to be warmongering, or an excuse for old men to relive dreams of dissoluteness. They knew the answer to any question they might ask about Anzac. It was the 'One Day of the Year', a sort of liminal space, if we talked anthropologically, a day when old men could clear themselves of the bonds they had collected—from family, from wives, from class, from respectability, from age—and enjoy the irresponsibility of the total institutions of which they had been members for a time.

The feeling was reinforced when we 'ethnogged', as they came to say, the Shrine. To them it was barren of sign and proclaimed the conventionalities of its symbols carved on its stone, in the majestic statues that had no majesty, in its formalism. Even the honour guard looked unreal. No intense goosesteps; no military rigidity; no frozen gaze; no shorn heads; just ordinary folk in the fancy dress of out-of-date uniforms. Not even glamorous; no hint of 40 000 Lighthorsemen charging over Egyptian sands; no sense of national possessiveness of the slouched hat and its feathers. 'Digger' was as foreign a word to describe what we saw, as 'metonymy' was to describe how we saw it.

The days that followed their visit to the Shrine were always bad and full of unconfidence. The argument that had surrounded the original building of the Shrine rose again in different forms. Why had not they built something practical? Where were the hospitals that might have been built? Wouldn't education have ended war more than monuments?

Things always changed at the Dawn Service on Anzac Day itself. No doubt the eeriness of early morning transport on near empty stomachs began it, or the sense of conspiracy, waiting in cars outside darkened houses. City-bred and with all the irregularity of the young at the other end of the day, greeting the dawn in an open space was a sort of pastoral experience. Paul Fussell in *The Great War and Modern Memory* (1975) wrote of this pastoral experience as being extraordinarily effective on men standing-to in the Flanders trenches looking to the east over enemy lines. At the Shrine, there was no light except the Eternal Flame and cigarettes glowing in cupped hands. The five or six thousand people who would be there made annual trysts with old colleagues, or clustered in prearranged groups. Most would divorce themselves from all that was to come in the rest of the day, and say they always came only to the Dawn Service. It was sacred, they would say. The crowd looked in the shadowy light like one imagined a stand-to might look like at dawn. The Shrine was just a shape against the sky, no rhetoric, no majestic statues.

The only ceremony of the Dawn Service was the playing of the Last Post by the trumpeter from the parapet of the Shrine and the single-line procession through the temple of the Shrine, each participant dropping a red poppy onto the Unknown Soldier's tomb. The silence, the half-darkness, the slow sad notes of the trumpet, the sense of community all made what Jim Boon would call a 'cultural operator', a moment of simplicity and synthesis in which the meaning of signs is known in their simplicity. All the texts of the symbolic action were hidden save for these few sounds and sights.

The relics of this solemnity lasted through the procession, although in the early years of our attendance the solemnity was broken a little by the request to all the women present to enter the Shrine at the end of the procession after the men. It was not a public request. Two women in uniform pulled women out of the line and asked them to wait. This was a shock for most of the students, but none protested, no matter how much they wrangled later with the cultural relativism of the request and their obedience. We never got a chance to ask the women in uniform about their feelings, and we were left with Gramsci in his prison to wonder at the hegemony of it.

Being last in the procession we were not quite prepared to find that everybody had disappeared on leaving the Shrine. We had to learn, in the first years at least, what it meant. We always planned as part of our reflective experience to spend the hours between the Dawn Service and the beginning of the march at 10 a.m. discussing and collating what we had seen and felt. As we walked away in that first year we discovered where all the others had gone. Down at the barracks on St Kilda Road, the boulevard over which the Shrine stood, a noisy, playful crowd had assembled around trestle tables. 'Ladies' in aprons, who had done it so often before for the 'men', were serving tea out of large enamel pots into massive old railway cups and saucers. The tea was strong, stewed, sweet and milky. It was a scene from hundreds of wartime railway stations and wharves, and relished as such by all who were there. There was much play of old roles—saluting, standing at attention talking to officers, nick-names, and stories that must have been told a thousand times and still raised a laugh. There were the perennial and expected practical jokes: a Rolls Royce, hired annually, would take away the scruffiest. Memories were frozen not in stone and gold letters, but in all the cued exchanges, in familiar gestures and language, in the taste of the over-brewed tea.

We could walk away with them and make our queries. So many times, as if it were a piece of gospel truth, they told us they celebrated Anzac for the gallantry of the defeat at Gallipoli. They would tell the young faces of our group as if they could not know what a peculiar sort of victory it was to have been beaten and yet discover an Australian identity. I would have to say, out of my knowledge of how these young men prepared for war in 1914, that the intensity of pride in defeat was matched only by the intensity of the sense of innocence and of the purity of their motives in going to war. The evil of the war was none of their making, they thought, but the brilliance of it was.

We discovered that assembling for the march was its most important moment. As the old units began to cluster in their assigned places, the empty calendar of their lives was filled with stories of the last year, or of the last several years if attachment had been irregular. It was the networking of their communications about the recently dead, of fortunes made and lost, in the certain knowledge that the news filtered out to a wider circle of those who would not or could not attend. Widows and sons would take somebody's place. Medals are not buried with the dead as in bygone warrior cultures. They are handed on. Grandchildren, awkward in their self-importance, would be there all bedecked. All could look the length of the march and see youth and middle years and old age in a line. Or they could look at their own unit and see their numbers dwindled like sand in an hour-glass. We had no doubt, as we watched and listened, that the years of their war experience had put their lives in step, made of it all a march. Anzac had little cyclic about it, or renewing. Time marched on, on a memory.

On the fringes of the crowd that watched there were always other, caricatured 'diggers', out of their units, usually showing their medals, but always showing signs in their dress, or in their gestures, or in the things they said, of not being part of the rest. Sometimes their otherness could not be avoided if they caught an eye. Sometimes they were so distant within themselves that they did not have an eye to be caught or to catch.

The march never ended in any assembly or parade. The different units simply approached the Shrine, turned left and quickly dispersed to their various reunion places. This was the occasion for which the organising committees had spent so many hours planning. Sometimes they prepared special entertainment, bagpipes, or had a special guest.

Always at some stage they broke off into the formal procedures of a parade-ground or a quarterdeck to listen to some words from their officers, or have a message mediated by a sergeant major. There would be reminiscences and banter. There would be a reminder of already known histories. In another rhythm, with another lilt, these histories could have been a chanted legend or a mythic genealogy. These formulaic narratives had their cultural operators, too, not blunted by repetition. None of it was blunted by repetition. Repetition of set forms liberated the group to make sacramental sense of the occasion. For the most part it was sacramental of a sort of military common sense. There was not much rhetoric, but much *realpolitik* about how the world works.

Back at the Shrine as the March ended, the socially élite, the politically powerful, the representatives of the structures of the State, the Church and Society formed a sort of model or map of proper power. They gathered in a square to salute the Queen and nation and to have someone spell out didactically the meaning of the day. The speaker was heard only with moderate sufferance by the rest of the crowd. Now that Anzac Day was really Anzac Half-Day, there was football, even races, or a pub to go to. There was enough restlessness in the crowd to suggest that this last act of the ritual was a private affair for the public figures. We did not like to go and ask these public figures if they believed it all or not, or whether they had a sense of any distance between the rhetoric and the reality. They looked patient, but at the end of several hours waiting for this their only part to play, they also looked a little bored. We guessed that for them it would have been a bigger sin not to have been there, than not to have believed.

Marshall MacLuhan used to distinguish between 'hot' and 'cold' media, the one overbearing imagination, the other fostering imagination. We began to feel that there were 'hot' and 'cold' sacred spaces, too. A Shrine filling the symbolic environment with formal, archaic images closed imagination down. A Shrine that was just an outline bounded by silence raised imagination up. None of us had seen the fields of ordered crosses in the Flanders cemeteries, but we sensed that they would raise our reverence and our pain like the Last Post at the Dawn Service. Some of us had seen the thousands of names of the dead carved in marble on the Canberra War Memorial and had been moved by them, although the ornateness of their setting took our mind's eye away from the enormity of their horror. I would have liked my students to have shared some experience of the Vietnam War Memorial in Washington. Its stark simplicity, the black bare poignancy of the names, the intensity of the attention brought by finding one recognisable name among so many would have persuaded them, I think of the dialogic element of ritual space.

In the end we found not much ideology or nationalism in Anzac Day, unless one listened to the speeches. And we felt, altogether, that the speeches were the last thing to be heard. Compassion was another thing. We found much compassion. There was enough compassion, I feel, to foster the hope that, in time, the 200 Years War with the Aborigines will have its memorial. But I tremble a little at what sort of dialogic imagination it will take to fill its sacred space.

SCHOOL AT WAR

MICHAEL CONWAY was the first boy from Xavier to die in war. He was shot through the head by a Boer sniper at Slingesfontein, South Africa, 10 February 1900. The letter of his commanding officer to his parents describing his death gave some assurance that it had been quick and painless. The letter encourages his mourners to believe that Private Conway had 'died as a brave man and a soldier, a favourite with all'. It was the first of more than a hundred letters which commanding officers were to write to parents and schoolmasters over the years about young men whose sudden, violent deaths needed some special marking. 'The butcher's bill was heavy', wrote another boy from the South Africa front. And he told of sitting on a hillside lately won from the Boers in torrential rain, surrounded by the grotesque horrors of the dead and dying. The perennial problem of the survivors was how to rescue what was personal and special from the massive impersonality of death that scythed men's lives away like so many heads of wheat.

There were not many boys of the school in South Africa, only a dozen or so. They had gone with the Victorian and West Australian companies, or had come from the other direction in the Imperial Army; or they had been by chance at the Cape when the war began. Some of these last had wandered on, unsuccessful, from the West Australian goldrush. They had few uncertainties. Charley 'Legs' McKenna, whose death had been prematurely announced in the obituary columns of *The Xaverian* the year before, wrote a letter from Mafeking describing the siege diet. 'I like donkey best of all! He is so tender. Mule liver is also very nice. I like horse only as German sausage. Plain sirloin of horse is not at all nice!' He also complained of annoying letters. 'We are eagerly awaiting news of our relief and somebody writes asking to have a set of our siege stamps sent out.' Charley survived the Mafeking siege and the Boer snipers, but was not so lucky the second time around. He died behind the front in Flanders in 1917.

Among the photographs of these years is one of Percy Fitzgerald, dressed in the uniform of a Captain of the 11th Hussars. Like so many school photographs, it froze a moment in Percy's life. For years he would peer out of the school magazine resplendent in his bar-braided tunic, his cavalry boots gleaming to the thigh, left hand on his sword, right hand holding his Hussars helmet. The Fitzgerald family had lent a touch of Irish aristocracy to the school. Percy himself married Millicent, Duchess of Sutherland, in 1914 and became a member of the general staff and aide to Sir John French. He added many Mentions in Despatches to the DSO he earned in South Africa. In 1900 he wrote back to the school from Ladysmith, a 'tin-pot' town he said, with a river and a graveyard as its only prominent features. Captain Fitzgerald thought it was like sitting in the bottom of an egg cup with the Boers' artillery on the rim. It was a 'shameful' position to be in after the Imperial Army had just routed the Boers, and the Gordons and the Dundees had shown them cold steel. He wrote with much prescience that, being an adjutant of such a fine regiment in such gallant engagement, he could expect 'any kudos that may be attached to the post in after years'. But he also tried to explain how the passions of battle took possession of him—how he galloped like the 'd---l' to deliver messages for his general, put a wounded soldier on his saddle under fire and walked back through the shells with the plunging horse. 'There was no special pluck on my side. One has got so callous to being fired on that I never had any hesitation about getting off and helping the poor devil.'

Nineteen hundred was a year in which the school shared all the certainties of the rest of the country. The boys had ended the last year of the old century with a quarter of a million other Victorians by farewelling the Tasmanian and Victorian contingents off to the South African War. The school chronicles recorded that they shouted 'Vive l'Angleterre,'

'Vive la Reine,' and 'Vive la Patrie' for a whole week. Why they had been so patriotic in French is unclear, unless they had succumbed to some plot set afoot by their French masters. At their Speech Day when Master G. Ralph had rendered the Polonaise on his violin and Masters Armand de Possel and C. Burke Gaffney had duelled with foils for six or eight minutes, Master H. Kirby recited 'The Midnight Charge' of Clement Scott. At the final words,

> Then pass the blessing—the lips between
> 'Tis the soldiers' oath—God Save the Queen

the whole Great Hall burst into enthusiastic cheering.

The first year of the new century itself was full of changes. The federation of the Australian colonies was about to be consummated, and the debating societies turned to constitutional issues. Even the Old Boys of the Associations of Xavier and St Patrick's caught the federation bug, for the moment at least, and joined company. They asked each other, when they came together, why there were not more politicians in Parliament from the school. Among the boys, the more literary looked for a poet whom they could dub Australian, Christian and noble. Adam Lindsay Gordon, with some difficulty, fitted the bill. He seemed to have a romantic gaiety which was nearly Celtic. This bonus made up a little for his poor score on morality.

The most important new event of the new century for the school was its incorporation into the Public Schools on 26 April, 1900. Since the days when the colonial government had given the various church denominations an educational grant, purportedly in proportion to their numbers in the community, St Patrick's College had been the single Catholic school among the Public Schools. They were 'Public Schools' because they had been established by public money. Xavier and St Patrick's had joined together to field sporting teams since 1878. But the Public Schools Association had become restless with this divided system and, with the agreement of St Patrick's, offered the college at Kew a place in the Public Schools.

The change in status made little or no difference in the organisation of the school. In fact, the authorities at the school were at pains to persuade parents and boys of the distinction between the Public School that Xavier was becoming and the Public Schools of the English tradition. That tradition, it was felt, was known to all through the mythologies of school life and the stories of Tom Brown's School Days. There was and would be no 'fag' system at Xavier, the school prospectus assured parents. In the Jesuit system of education, they said, boys were never left completely to themselves. Surveillance was seen as a proper counter to fagging, 'so detrimental to boys of timid natures and delicate constitutions.' William Keane, himself one of the more brilliant scholars at the school and destined to join the Society of Jesus, wrote an essay on the difference between the English Public Schools and the Public School that Xavier had now become. The great difference, he thought, was the lack of tradition in Australia. In England every action of daily life, good and bad, was guided by traditions that were firm and unavoidable. They served English youth in helping them to distinguish what was correct from what was not proper. In Australia, especially because of the dominance of day pupils in the Public Schools, the home developed the boys' chief traits, not the school. An Australian youth, he wrote, is under his own control.

There is a slight wistfulness in young William Keane's appreciation of tradition. It is as if the patriotic cheers for Queen and Country as well as the excited promise of a new century and a new Public School status rang a little hollow. He was persuaded that his colonial education was only a pale reflection of more real, more lasting ways.

In keeping with the martial spirits raised by the Boer War—indeed with the grumblings of the boys that the school had not been able to participate fully in the grand send-offs because they had not cadets—the new century saw the establishment of a College Cadet Corps. The second division prefect, Mr Bernard Page, SJ, himself to become a military chaplain in the Great War, was the chief instigator. Major Alexander Lucas was contracted to drill the corps. He was paid £20 per annum, and lunches on Wednesdays. In the time-honoured tradition of these institutions, the cadets were immediately dubbed 'tin soldiers' ('chocolate soldiers' in later years). The principal excitement of the first months was in getting a uniform and in creating officers. Two lieutenants, C. Burke-Gaffney and C. Gavan Duffy, both with more poetry in their veins than martial spirit, acquired gilt-faced captains' tunics and swords. They cling determinedly, if awkwardly, to the swords in the first photograph taken of the sixty bright-faced cadets. Not many of them appear to be more than eleven or twelve years of age. The names of these 'tin soldiers' are not given. A dozen of them hold rifles in a most unmilitary fashion. One suspects that there were no more than twelve rifles in the armoury. The school chronicler reported that there was more than usual eagerness among the troops to be seen in town or in Kew in their uniforms.

The College was attacked in manoeuvres on a number of occasions. The Corps marched bravely out to Heidelberg, and sorely back. School's honour was restored and happiness discovered when the cadets were allowed to parade in Melbourne streets in welcome to the returning soldiers of the Boer War. It was not the last war that many of these boys would experience. The holocaust of the Great War was fourteen years away. The empty, half-joking phrases of 'getting into fighting form' and 'fighting for Australia and the causes of Her Majesty' would become true enough. They did not know it, but from the year 1903 the cadets were filling that great human pool from which the heroes and the dead, the wounded and the survivors would come.

The years between the Boer War and the Great War were important years for the school. At the end of 1899 there were 119 boys. In 1914 there were 234. In the first years of incorporation into the Public Schools numbers jumped nearly fifty per cent to 160. That peak had been reached in 1890 at 166, but the depression of the 1890s had driven the number down to 89 in 1897. More significantly, during this period the number of day boys first came to equal the number of boarders in the school, and then topped them. Until 1895 the boarders usually doubled the day boys in number.

The years also coincided with the terms of office of two strong rectors, Father Keating and Father O'Dwyer. The young Frank O'Keefe began his long love affair with the school in 1906. Sixty years later when he scrawled his memories of those years on the backs of envelopes, his first remarks about Father Keating were in—what else?—verse.

> Loving and loved by all
> An easy mixer with great and small.

But the things that he remembered of Father Keating were that he had introduced the boy prefect system, that for £300 he turfed in an oval for the juniors, and bought half of the Kew Mechanics' Institute to use as a pavilion. For good measure, Father O'Keefe added that from the steps of this new second division pavilion

> Without a ladder and without glasses
> One may see farther than the 'Ackney Marshes

For Father O'Dwyer he singled out the encouragement he had given to the editor of the *Xaverian* (himself), to collect a catalogue of the names of all the boys who had been in the school. He was also encouraged, with the help of his brother Stan, to erect School Honour Boards. This last task took some imagination. There had been no 'Captains of the School' for the first twenty-five years; nor duxes of the school, for that matter. And no one had thought being captain of the cricket team, or of the football team, was important enough to record. The gold-lettered Honour Boards which Frank O'Keefe engineered were, like all mythologies, not so much about the past as about the present. 1900 to 1917 were gestation years of 'School Spirit'. Boy prefects, captains, duxes, honour boards appear. It was the period when the 'past' was offering its reflections to the 'present' in reminiscences. Every year during this time someone 'Looks Backward' as if a sense of the school's growing greatness made yesteryear's trivia worthy of memory.

Above all it was the period when overwhelming defeat in sport had begun to lessen. Somewhat to their surprise, the School XI won their very first premiership match as a Public School against Geelong Grammar in 1901. (Grammar, it might be said, was caught on a wet wicket in their second innings.) For the next five years neither a cricket nor a football team won a single match against another Public School. Then in 1906 Xavier won one football match and one cricket match. It was a real beginning. There was not another year in this period when the school did not win some match in either football or cricket. Indeed in 1910 both teams won their respective premierships, and an excited Old Xaverian Association presented the school with an oak-framed photograph of the members of the XI and the XX.

Father Eustace Boylan used to say that 1906, the year in which the teams each won a match and in which the school rowed for its first Head of the River, was a turning point in the school's history. That year he wrote a school song, 'Black and Red', to a French air, and the music master, Mr Victor Zelma, transcribed it. When it first appeared in print, its writer had to explain away his poetic licence in changing the accepted colour cry of Xavier from 'Cardinal and Black' to 'Black and Red'. But the 'School Spirit' had not yet become incarnate in colours any more than it had in mottos or badges. '*Nil nisi justum*' ('Nothing unless proper') and '*Fortes fortuna juvenat*' ('Fortune gives strength to the strong') were mottoes that prompted plenty of poetry at the time. '*Sursum corda*' and the present college crest won out in 1910. Hearts had no doubt *been* lifted by the double premiership.

Father Boylan had a philosophy of school songs. He had, he wrote in later years, 'a profound contempt' for mere academic music, which however excellent for a small tea party, or for a calm evening in a drawing-room, utterly lacks the red-bloodedness of a genuine school song'. For that matter he was a little sceptical of Father Frank O'Keefe's musical abilities, if admiring of his enthusiasm. 'It would be an exaggeration to say that he was tone deaf', he wrote of 'Kister' O'Keefe, but he was absolutely rhythm deaf. He could not distinguish between one time and another, and had no conception of metre.' He thought that most of the songs which Father O'Keefe sponsored were failures. They were good 'fill-up stuff' but not really successful songs. Even the 'Rowing Song' by James B. Byrne did not come up to Father Boylan's standards. For him there were really only two songs: 'Black and Red' and 'Xavier's Through'.

It is difficult for us, who live in an age when it is impossible to write or even agree on a National Anthem, to conceive of words about a school or about a sports event that are not mawkish, overly sentimental or expressive of exaggerated emotions. A later generation of boys might remember Father O'Keefe, a bent old man, a beret of what appears to be two old black socks on his balding head, deafness added to his rhythm deafness, thumping a tinny piano in the echoing depths of the Great Hall.

They would have sung his school songs, then, a little cynically. Or they might have sung them more vigorously, but with the same cynicism, under the beady eye of Father Montague as he led them in some warm-up for a football match or the Head of the River. Or they might have sung them as interludes in the practice of war cries, or what seems now the football coach's last mad resort. 'The B Plan,' 'The B Plan,' 'The A Plan,' 'The A Plan,' the boys would shout in unison, as if informing the minds of their lagging heroes about tactics would change the realities of their fumbling, losing ways. Somehow, in the hands of O'Keefe, Van Prooyen and Montague, the school song had Kafkaesque qualities that Father Boylan never dreamed of.

'Black and Red' was written between the Boer War and the Great War. 'Xavier's Through' was written in 1917 by Miss Majorie Quinn, niece of the poet Roderic Quinn. It was put to music by J. Hugh McMenamin (1893) with the hope that it would 'foster *esprit de corps* by a rhythmical record of Xaverian deeds.' Both songs have a point in a chapter on wars.

First, let it be said that any poet is going to have trouble with the word 'Xavier'. William Keane, in launching the badge and motto in 1910, told the 'sons of Xavier' to 'lift up your hearts—young hearts, to God your Saviour'. Father Boylan wrote of those 'who march beneath the Black and Red Flag of Xavier' as being 'marked by their sweet and calm behaviour'. 'Kew' was a much safer word:

> March, boys, march for Kew
> All prepared to die or do.
> With hearts all steady and true,
> Both the old boys and the new;
> Be the foeman many or few,
> Let us face the task before us
> With united ranks and true,
> And the old flag floating o'er us!

Words in songs of this sort, in a sense, do not matter. It is the tune and the singing that stir the feelings and reflect the memories. The hyperboles in the verses probably do not matter as much as the nostalgic sense of comradeship or loneliness, of excitement or disappointment, of triumphs and failures. Dying or doing, marching for Kew, facing foes, uniting ranks, steadying hearts—all are extravagant ways of talking about hoping to win the football match.

> When the blasts of war
> Call loudly from afar;
> They're up with hearts aglow,
> They long to meet the foe.

This is an excited way of saying that Tim Collins bowled the first ball, Mick Mornane won the toss, or Jack Rowan strokes the crew. But then again that same Jack Rowan, stroke of the first crew and dux of the school, described the 'glorious and well fought field' of the school's first Public School football victory. He spoke of the 'joy of the moment . . . We have tasted the sweets of victory, and our enthusiasm knew no bounds!' 'School Spirit' demanded extravagant and martial phrases. And in that time between the wars, when there were no wars, it did not seem out of place to sing:

> Oh, when the battle sweeps along, fierce and strong,
> And when our luck is for a moment declining,
> Like heroes let us gaily meet our defeat—
> No wailing, no womanly repining.
> But raise again o'erhead
> Our standard Black and Red,
> And if 'tis stained with gore,
> We'll love it all the more;
> As if our ranks we close,
> Once more to face our foes,
> We fling them back defiance proud and strong.
>
> CHORUS:
> As we march, boys, march for Kew,
> All prepared to die or do . . .

It was a song they were not embarrassed to sing with a more direct and immediate meaning. Indeed, as we shall see, they sang it with a few tears—a Xavier flag in one hand and an Australian flag in the other—on the night of 10 September 1915 when they were sent off to war. The rhetoric of facing foes and doing-and-dying seemed more natural then.

Miss Majorie Quinn's 'Xavier's Through' had a more jarring note. It celebrated the school's championship football team which, under its captain, Ed Hood, had defeated every other Public School:

> The tale of how the boys of Xavier College won
> The Championship in nineteen seventeen,
> Will be retold in song and verse for evermore.
> To keep the meaning of that triumph green,
> The fearless Xavier boys with shouting filled the air,
> As forth they went upon the Champion's Day;
> With courage and with care, with brilliancy and skill,
> Right to the goal the Eighteen stormed their way.

But this was 1917. The war was two years old. Already thirty boys of the school had been killed. Some of them had belonged to the first premiership team of 1910. The young Daniel Mannix had just become Archbishop of Melbourne and 'triumph green'—which Miss Quinn had innocently referred to—had, to many Australians, a sinister ring. After the Irish Rising of Easter, 1916, there were many who suspected Catholics of disloyalty. The Jesuits at Xavier were Irish. In 1917 only Fathers Frank O'Keefe, William Baker, Mat Egan and Mr Gordon Rourke were Australian-born. The other nine Jesuits were born in Ireland. Despite the school's membership in the Public Schools, boys and masters came under the same suspicion as other Catholic institutions. In 1917 when Xavier had won the football championship, the headmasters of the Public Schools had cancelled all Public School premiership sport. In a city somewhat deprived of football and other sport by the war, the public had come to be keenly interested in Public School sport. In 1916, friction and bitterness between the schools had become very noticeable. In February 1917, the headmasters agreed to do away with the year's premierships as well as rowing if any 'regrettable incidents' occurred. It seems that 'war cries' were the occasions of trouble. The boys had invented 'war cries' which were directed not so much at team support as at denigration of the other school's team. The practice had also grown of attending in school groups the matches between schools other than one's own and lending vocal and physical support to 'friendly' schools. The time-honoured trek from goal to goal at the end of quarters had become pilgrimages of peril and confrontation. The rowing competitions passed off without incident that year, but the headmasters still hoped for a venue where the crews could compete six abreast rather than in heats. The heats fostered alliances and divisions among the supporters. Cricket was innocent enough. In the last round of the football, however, when Xavier had played Scotch for the championship and won, a 'regrettable incident' did take place. It was at the Melbourne Grammar–Wesley match two days later. 'Old Boy', the sporting commentator of the *Australasian*, thought it only 'a bit of a breeze' in which Scotch boys shouted the Wesley 'war cry' and Wesley boys and Melbourne Grammar boys stood outside the MCG and glared at one another. 'War cries' had also been shouted at the Scotch–Xavier match, and boys had stood around shouting at one another. The headmasters met and decided that a 'regrettable incident' had taken place and cancelled all competition sports. When the captains of the different schools wrote asking that the ban be lifted, the headmasters replied: 'Playing at hats here in Victoria seemed repulsive when hundreds of letters told how the real brotherhood of all Public School boys was being shown under other skies and tested as it never had been before.'

There was grumbling in the school but also relief that what had been won would not be taken away. Outside the school, the issue was looked at in a different light. The *Mining Standard*, a newspaper of the day, was critical of the 'war cries', but reminded its readers that Xavier College teams were composed of boys much older and bigger than those that represented other schools. They were 'men playing boys'. Boys elsewhere, it went on, 'get away from the school and rush to war'. But

Xavier had a different standard of honour and patriotism! Even if an age limit were imposed, the *Mining Standard* believed, it would not be honoured. 'Experience of the sporting methods of Xavier College has not been such to inspire confidence.'

They were bitter, harsh words. It would not have helped for the rector, Father O'Dwyer, to explain that for a number of years he had advocated the prolongation of school for one year after matriculation. They were hard times. Men and boys had to justify why they had not gone to war. One Xaverian wrote to 'Old Boy' in the *Australasian* complaining that as a 19-year-old boy he could not get his parents' consent to join the army. What would he tell his friends after the war? He added, almost as an aside, that his brother had been killed at Gallipoli. 'Old Boy' himself felt that the sporting pulse and the moral pulse of the community were pretty much the same thing. He relished the Public School spirit that produced good athletes and good soldiers at the same time. 'The lessons of unselfishness, loyalty and devotion to a cause learned at the nets, or on the river, in the football field or on the tennis court have been valuable in that sterner game in which so many thousand Britishers have given their best . . . The fellow who has shepherded you or for whom you have shepherded in the ruck, the batsman who has held an end or, by some brilliant hitting, has pulled a match out of the fire, the "No. 7" who has backed his stroke up in a desperate finish—these are the men for the trenches or the charge.'

'Old Boy' kept a count of Public School boys who had enlisted. At the end of the first year of the war, he calculated: Melbourne Grammar, 980; Scotch 860; Wesley, 675; Geelong College, 360; Geelong Grammar, 300; Xavier, 300. As the war proceeded and he faced the 'dark disgrace' that men would have to be conscripted for the war, he delighted to point out that those whose weekly exploits in sport he described had been the first to enlist. They had belonged to the Public School community 'in which right is recognized as paramount, where each boy regards the honour of his school as in his keeping, and where failure in the individual throws discredit on the whole.'

> The battle raged and waned,
> With fortune good and ill,' wrote Miss Quinn,

'All up and down and round about the field;
But, tho' the foe was stern, he could not hope to win-
Taught by Xavier's love and watchful care,
We know not how to fail.

Between the wars the school was discovering a new rhetoric to describe itself. To lose was ennobling when there were occasional wins. Virtue in victory had a certain catholicity without being Catholic. Being recognised as a Public School whitewashed the green of being Irish. The Great War that was upon them was more important for the school than anything that had happened before. It was the first real sign that being a Public School had made them different. The school went to war in 1914 with excitement and enthusiasm. The actual news of the war came in the middle of a football match against Melbourne Grammar at the MCG on a wet Wednesday afternoon. Boys stood silently in the rain at the ground grasping at the news-sheets that were being distributed. The two teams played listlessly and carelessly, Xavier apparently more so than Grammar, because they lost. All the talk as the boys returned to school was about whether two hours of drill would become a daily necessity. Almost immediately a large war map was created in the Hall, and strife developed in the newspaper clubs as members started their own personal scrapbooks, to the detriment of supposedly communally-owned copies of the papers. Indeed, drills and parades and 'military operations' sharply increased. Thursday afternoons were decidedly physical: 3:30 to 5:30, drill; 6:00 to 7:00, dancing. The first sacrifice to national necessity was the swimming pool. The work just begun on its construction had to be cancelled.

For the community outside the school, those first bloodless days of the war were filled with stories of young men and old rushing to service. Clive Conrick, who had been at Xavier in 1901, captured headlines with the story of his determination to join the forces. As soon as war was declared, he rode his horse 460 miles from his father's station at Nappa Merrilands to Hergot Springs in South Australia. From there he took a five hundred mile train trip to Adelaide. In Adelaide he found the South Australia contingent already full. He cabled Tasmania and discovered the same situation there. He then cabled Sydney to be told that if he could get to Liverpool at his own expense he could join the New South Wales contingent. Clive Conrick had many more miles to go. He went to Egypt with the Light Horse, and he was at Gallipoli until the evacuation. He returned to the Camel Corps in Egypt and, on the disbanding of that corps, he joined the Flying Corps as an observer.

In the midst of all this excitement, everybody itched to do something. They longed, if nothing else, to urge one another on and to celebrate their own motives and certainties. The Old Xaverian Association organised a Smoke Night just after the war's beginning. It was meant to mark their esteem for those who had joined the services. Two hundred men packed the boys dining room. They sang the national anthem loudly and strongly. With a little less certainty, one suspects, they followed Dr Edward Ryan in his rendition of the 'Marseillaise'. (The beginning of the war was made more memorable for this famous son of Xavier, it was reported, for his having sired a daughter on the day that the guns of August first fired.) All the toasts to the King, to the soldiers of Xavier, as well as those of the Associated Public Schools of Victoria, and to the school were generously supported. As every patriotic speech ended, all jumped to their feet and applauded for minutes on end.

For the speech of the rector, Father James O'Dwyer, cheering from this gathering was prolonged. It was a careful speech. He spoke as an Irishman commenting on the justice of an English cause and on the propriety of Australian support for the war. He also spoke, as many other Jesuits could speak, of his knowledge of Belgium and of Louvain where he had received part of his training. He spoke of how Belgium's 'thrifty, industrious, pure-living, home-loving people' should not suffer at the hands of 'hordes of ruthless aggressors and [advocates] of military autocracy'. He played the part of a moral theologian, speaking of how the justice of the cause would mean that there would be no clash of conscience for those involved in killing. 'With a light heart our boys may go forth, with their cause satisfied by truth.' He dwelt on the obligations which Australians had to their Motherland. Australia had profited by the highest form of imperialism: she had been suffered to grow on her own lines. 'In the story of Empire, there has been nothing so unselfish as the relation of the Motherland to her Colonies.' He mused over what higher purpose this evil might have. It would 'search out, test and purify our civilization'. It would 'burn away the veneer that too much prosperity and generations of comfort had spread on the high qualities of the race'. It would seal Australia's nationhood. As Lawson had written: 'A Nation is born when the shells fall fast, or its lease of life renewed'.

To the boys going away, Father O'Dwyer had a special word. They had learnt of life at school. Courage, discipline, self-restraint and co-operation—they had learnt these on the playing fields. They would thus face odds gallantly, hold their opponents in respect, and practice self-control. 'If I wished to teach soldierly qualities, I know no finer training than that which the struggles of our Schools Association gives its members.' So he proudly sent them off; told them that the school would proudly welcome them home and, for those who fell by the way the school would just as proudly cherish their memory.

Lieutenant M. B. Ryan was the senior officer there that evening. He was a little overwhelmed at being at the centre of the stage onto which he was so suddenly thrust. He said a few words as he held the small school flag and Union Jack that each of the soldiers there had been given. They were simply discharging their duty, he said. It did not matter how they fared personally so long as they struck a few good blows for the Empire. Wherever they went, the memory of the school would be uppermost in their minds. H. B. Dickenson, once a rower for Wesley, stood up as representative of the other Public Schools. He told them of the Public Schools company that had been formed in the 5th Battalion under Captain Henry Carter of Wesley. The Public School spirit, he thought, was an ideal spur to action. 'They would not be without distinction when the hour to test them came.'

The time came quicker than they dreamed. At the landing at Gallipoli on 25 April 1915, Lieutenant Mick Ryan received a bullet through the shoulder, then another through the wrist, then one through the left foot, then one more through the left leg and another two through the right shoulder and arm. In this leadened condition and with the men helping him killed as they bent over him, who should appear but H. B. Dickenson. He helped to carry him back a mile and a half to the hospital ship. It was a story, said 'Old Boy' when he heard of it, 'that will be told whenever old Public School boys meet'.

When the evening at Xavier was over, all stood in a crowd on the main steps of the old South Wing. They shook hands with one another over and over again, not wanting to leave, aglow with the comradeship and sense of virtue of the moment. Some of the new soldiers were hoisted on shoulders and carried to the taxis that were waiting to take them back to the camp at Broadmeadows. It was a very special moment long remembered and spoken of in the staging camps of Egypt, and in the trenches of Gallipoli and Flanders. It prompted many to write back and have the *Xaverian* sent to them. They looked out for old school mates in the fighting lines and sent letters home telling how they met this fellow or that, and how they prospered.

Even now, seventy years later, these meetings were fixed by who knows what fixative in a man's memory. Old men, when asked to remember back, will conjure up a Justin Rowan, or a Maurice Cussen, or Xavier de Bavay, dropping off a lorry behind Armentières, in a hospital bed or camp on Salisbury Plains, popping into a dugout on the Peninsula. It was as if the chance meeting of men who had shared familiar places and relished known nicknames or a story made secure moments in the disordered insanity that had so disturbed their lives.

In September, 1914, the boys at school were a little bemused by this patriotic 'function'. They only remarked that it took a full week to get all the chairs back into their right places. For those who had to confront their own decision already made or to be made, there was nothing mawkish in their tears or in their being so certain about the rightness of their cause, nothing unseemly in the warmth they sparked in one another.

Joseph Peter Lalor was the first of a new generation of the school to die in a new war. Joe Lalor was the grandson of Peter Lalor, the hero of the Eureka stockade. Only slightly taller than his famous 5'1" grandfather, Joe was a restless soul who left school midway through his final year and made his way to work on the London docks. From there he joined the French Foreign Legion, 'an environment which', said the Archbishop of Perth in Joe's panegyric, 'was at no time remarkable for its religious fervour'. He used his experience to good purpose and returned to Western Australia to be an instructor in military matters as well as a military journalist.

Joe Lalor was a captain in the army by the time war broke out. On the morning of 25 April he was in the attack on Sari Bair. Sword in hand, he led his section up the slopes to find first his colonel and then his major killed in front of him. In that long, desperate day, he and his men first took the spur of the hill, then defended it and lost it. The Anzacs, it was reported, found Joe Lalor next morning on a quiet, deserted spur, dead from shrapnel, surrounded by six Turks shot to death and a seventh killed by the sword.

It was a gallant death, the sort of death Australians at home thirsted to hear about. Poets played on the symbols of Eureka and Gallipoli: 'For the people at Eureka, for the king at Sari Bair.' Journalists dwelt on his small stature and the contrastingly magnificent physique of the Turk. 'His body looked small, men say, beneath the great bulk of his enemy, but truly it was the inhabitation of an indomitable spirit.' They quoted with approval the words of his family, as if they made sense of the senseless: 'I'm glad to know that he went out that way. It would have been the way he would have chosen'. The school, and with it Catholic Australia, found a deeper comfort in their hero. Joe Lalor was *Australian* and *Catholic* and *Irish*. Dying gallantly on what was already being acclaimed as the true birthday of the nation, he legitimated their cultural and religious differences. They broadcast his piety, his weekly confessions, his last communions, his novenas, the rosaries he organised for his men. And they proudly proclaimed that between independence and loyalty, between heroics and religious conviction, there were no contradictions.

Before 1914 was over more than forty Xaverians had joined the services, and in that year photographs of the men in uniform were added to the solemn, formal photographs of the 'Past' that graced the pages of the *Xaverian*. Occasionally, especially if they were young officers, they look out of the pages in smart, well-fitted jackets and jaunty caps and sparkling belts. For the most part, they have a very unmilitary quality. The crumpled, rough cloth of their jackets buttoned to the neck seems to sit uneasily on their shoulders. The slouch hats sit squarely, fully, nothing jaunty or puckish. They find it hard to get the right facial expression. Jack McQuade, looking like a Sergeant-Major's nightmare, stares out of the page with a half-proud, half-deprecating grin on his face. He looks as if winning his 'race' to be an early volunteer was his own private joke about the seriousness of life. France Slaweski, brother of Boleslas, was still seeking to revenge the outcome of the Franco-Prussian War of 1870. He tried to join the French army but was accepted as a masseur in the AIF Medical Corps instead. He chose to be photographed sitting in a crumpled uniform on a horse. It was a short-legged steed, as burly as France himself; it had more potential as a brewery nag than a lighthorse. Clarence O'Brien, in his photograph, looks more like the bank clerk he had just ceased to be than a soldier. But the disguise did not secure him from a wound in the first landing at Galipoli. As a member of the Public Schools Company, he recorded that he was rescued from the hands of the Turks by a boy from Scotch. Perhaps the soldier from Scotch was a member of that boatload of F Company which Mr Anderson, the headmaster of Wesley, reported as having debated the merits of the various crews about to row the Head of the River in Melbourne, while they waited in the dark off the beach at Gallipoli.

Six other Xaverians were killed on Gallipoli. They were Norm Blackie, Noel Gambettà, Rupert Hepburn, Horace Thompson, Keith McIlwaith and Sydney O'Neill. Major Frank Murphy died of meningitis caught in the trenches. They all seemed to die less symbolically than Joe Lalor. No doubt their names are carved and written and emblazoned in a dozen places on national monuments, on small memorials in country towns, on honour boards in schools and clubs and regimental dining halls. For the living, coping with heroes who die in large numbers is never easy. Before the war ended, fifty-three Xaverians had been killed, one in eight of those who had enlisted ('listed, as the easy phrase of the day put it).

The school coped with these deaths by establishing an honour roll on which the names were inscribed as the killings occurred. The board was too small by far. How does one betray one's pessimism with generous space for the as yet unkilled dead? As each death was announced, the rector or one of the other priests would identify the name for boys who did not know the soldier, and a Mass would be said for his soul. If family and friends had requested it, a number of masses would be said. At the end of the year, the *Xaverian* would highlight the name in dark print in the list of those 'With the Army' and mark the name with the stark inscription of 'killed'. If there were details to be known of the death these, and such letters as commanding officers, parents or friends had written to the editor, would be printed. If there were a photograph, it would be printed, edged with black lines. And, of course, when the war was not three months over, the Old Xaverian Association resolved to erect a Memorial Chapel to '(a) commemorate Old Xaverians who had fallen in war (recently and happily come to a close); (b) to celebrate the joys of peace; and (c) last but not least, to worthily mark the golden jubilee of the school which was fast approaching'.

In the school year of 1915 and with the first and second expeditionary forces in Egypt and then in Gallipoli, there seemed little impact of the war on the life of the school itself. Some masters commented that there seemed something wanting even though the routine of the school was continued. There was a lack of interest and enthusiasm in games and sports. The senior debating society began its year with a debate on the motion that 'The execution of Charles I was neither a crime nor a blunder'. The House protested that Charles was badly done by. A month later they enthusiastically rejected the motion that there was too much sport in Australia. But by the end of the year they were debating more pertinent topics. The votes on whether the 'war had made a review of the White Australia policy necessary' was equally divided. The motion which was beginning to be debated in the community as well at the time, 'It is only by conscription that a modern nation can effectively defend itself' was lost by only one vote. The rector, Father O'Dwyer, presided over this last debate. He chose only to give helpful hints on the art of speaking. But Father Eustace Boylan spoke to the issue itself, and the minutes record that the whole debate flared again with new speeches from the floor. The juniors debated only twice that year: once on the perennial question about the relative merits of city and country life; the second time more provocatively, 'That the Allies should adopt German methods of warfare'. By 41 to 7 the House voted that indeed the allies should use the methods of 'Teutonic frightfulness' of gassing, blockading, murdering and piracy to conclude the struggle quickly and successfully.

The preoccupation of the schoolboy was with very mundane things. Lorne Greville's turtle, brought from the Murray, excited the school chronicler the whole year through with its housing and eating problems. Boarders let patriotism brighten the darker side of their cultural natures by wangling seats to the 'Belgian concert' at the Hawthorn town hall. Or they sacrificed a little human respect by proferring 'manly bosums' to 'Kew ladies' to pin Belgian flags on. Archbishop Carr, thinking to gain a little moral profit from the martial spirit abroad, established the Knighthood of Our Lady of the Southern Cross at the school. Its object was the honour and defence of women:

'The protection of the weak and, more particularly, of the weaker sex, is at once the duty and the privilege of the true knight. Nor is the duty confined to home, or kindred, or native country. It is extended to every place where the honour of God, the defence of the weak, and the respect due to women calls for its exercise. All who are willing to uphold the duties and responsibilities of married life, to protect the purity of the young, to put a stop, as far as opportunity may allow, to every word and act calculated to offend modesty and injure innocence are invited to become sharers in this new spiritual crusade. The members will be distinguished by the ceremony of initiation, and by wearing a distinctive badge appropriate to the Order. Each candidate makes the following promises:

1. As a true knight, I promise to practice in public and in private, at home and abroad, the virtues of the knightly office.
2. To promote the faithful fulfilment of the duties of the married life.
3. To shield from harm and stain the dignity and purity of women.
4. To suppress by every legitimate means all indecency in word and action.

5. To exhibit towards all, male and female, a chivalrous courtesy.'

The good archbishop himself was about to go to his reward, and the knighthoods seem to have been conferred only once. And that is as good a reason as any to record for time immemorial that they went to Father McGinnis, Th. King, N. Hehir, Jno. Corry, Leo Tighe, G. Higgins, A. Fynn, Th. McLelland, J. San Miguel, A. Welshman, Jno. Ryan, Edw. Casey, K. O'Day, M. O'Brien, Ray Parer and Vivien Oxenham.

It is not possible here to give the stories of those 410 Xaverians who enlisted or even of those fifty-three who were killed in the Great War. Of a probable 400 men under thirty-five years of age in 1914 who had been at the school, about seventy-five per cent enlisted. This seems a high proportion and justifies the anger they felt at the accusation that as Catholics they were not fully behind the war. That they were sensitive to the jibe is shown in the frequent references they make in their letters to their continued, if at times unsuccessful, efforts to get into the army. Their enlistment is rarely registered in the *Xaverian* without reference to the financial sacrifice they made by voluntarily giving up good positions or selling out their properties. At least sixty-nine of them received commissions, a slightly higher rate than the national average for Catholics in the forces at this time. We know of forty-four men being wounded in addition to the fifty-three men who were killed. This is under the national average for casualty figures, but the Xavier figures are by no means reliable. The highest rank reached by a Xaverian during the war seems to have been Brigadier-General. This was Harold Cohen. There were several colonels. Among them were A. Jacobson, H. Byrne and J. Clareborough. In all, thirty Xaverians were decorated: Military Medal, seven; Military Cross, twelve; Distinguished Service Order, seven; Distinguished Conduct Medal, seven; and Distinguished Service Cross, one. Six Xaverian priests became chaplains. Most of the college boys, of course, joined the Australian services. Yet twenty-two men joined the British army in England, Jacques Playoust, Rene Chaleyer and Andre Prenat had continued Xavier's French connection by joining the French army. Jacques Playoust endured four months of the horrors of the French army's fighting at Verdun. He had been buried alive as the result

253

of an artillery siege, but he wrote that he was happy to be a '*simple soldat*'. There were other foreign enlistments in New Zealand, Canada and the United States. Almost all who joined the services in Australia joined the army. Only nine men went to the navy. Twenty-two joined the Air Flying Corps.

'Poor Noel . . .', 'Poor Cedric . . .', 'Poor Gervase . . .'. These were ominous phrases between 1915 and 1918. They signalled the news that another man was dead and presaged the story of how a bullet, or a piece of shrapnel, or a bomb, or a mine, or a shell had closed another lottery of life. Not many men could find words to describe what they saw and felt. They mostly skirted on the periphery of their own lives. They laughed at the mad bazaars of Cairo, or the bizarreness of being encamped under the pyramids. From the mud of Flanders, they would write of pilgrimages to cathedrals, museums and historic monuments. Or they would delight in locating places in their reader's imagination, comparing the bridges across the Nile to Prince's Bridge, or the bazaar to Eastern Market, or the beaches to St Kilda.

But there were moments when they expressed their dismay. Archie Gambetta wrote about the death of his brother Noel:

'We were standing within two feet of each other chatting about home, when suddenly a stray shot struck poor Noel. He simply gasped, and all was over. It was a fearful shock, but in calmer moments I had (and you, too, will have) the consolation of feeling that he went through quickly yet prepared, and in the grace of God, for he had been to Holy Communion just two mornings before. We buried him at Brown's Dip, Lone Pine, putting up a small cross to mark the spot where he lies in the little cemetery. May he rest in peace.'

When Ced Hunter was killed by a piece of shrapnel as he cooked his mates' breakfast, his friend's whole world fell apart. He wrote from the mud-filled dugout beside his guns:

'I cannot tell you what his loss means to me. Today, the first day we have been separated since he came to the 10th, has been utterly desolate, and I dare not think of the many days before me. We were friends at school and, afterwards, over here, we were inseparable. We slept in the same blankets, used the same mess-tin—everything either of us had belonged to both—money, clothes, everything.

If I bought tooth paste, it was Ced's as much as mine; if Ced got a parcel from home, I opened it if he happened to be away. And, in the same way, we shared our news from home. Often, lying in bed with shells screaming over our heads, we would yarn till early morning of the good times we had at home, and the better times we would have when we got back—if ever we did get back.

Always he spoke lovingly of you and worried because you would be anxious for his safety. I know that when things were at their worst his letters to you were their most cheerful. In the battery he is missed as none of our other dead have been missed since we came to France. Everyone with the battery was his friend and, for a friend, he would do anything, as I know well. Poor Ced! We had hoped to be wounded together, and spoke of what we would do when we got to England. And indeed it seemed unlikely that one of us could be hit and not the other, since we were never apart. I will always be proud of the fact that the Corporal of the Signallers always took us with him on any job involving extra risk. Ced always volunteered because he was afraid of nothing and liked the excitement, and I because I wanted to be with Ced, and because I drew courage from him. I feel as if I shall never volunteer for anything now that he has gone—clean, honourable and brave and loyal. I shall never have a friend like him again. It seems almost insincere to offer you words of consolation. And yet it would be some comfort to know that he died in the way he would have chosen: died the hardest death a man could wish for: died swiftly and without pain: died young and strong and brave, giving his life for an ideal; and above all, died in the grace of God for I knew him most intimately, and am certain as one may be of anything on earth that he is at this moment safe in heaven.

It hurts me to think of your great sorrow. In this awful war it is, as Ced knew, and as I know, our mothers at home who pay the greatest price—in fear and anxiety for our safety while we live, and in grief when we fall. But Ced would have wished you to meet it bravely and proudly, as the mother of a soldier and a very gallant gentleman, and, if it should be my own turn next, I look to you to comfort my own dear mother and lend her some of the courage which Ced's mother must have. Almost I find myself envying Ced. He is at rest and in peace after twenty weary war months, with all the privations and hardships inseparable from such a life, and I am left to carry on deprived of the sunshine and strength his very presence gave me. Never mind, I suppose he can help me on high just as well, and better, than on earth. That he may do so—especially in gaining for you all comfort and consolation in your hour of sorrow—is the heartfelt prayer of one who loved him in life and does not forget him in death.'

Eric White had been the very first Xaverian to join the army. He had been secretary of the Old Xaverian Association and of the Boat Club, and he kept up his Public School ties in F Company of the 5th Battalion. He was wounded in the first landing at Gallipoli, invalided to Egypt and then to England. He returned to Gallipoli just in time for the evacuation. Death caught up with him in France in July, 1916. He looks out of the pages of the *Xaverian* as a very uncertain soldier, his tunic too wide and his sleeves too long. His mates in the Old Xaverian Association wished him farewell with the promise that they would make him secretary again. They warned him that though it was 'a long way to Tipperary', he should 'Sursum Corda'. He himself played the very proper secretary at the front and in hospital. He recorded the names of all Xaverians he met. From his hospital bed in England and with his eyes sore and tender from the effects of an explosion, he told of the 'boom' that Australians were enjoying in England. Everybody wanted to talk with them. They were still basking in the glory of Anzac. For himself the fine feelings of war had now to be weighed against his experiences of life at the Peninsula. He told himself not to be downhearted, because he had been lucky while so many others had gone to their deaths. He noted those who had been killed around him—Keith McIlwraith, Joe Lalor, Norm Blackie of Xavier, and Jack Newbury of Wesley. There were others like Clarrie O'Brien, Austin Hepburn, George Capes, Mick Ryan, who were all filled in varying degrees with lead. At the hospital he persuaded his commander, Lieutenant W. L. 'Bird' Heron of Melbourne

Grammar School, to overcome his scruples about his health and send him back to the front. He was killed a few months later at Paschendale. His platoon commander, himself dead a week later, bounden by that sad duty of marking a personal passing in the midst of massive murder, wrote to his mother. He told of Eric's sense of duty, of the admiration the men felt for their corporal and the sad loss he would be.

The letters traverse familiar and similar grounds. They laugh at the antics of bathers 'swimming faster than Frank Beaurepaire' when 'Beachey Hill' lets fly at Anzac Cove. They swagger in a Paris march, take kindly to being a hero in Tipperary, confuse the locals in Piccadilly with their accent. Frank Keane cabled 'Well played, Xavier' from Flanders fields when he heard of the 1917 championship. George Kirby organised an orchestra of violin, piccolo, mouth organ and tin whistles to serenade the Turks in the Palestinian desert. The flyers among them lived unreal lives of dash and flurry. Jack Cussen reported that pilots were given 'tickets' after only three hours of instruction and, as if to persuade the authorities of the wrong-headedness of their policy, 'bent' his 'Avro' when he caught its skid landing at too sharp an angle. Raymond Parer, one of the Knights of Our Lady of the Southern Cross, was forced to land not once but twice in the middle of schoolgirl picnics, and was forced to stay for tea and tell which was the prettiest. Jack Kerry floated in the dark over London in a basket balloon testing the search light system. He chuckled about 'tootling' over house tops trailing a long rope, and terrifying the inhabitants of villages.

In the trenches, waiting to make a 'rush', immured in filth and unspeakable slime, watching the mad misfortune of others, not many found words for what they saw. When they did, they held those who do not know what they knew mesmerised with the simplicity with which they speak of the unspeakable. Frank Loughnan, Leo Meagher, Jim Fitzgerald belonged to those years at Xavier of which Father Eustace Boylan spoke as new beginnings and no doubt were among the first to sing his song. Since those days they learned new meanings for 'foe' and 'battle' and 'flags'. Here is what they said: first Leo Meagher from beside his artillery behind Paschendale; then Frank Loughnan from Lone Pine; then Jim Fitzgerald after being wounded in Flanders.

Leo Meagher from Paschendale:

'Since I last wrote to you another move has taken place, and now we are just behind the line where the fiercest and most bloody fighting has taken place. We are being held as a reserve to be thrown in at any moment, and we are under orders to be ready to move at a very few minutes notice. Ground is being gained here, but at what cost to both sides. I sleep o' nights in my blanket—soldierly fashion—on the field underneath the muzzle of our gun, and as I lie there and listen to that incessant relentless bombardment which never, never ceases, I have to breathe a prayer for those hearts of steel which are enduring such an ordeal. I have seen them coming back—streams and streams of wounded— and all of them joyful—some even singing with abandoned joy, at being delivered alive out of the inferno. They get no time for sleep, biscuits are their food, water a luxury, because all the water out there is poisoned, and transport is extremely difficult. Thus sleepless, starved, dirty, blood-stained, and parched with insatiable thirst, they are battling there hand to hand, backing their way by sheer force through the most amazing defences. The artillery, too, are all out in the open, close to their infan-try, firing like blazes till they get blown out or till darkness descends and enables them to choose another position to start afresh. They tell me here that the artillery bombardment is more intense and concentrated than it ever was at ————. French soldiers say that, and if it is so, it means that human eyes have never before seen anything to equal it in this world.

You are quite wrong in your opinion that artillery, especially field artillery, is five or six miles behind its infantry and, therefore, as you say, in no danger from gas, and field artillery are rarely further than two or three thousand yards in rear of infantry. Here, in fighting of this kind, they are rarely as much as 1000 yards behind. Field artillery, you must remember is very small metal, and mobility and close contact with its own infantry are its salient features. Thus often here the field guns are just behind the infantry, and at times are taken up right behind the trenches. Also the gas they use is most poisonous and deadly, and is as effective at 4000 yards as at 100 yards. Furthermore, the Germans have heavily and continually used gas in shells against our artillery. They used it against us at our last position, but here they make a habit of it and use both poisonous gas and lachrymatory [which] shells are large, and of long range. (This particular gas was projected from cylinders and floated across country), and though by then it was not deadly, yet you can imagine the tenacity and body of the hideous stuff by the fact that at that prodigious distance it rusted to black almost the newly-polished harness, and blighted crops and green stuffs in its passage. Oh yes! gas is a very real and deadly danger, and none of us ever walks a yard without our gas helmet over our shoulders. In fact, here in France the gas bag with the helmets in is as much a part of the troops' equipment as boots and trousers are. Bitter, bitter experience has taught us a lesson in this, as in everything else, and as regards the fighting here the ground we're on here seems pitifully small to the sacrifice made to gain it, but no doubt the situation has its tactical advantages, and the bloodthirsty and deter-mined onslaughts, continuous and merciless as they are, must do much to crumple up the enemy's morale. Their defences are astounding—in some cases they are deep dugouts 20 feet deep, lined with two feet of solid concrete and innumerable rows of sandbags in which the enemy infantry take refuge when the bombardment commences. When our men, in the face of the most intense fire—our men having ceased, its work of destruction done—advance and leap into the remains of these battered trenches, they bomb and bayonet the Germans who are hiding deep down in the bowels of the earth.

I must tell you that an hiatus has occurred in this letter, and for several days I have not touched it. It is July 30th now, and oh! what a change the last four days have made. We got move orders on the night of the 26th, and soon came right up into it. I would not have missed this for worlds, though it's horrible and hideous. What a battlefield it is. We have come right through those historic villages and woods, from which the Germans have been driven, and are now away beyond their third line. The fighting is fierce, bloodthirsty and incredibly bitter. What a battlefield this is, battered trenches, heaps of debris where villages once were, thousands of empty shell-cases all over the field. Innumerable great shell holes pit the earth, in many cases from six to ten feet deep. Millions of shells have fallen here, and it is as though the ground had all been ploughed up by a gigantic and superhuman furrow. Walking at night is difficult and dangerous, for at any moment you pitch on your face into some big unseen hole. Broken rifles and bayonets, shattered shells in myriads, water-bottles, bandoliers, and every kind of equipment lies scattered on the field, where they have been abandoned by their owners in a hasty retreat. Worst of all, and hideous to relate, rude graves with a board for a headstone, and the name of the fellow scribbled in indelible pencil, are quite common.

I have been here four days now. My full impressions (written in my brain as they ineradicably are) I shall give you when next I see you, if ever that happy time should again arrive. Every night we've been here, there has been the most fearful and determined fighting, and it would be entirely useless to try and describe it to you. The thunder of countless guns, large and small, makes hearing one another's speech quite impossible, and a signal by means of a lamp even at a distance of 10 yards is necessary. The very earth seems to rise and fall with the concussion, and 'hell' is a word the significance of which has been too much depleted by constant usage to adequately describe the demoniacal nightly scenes which occur here regularly. Flashes of guns, the noise of a million devils in agony, green and red rockets of distress, white flashes from the trenches, the thick haze of smoke, the constant whining, screaming and roaring of shells overhead make up a conglomeration of terror, wonder, distraction, exhilaration and unreality which must be encountered to be believed. We have been heavily shelled here with huge devastating shells, and inside of 24 hours after arrival our battery had suffered two casualties. Neither was, fortunately, killed, one man getting a piece of shell through his hand, and another a large hole in his leg. The brigade has suffered a number of casualties since, but the losses of the indomitable infantry are still heavier, and it gives me a certain grain of very human satisfaction to be near them helping them somewhat to bear the very greatest of trials and crosses this world could hold for anyone. I've had some fairly narrow squeaks, but by dint of flinging myself on my face into some convenient shell hole in the filth and dirt, I have managed to dodge all Fritz's most earnest efforts. Many more things I could tell you, but the noise of fierce and continuous strafing are not, as you may imagine, conducive to letter-writing. However, some day, please God, I shall be able to tell you all about one of the most historic battlefields of modern and, indeed, ancient times. Don't worry if you don't hear from me for some time. Probably I won't have time to write much. This has taken nearly ten days to complete. I'll be all right. I'm well, better than ever I was—only sunburnt and dirty. Give my love to all at 'Ikerrin'. They have been very good to me in more ways than this world dreams of. Some day I'll thank them as they deserve.'

Frank Loughnan from Lone Pine:

'Things are going just the same here. We are quite old hands now. We are beginning to know our way about in the trenches. Well, I have had quite a little experience up in the firing-line during the last forty-eight hours. Keith and I were detailed to go into the bomb pit and throw bombs into the Turkish trenches. So you can imagine we are not very far away from them. Of course, they throw bombs back at us, but they very seldom get right into our pit. If the bombs come in, you throw a blanket on them and duck for your life. The blanket smothers them, and they don't do much damage if the blanket is well over them. Everything was going on well till the morning of the second day. It was our shift, and one of the chaps who was throwing the bombs held on too long, or perhaps there was a faulty fuse. Anyhow, the thing exploded in his hand. He was killed, and one other, while several were wounded. Such things are incidental to bomb-throwing. Well, that was the start of it. Our engineers were putting in a sap which started from the bomb pit. They were going to sap right under the Turks' trenches, and then blow them up, but Mr. Turkey was there before them. The Turks were tunnelling too. Our fellows struck and opened the top of the Turkish sap when they had gone about twenty-two feet. They blocked the hole up with sandbags, and sent me down the tunnel with a revolver to keep guard.

While patiently waiting there, I could hear the Turks digging away and talking to each other, and there was I sitting over their heads and expecting to be blown up at any minute! After about two hours the sand bags began to move, then one was taken right down to the lower tunnel. I could not see anyone, but I could hear them quite plainly. Then another one was pulled down, and in the semi-darkness I could see into the Turks' tunnel. It was too dark for me to see anything distinctly, but I thought that I could see some one move, I fired and came out. I reported the matter to our fellows in the bomb pit, and they brought the engineer down, and we went into the tunnel again. Everything was just the same, except that more sand bags were gone. We came out again. My time was up then, and I was relieved.

About an hour afterwards our lieutenant was shot. He had crawled down the tunnel, and the Turks shot him with a revolver. He was the whitest man ever made. We were all very much shaken up at losing him so soon after landing here.

Well, the place is blocked up with sand bags now at the face, and a loophole is left. A man is there in guard, and keeps firing down the sap with a revolver in case a Turk should crawl up and put a charge in to blow the pit up.

In the pit Keith kept on throwing bombs, while I remained on guard with the revolver. I thought that the place was going to be blown up any minute, but it is still in the same place. I don't relish going into that pit again, but if detailed for the work, of course I'll do it.

P.S.—I have not had a wash or a shave for over a week, so you can imagine what I look like.'

Jim Fitzgerald from Flanders:

'At seven the first wave went over the top, and the others, four in all, followed at minute intervals. I was in the last. I had gone only about 150 yards in the open when it seemed as if a horse had kicked me in the left arm, and at the same time as if red-hot needles were being driven into my hip. I went on, but having gone a few yards, I fell, and then I noticed my arm hanging loosely and the blood oozing over my boots. Within reach of my other arm I saw a water-bottle, and was soon having a long drink. I had nearly finished it when someone called out: "Hey! mate, give us a drink!" and looking behind I saw a chap crawling painfully up to me. His leg was broken, and he was very glad to get the drink. Then I put my head up to have a look round, but two sharp 'pings' from a sniper's rifle made me duck it down again. After half an hour of waiting I started to crawl back, not daring to rise. At last I got to the barbed wire, and someone caught me as I slid over the parapet, and soon I found myself with a big lot of other wounded in a small dugout. Afterwards we were moved out to the back of the trench, hard up against a wall. Whilst there a 'nose-cap', or 'double-header', burst near, killing one poor fellow, blowing the shoulder off another, and putting two more holes in my left leg. I just said my prayers and waited for another shell to finish me. An officer came along and ordered every fit man into the front trench, as he expected a charge, but the remnant of fit men in those parts would have been poor protection had the Germans come on. About 4 on Friday afternoon my stretcher came, and I was soon in an ambulance on the way to the dressing station where I got a hot drink, had a good wash, and was given first aid. Then we were taken to the Canadian Hospital at Boulogne, and afterwards I found myself at Sheffield. Our Division suffered heavily in this engagement, which was its first in France. A large number were hit during the bombardment, and more during the charge. We took the first line, and held on all night. But the first trenches were flooded, and those who were badly hit were drowned. As there were no supports, the Anzacs had to retire on Thursday, and the position was just the same as before. The Germans seemed to know all our plans. They sent us word on the 17th, 'Advance, Australia, and take us if you can'. On the 20th they sent over again, 'Two days too late, Anzacs'. We caught two spies in our trenches and, of course, they got short shrift.'

Letters are strange personal reliquaries of men's lives, signatures on events that happen only once and in totally particular ways. Letters written about the war make sad, awful reading. The reading of them, I must confess, stirs my tears and makes me angry and frustrated that I can rescue so few of them from the anonymity of honour rolls and national monuments, or snatch for them so few moments time, for them so meagerly meted out. 'Poor Gervase' Edgeworth-Somers, for example, was killed in the last month of the war at the age of nineteen. His brother Noel had been killed before him at Gallipoli. His commanding officer had written bluntly to Dr Somers while Gervase was in camp. 'Your boy is making a fine soldier, but you must face the fact that for one of his type there are only two things—rapid promotion or death.'

For Gervase, it was death. His mother wrote these lines just after Armistice Day.

> Though I rejoice and watch with proud
>   Dimmed eyes,
> The flag my sons have died for float
>   Against the skies.
> You will forgive and understand, who
>   have no death to mourn,
> That though I share your pride and joy
>   I feel forlorn
> When other mother's brown faced sons march by
>   With soldiers tread
> (Dear gallant boys, I love them all, yet then
>   I mourn my dead)
>
> One near Aegean seas sleeps well;
> The wild thyme scents his grave.
> One sleeps in France; in dreams
> I see red poppies o'er him wave.
> Rejoicing, I watch with you today
> The flag they died for float against the skies.
> Victory is ours, and if my tears fall fast,
> You will forgive—no brown-faced sons of mine march past.

Postlude

Soliloquy in San Giacomo

I AM at mass in San Giacomo's in Bellagio. Donna is beside me. We share a faith. How much we share we do not dare to ask. On the edge of faith is death and parting. It is hard to say there is a future life, when living is such communion. Our witness is to now and how much larger than itself is every minute. These precious minutes are not made larger for thinking that they will last forever. They will not. Even if they are only changed, and not taken away, the change holds no joy. It is only the same that I want forever.

In this Italian church, Italian words wash over me. Their ambience is my symboling, not their individual meaning. I baulk at credos in English, but not in Italian. In English, I begin to wonder at my honesty. My mind goes laterally to the ways I believe, not to what I believe. In Italian believing has no words, just a sense that something of what I do is true. In Italian, I know that other believers are the same, for all their differences. I catch the distance between their selves and their believing words— in the distraction of their eyes, in the hunched silence of the old, in the twisting curiosities of the young. Maybe what those Latin traditionalists say is true. The language of religion is best a mysterious language. I doubt, however, that it should be dead.

There is something new in this religious experience. The priest in his green post-Pentecost vestments is flanked by two young girls at the altar. They wear white copes which they flounce around their jeans. The Pope will have women priests before he knows it. But not much femininity here. Officiousness has no gender. Their big-sisterly preoccupation with assorted altar persons and what these minions should be doing now and next does not augur well for gendering Church rules in other ways.

The priest between them has softer eyes, gentler hands, even if his chin and jaws are shaded macho black. He looks like a Jesus statue, were his beard more curlicued, his locks more flowing. Maybe this is the Italian stamp on Catholic belief. Maybe all our faiths are plaster-moulded with sweet images. Mercifully, this twentieth-century Italian glitsch is in the dark all around us. Votive candles rescue them a little, enough to see a Virgin's dainty foot crushing some poor serpent's head, enough to see the bloodless gore of a Sacred Heart all afire.

Dear God, should I feel guilty at these distractions? Or should I say in present circumstances that it is my duty to be spectator to my thoughts? Are these faithful around me having semiotic excursions, too? Or are they happy to find some metonymy in this kaleidoscope of metaphors of your presence? Lambs, pelicans, fish, doves—snakes, griffins, horns and hoof—the menagerie of divine and devilish presence is large and no doubt fashionably changing. There is an archaeology of faith around us. The pulpit, older by centuries than anything else, is all writhing grotesqueries. The ageless struggle of the Word with evil in human souls is caught in stone forever, or as much of forever as earthquakes, wars, fires and architects allow. But the clutter of other signs is large. The church is a deposit of creeping symboling and each symbol loses its staged effect in the presence of others. Even the floor climbs higher to the ceiling. The renovators will not like the clutter. When the church is dead and becomes museum for being heritage, they will strip it to some pristine simplicity, so that we can gape at it and think how beautiful it was to believe with such economy. Meanwhile, being modern and being, as Pope John XXIII said as he set us free, 'at the end of the road and the top of the heap', we have to believe in a cluttered way.

There is incense now, swirling around the candles being carried by small persons. From the tops of heads somewhere beneath the pulpit ledge come a succession of light-voiced invocations, and there is a flutter in different corners of the church as families realise that it is their child that is calling on us to 'Pray to the Lord'. Sundays must be a busy time for the Lord as he unravels the tangle of our minds and the contradictions of our requests to give us what we really need and sometimes what we want. I bet in this Italian world, he takes Mondays off, to four o'clock at least. Is God Italian? Is She Mother? Black or white? Me or you? How exact the mirror of our reflections? Is there anything else than ourselves to be seen? How can I be so relativist and still believe? I know. The Devil is an empiricist philosopher. Are you certain that you are relativist? he asks, and thinks he has me. His horns are his dilemmas. That's his private hell.

It is time for giving. There is a bustle among the altar persons as they process with a silver cup of wafers and cruets of wine and water. We are an undisciplined lot. We kneel and stand and sit in dribs and drabs. Time was when our bodily movement was our principal contribution to the liturgy, and we knew by the rhythm of the silences and the sounds of the bell when to reverence, when to listen to our heartbeats. Someone should tell the priests about lovers and their silences. Maybe it is true of believers too. Anyway we know enough to sit and give and fumble in our pockets and our purses. Innocent children come to take our money. Remember how it used to be? A mafia of ushers, the clink of money-changers in the temple. Always a problem of symboling, this giving business; a little grubby to put it on God's altar; a little grabby to race it off to the sacristy safe out of thieving reach. Inflation has stopped the clinking of coins. One wonders what use the Lord puts Adam Smith and John Keynes to now.

This commercial break, like all commercial breaks, interrupts the narrative. I catch the priest dripping a little water into the wine in the chalice. He does not do it with a scrupling gesture to catch a single drop. He does not have one of those little one-drop spoons. He is probably not old enough to have been plagued with all the old debates of when did wine become water with these drops, and if water would it turn to Blood? If it didn't, would the mass be valid? Would the faithful have fulfilled their Sunday obligations? Would the souls in purgatory for whom it was offered benefit or not? This was no deep problem of how Calvary could be repeated so often, for which, having the answer wrong, so many have been burned. This was a much more trivial pursuit of tortured souls making arithmetic of their beliefs. I do not see the priest scrupling very much at all. All that rubbing and scraping to dry the sacred moisture and to collect the sacred crumbs. Whatever happened to those little saints who gave their all to stop some accident of desecration? Whatever happened to all those nuclear fissionists among the moral theologians who calculated the physics of our fastings and the arithmetic of our sinnings? What do these transformations of these transubstantiations mean? There are some, not I, who are nostalgic for the security these insecurities gave. I wonder what the transformations mean. I wonder what the transformations do.

Whatever happened, for that matter, to all the allegories that filled the air like angel choirs. That dangerous drip of water: it was the water that flowed from Jesus' heart when the soldier pierced it with his lance. Holy pictures filled our missals, like baseball cards. We collected these images of the crucified and the chalices of his blood and water. Had some anthropologist come and asked us what we meant by doing this or doing that, we had some meaning of it to recite. Our spiritual landscape was full of stories. Not so much, M. Lévi-Strauss, about jaguars and honey, as about the ways in which this action or that material object, this space or that timing, represented a moment in the life and death of Jesus Christ, especially in his moment of sacrifice. Allegory as a mode of explaining signs has been frowned upon by the church for a thousand years. Allegory too easily got out of ecclesiastical control. Allegory is too vernacular for a Latin church. I note, however, how didactic is this Italian priest. His Sunday leaflet is full of instructions of the dramatic structure of the mass, the meaning of its clusters of signs, the relation of the readings to the liturgical year. It is a dangerous touch of conventionality and make-believe. A ritual that needs to be explained is no ritual at all.

The altar persons are assembling again, this time with candles twice as large as any one of them. Keeping the candles alight is clearly some sacred trust. Their assembling signifies the climactic part of the mass—the consecration. As it happens, my mind is full of Kenneth Burke and his logology of religion. The 'word'—*verbum*—he says, in St Augustine is taken for a force—*percussit*; the word strikes. The consecration is the moment of force in the mass. Priests in time past arched their bodies, rounded their lips, gathered their spirits and imprinted the words on the large white wafer in their hands—'*Hoc est enim corpus meum*', 'For this is my body'. It was a logological moment par excellence. Were the words imprinted separately and individually—*hoc* (this) . . . *est* (is) . . . ? Or were the words a sentence—*hocestenimcorpusmeum* . . . pushed explosively into the bread as if the awesome power of being Christ and saying 'this is my body' should not belong to ordinary men. It was the theatrical moment of the priesthood. Silence enclosed worshipping gestures. Then the jangle of bells sent shivers down doubting and distracted spines.

Today's performance is more narratological than logological. No bells, no silence. Its ordinariness denies the grandeur of all those large candles being held by these little people. It has come and gone between a rather unconvincing 'Hosanna in excelsis' and a dissipated 'Great Amen'. The 'Lord's Prayer' is rattled off and awkwardly we give the 'Kiss of Peace'. Coming from a non-tactile culture, I am a little disappointed in this Italian 'Kiss of Peace'. For many years I have made pedagogical capital out of this 'Kiss of Peace'. It is my moment in my ethnography courses to explain the difference between sign and symbol, metonymy and metaphor. The Catholic Church, I will say, looking to change the significance of the eucharistic liturgy a little away from sacrifice to communion, dredged up this old gesture of the 'Kiss of Peace'. In a culture as stiff as ours, it could not be a real kiss. It had to be a handshake. Now handshakes are very sacramental. There are happy handshakes, sad handshakes, congratulatory handshakes. They are signs; they effect what they signify in the doing of them. They *are* happiness, sadness, felicitation. But we do not have a 'Christ in the community' handshake. So when we give the 'Kiss of Peace' in a handshake suddenly we are awkward. We add solemnity and sincerity with all sorts of little inventions—double clasps, soul-searching looks. Or we are shy and quick and distant, as the consciousness of our conventionality makes of our gesture not a sign but a symbol. We work out the meaning and in that adscription catch our own inventiveness. Italians are not so tactile as I thought. We smile, we nod. Our 'Peace be with you's are a little strained, as if we have untangled 'goodbye' into 'God be with you' and made something religious out of something ordinarily secular. There is something soothing in its universal character, however. The 'Kiss of Peace' is Italian, American, Australian, German, young, old, male, female, pious, agnostic. The innocents who took our money are back again. Swiftly, limply, they 'kiss' us all and fly back to the altar, almost before you can say 'Lamb of God, who taketh away the sins of the world! Have mercy on us'.

So it is communion time. Raggedly we take our wafers. Some in left hand, some in right. Some on the tongue. A revolution, here, in ritual behaviour. I remember the fasts and the scruple whether toothpaste or a drop of water broke them. The rewards of early morning mass were substantial—breakfast halfway on time. I remember all the agonies that adolescent bodies created for the pious, the hells to which one was doomed by unconfessed 'mortal sins'. I remember the sin it was thought to be to let the Body of the Lord touch one's teeth. Even now as I move away from the communion rail—a cloth held by two curious innocents—I feel it is a radical gesture to chew the wafer. My meditations, anyway, are distracted by my twisted anthropology. Left hand:right hand—death:life. All the cultures in my head confuse me. Perhaps I should have taken the Bread of Life on my tongue.

The thousands of these communions in my life, for all their scruples and their arithmetic, have been sweet. Not mystic, I think, but sometimes moments of discernment, of cleared vision, occasionally even of a little breathless love. Why should I laugh at that? Why should I turn it upside down and say it is the effect of something else? Of deluded ambitions? Of subliminal class and sex? I have said to myself and to anybody who would ask, that I would like to describe religious experience as it is, not in terms of something else. It is an arrogance and sometimes a bore to begin with oneself. But I do not know where else to begin, where else to find the same, where else to find the different. Perhaps I should write a poem and by that be honest to my particularities. But then again, I do not think my narratives of what it is to believe and hope, to be guilty and sad, to be sure and doubting—in different space and different time—is something less than a poem. Or should be.

REFERENCES

Abbott, J. L. 1982, *John Hawkesworth, Eighteenth Century Man of Letters*, University of Wisconsin, Madison.

Adams, H. 1947, *Tahiti. Memoirs of Arii Tamai*, ed. Rob. E. Spiller, Scholars' Facsimile, New York.

——1964, *Mémoires d'Arii Taimai*, Société des Océanistes, Paris.

Agnew, Jean-Chistophe 1986, *Worlds Apart. The Market and the Theater in Anglo-American Thought*, 1550–1750, Cambridge University Press, Cambridge.

Allen, R. G. 1962, 'De Loutherbourg and Captain Cook', *Theatre Research* 4: 195–211.

——1962, 'Topical Scenes for Pantomime', *Educational Theatre Journal* 17: 289–301.

——1966, 'The Eidophusikon', *Theatre Design and Technology* 7: 12–16.

Ankersmit, F. R. 1989, 'Historiography and Postmodernism', *History and Theory* 28: 137–53.

——1990, 'Reply to Professor Zagorin'. *History and Theory* 29: 275–96.

Ardener, Edward 1982, 'Social Anthropology, Language and Reality', in D. Parkin, (ed.), *Semantic Anthropology*.

Arpad, J. 1977, 'Immediate Experience and the Historical Method', *Journal of Popular Culture* 11: 141–54.

Avineri, Shlomo 1968, *The Social and Political Thought of Karl Marx*, Cambridge University Press, Cambridge.

Bakhtin, Mikhail 1984, *Rabelais and His World*, trans. Helene Iswolsky, Indiana University Press, Bloomington.

Bann, Stephen 1984, *The Clothing of Clio: A Study of the Representation of History in Nineteenth Century Britain and France*, Cambridge University Press, Cambridge.

273

Barish, Jonas 1981, *The Anti-theatrical Prejudice*, University of California Press, Berkeley.

Barthes, Roland 1977, *Roland Barthes by Roland Barthes*, Hill and Wang, New York.

——1986, 'Diderot, Brecht, Eisenstein', in Philip Rosen (ed.) 1986, *Narrative, Apparatus, Ideology*, Columbia University Press, New York.

Beaglehole, J. C. 1967 [1776], *The Voyage of the Resolution and Discovery 1776–1780*, Hakluyt Society, Cambridge.

Benjamin, Walter 1955, *Illuminations*, Schocken Books, New York.

Berger, John 1972, *Ways of Seeing*, Pelican, London.

Berkhofer, Robert E. 1973, 'Clio and the Culture Concept: Some Impressions of a Changing Relationship', in *The Idea of Culture in the Social Sciences*, eds L. Schneider and C. Bonjean, Cambridge University Press, Cambridge.

Biersack, Aletta (ed.) 1990, *Clio in Oceania*, Smithsonian Institution Press, Washington.

Blau, Herbert 1982, *Take Up the Bodies. Theater at the Vanishing Point*, University of Illinois Press, Urbana.

Bligh, W. n.d., Drawings, Mitchell Library, Sydney, PXA565 f18, f19, f52.

——1937 [1785], *Log of the Bounty*, Golden Cockerell, London.

——1976 [1791], *Log of the Providence*, Genesis, London.

Blunden, Edmund 1989 [1928], *Undertones of War*, Folio Society, London.

Boon, James 1973, 'Further Operations of Culture in Anthropology', in *The Idea of Culture in the Social Sciences*, eds L. Schneider and C. Bonjean, Cambridge University Press, Cambridge.

——1982, *Other Tribes, Other Scribes*, Cambridge University Press, Cambridge.

Bourdieu, Pierre 1977, *Outline of a Theory of Practice*, Cambridge University Press, Cambridge.

Bougainville, Louis de 1967 [1772], *A Voyage Round the World*, Da Capo, New York.

Bowen, Abel 1816, *Naval Monument*, New York.

Brannan, John 1823, *Official Letters of the Military and Naval Officers of the United States in the Years 1812–15*, Anno Press, New York.

Brown, Richard H. 1977, *A Poetic for Sociology*, Cambridge University Press, Cambridge.

Brown, Richard Harvey & Stanford M. Lyman (eds) 1978, *Structure, Consciousness and History*, Cambridge University Press, Cambridge.

Bruner, Edward M. (ed.) 1984 *Text, Play and Story*, American Ethnological Society, Washington.

Burnim, Kalman A. 1964, 'David Garrick: Plot and Practice' in Gassner and Allen 1964: 1011–34.

Buttimer, Anne 1982, 'Musing on Helicon: Root Metaphors and Geography', *Geografiska Annaler 64:* 89–96.

Canary, Robert H. & Henry Kozicki (eds) 1978, *The Writing of History. Literary Form and Historical Understanding*, University of Wisconsin Press, Madison.

Carlson, Marvin 1984, *Theories of the Theatre. A Historical and Critical Survey from the Greeks to the Present*, Cornell University Press, Ithaca.

Carr, E. H. 1961, *What is History?* Penguin, Harmondsworth.

Carson, Rachel 1989, *The Sea Around Us*, Mentor, New York.

Chatwin, Bruce 1988, *The Songlines*, Penguin, New York.

Chesneaux, Jean 1976, *Pasts and Futures or What is History for?*, Thames and Hudson, London.

Clifford, James 1983, 'On Ethnographic Authority', *Representations* 1: 118–46.

——1988, *The Predicament of Culture*, Harvard University Press, Cambridge, Mass.

Clifford, James & George E Marcus (eds) 1986, *Writing Culture. The Poetics and Politics of Ethnography*, University of California Press, Berkeley.

Cole, Toby & Helen Krich Chinoy (eds) 1949, *Actors on Acting*, Crown, New York.

Corney, B. G. 1913 [1772], *The Quest and Occupation of Tahiti by the Emissaries of Spain during the Years 1772–1776*, Hakluyt Society, Cambridge.

Court of Apollo 1774, *The Court of Apollo, An Heroic Epistle from the Injured Harriet, Mistress to Mr Banks, to Oberea, Queen of Otaheite*, London.

Crick, Malcolm 1976, *Explorations in Language and Meaning*, Malaby Press, London.

Crosby, Alfred W. 1986, *Ecological Imperialism. The Biological Expansion of Europe, 900–1900*, Cambridge University Press, Cambridge.

Culler, Jonathan 1975, *Structuralist Poetics*, Cornell University Press, Ithaca.

De Certeau, Michel 1989, *The Writing of History*, Columbia University Press, New York.

Dening, Greg 1962, 'Geographical Knowledge of the Polynesians', in J. Golson (ed.), *Polynesian Navigation*, Polynesian Society Memoir 34, Wellington, pp. 102–53.

——1966, 'Ethnohistory in Polynesia', *Journal of Pacific History* 1: 23–42.

——1969, 'Thoughts on a Randy Censor', *Meanjin Quarterly* 28: 503–7.

——1973, 'History as a Social System', *Historical Studies* 15: 673–85.

——1974, *The Marquesan Journal of Edward Robarts, 1797–1824*, Australian National University Press, Canberra.

——1976, 'Violent Men: Post–Revolutionary Americans in the Pacific', in Norman Harper and Elaine Barry (eds), *American Studies Down Under*, ANZASA Pacific Circle 4, Melbourne, pp. 21–41.

——1978a, *Xavier: A Centenary Portrait*, Old Xaverian Association, Melbourne.

——1978b, 'Institutions of Violence in the Marquesas', in N. Gunson (ed), *Changing Pacific*, Oxford University Press, Melbourne, pp. 134–41.

——1979, 'Transculturalism and Marginality', in Jean Martin (ed.), *Counter-Predictive Research Outcomes*, Department of Sociology Research Monograph 2, Canberra, pp. 57–66.

——1980 (1988), *Islands and Beaches. Discourse on a Silent Land: Marquesas 1774–1880*, Dorsey Press, Chicago.

——1981, *The Marquesas Islands* (with E. Christian), Les Editions du Pacifique, Papeete.

——1982a, 'What's Local in Local History?', *Victorian Historical Journal* 53: 74–9.

——1982b, 'Sharks that Walk on the Land', *Meanjin Quarterly* 41: 417–37.

——1983, 'The Face of Battle: Valparaiso 1814', *War and Society* 1: 25–42.

——1984, *The Death of Captain Cook*, Mitchell Library, Dulcie Stretton Lecture, Sydney.

——1986, 'Possessing Tahiti', *Archaeology in Oceania,* 21: 103–18.

——1988a, *History's Anthropology. The Death of William Gooch*, University Press of America, Washington.

——1988b, *The Bounty. An Ethnographic History*, Melbourne University History Monograph, Melbourne.

——1989a, 'History "in" the Pacific', *The Contemporary Pacific*, 1: 134–9.

——1989b, 'Southern Cross/Northern Crosses', in John Hardy and Alan Frost (eds)*, Studies from Terra Australis to Australia*, Australian Academy of the Humanities, Canberra, pp. 233–43.

——1990a, 'ANZAC Day: An Ethnographic Reflection after Reading Bruce Kapferer', *Social Analysis*, 29: 62–6.

——1990b, 'Ethnography on My Mind', in Bain Attwood (ed.), *Boundaries of the Past*, The History Institute, Victoria, Melbourne, pp.14–21.

——1991a, 'A Poetic for Histories: Transformations that Present the Past'', in Biersack 1991: 347–80.

——1991b, 'Claptrap, Art and Science: Representation, Realisation, Reflection', *Melbourne Historical Journal*, 21: 95–103.

——1992a, *Mr Bligh's Bad Language. Passion, Power and Theatre on the Bounty*, Cambridge University Press, New York.

——1992b, 'Towards an Anthropology of Performance in Encounters in Place', in Donald H. Rubenstein (ed.), *Pacific History*, University of Guam Press, Guam, pp. 3–7.

——1993, 'The Theatricality of History Making and the Paradoxes of Acting', *Cultural Anthropology*, 8: 73–95.

——1994, The Theatricality of Observing and Being Observed: 'Eighteenth–century 'Europe' 'discovers' the ? century 'Pacific', in *Implicit Understandings*, Stuart B. Schwartz (ed.), Cambridge University Press, Cambridge, pp. 451–83.

——1995, *The Death of William Gooch. A History's Anthropology*, Melbourne University Press, Melbourne.

Dening, Greg & Doug Kennedy 1993, *Xavier Portraits*, Old Xaverians' Association, Melbourne.

Dewey, John 1934, *Art as Experience*, Minton, New York.

Dibdin, Charles n.d., *A Complete History of the Stage*, privately printed, London.

Douglas, Sir Howard 1851, *A Treatise on Naval Gunnery*, 3rd edn., John Murray, London.

Driessen, H.A.H. 1982, 'Outriggerless Canoes and Glorious Beings', *Journal of Pacific History* 17: 3–28.

Egan, Clifford L. 1974, 'The Origins of the War of 1812: Three Decades of Historical Writing', *Military Affairs*, 38: 72–5.

English Alphabet 1786, *An English Alphabet for the Use of Foreigners; wherein the Pronunciation of Vowels or Voice–letters is explained in twelve short General Rules with Several Exceptions as abridged (for the instruction of Omiah) from a larger work*, London.

Epeli Hau'ofa 1994, 'Our Sea of Islands', *The Contemporary Pacific*, 6: 147–63.

Epistle from Oberea 1775, *Epistle from Oberea, Queen of Otaheite to Joseph Banks Esq., Translated by TQZ Esq., Professor of the Otaheitian Language in Dublin and of all the Languages of the Undiscovered Islands in the South Seas*, 3rd edn., Almon, London.

Epistle from Banks n.d., *Epistle from Mr Banks Voyager Monster-Hunter and Amoroso to Oberea, Queen of Otaheite*, London.

Evans, Henry Clay 1927, *Chile and its Relations with the United States*, Duke University Press, Durham.

Evans-Pritchard, E 1940, *The Nuer*, Oxford University Press, Oxford.

Fernandez, James 1986, *Persuasions and Performances. The Play of Tropes in Culture*, Indiana University Press, Bloomington.

Ferris, Timothy 1988, *Coming of Age in the Milky Way*, Doubleday, New York.

Feuer, Lewis S. (ed.) 1969, *Marx and Engels*, Fontana, London.

Foucault, Michel 1975, 'Entrétien sur le prison: le livre et sa méthode.' *Magazine Littéraire*, 101: 33.

Fowler, H.W. 1965, *A Dictionary of Modern English Usage*, 2nd edn, Oxford University Press, Oxford.

Freeman, Derek 1983, *Margaret Mead and Samoa. The Making and Unmaking of an Anthropological Myth*, Australian University Press, Canberra.

Fried, Michael 1980, *Absorption and Theatricality. Painting and the Beholder in the Age of Diderot*, University of Chicago Press, Chicago.

Fussell, Paul 1975, *The Great War and Modern Memory*, Oxford University Press, London.

Gabler, Neal 1988, *An Empire of their Own: How the Jews Invented Hollywood*, Crown, New York.

Gadamer, Hans-George 1982, *Truth and Method*, Crossroad, New York.

Garitee, Jerome R. 1977, *The Republic's Private Navy*, Mystic Seaport, Middleton.

Gassner, John & Ralph G. Allen (eds) 1964, *Theatre and Drama in the Making*, Houghton Mifflin, Boston.

Gay, Peter 1975, *Style in History*, Jonathan Cape, London.

Gebser, Jean 1984, *The Ever Present Origin*, Ohio University Press, Athens, Ohio.

Geertz, Clifford 1975, *The Interpretation of Cultures*, Hutchinson, London.

——1983, *Local Knowledge*, Basic Books, New York.

Genovese, Eugene & Elizabeth D. Fox-Genovese 1976, 'The Political Crisis of Social History', *Journal of Social History* 10: 305–19.

Gore, J. 1766, Logbook of HMS *Dolphin*, Aug. 21, 1766–October, 1767, Mitchell Library, Sydney, B1533–B1534.

Gossman, Lionel 1978, 'History and Literature. Reproduction or Signification', in Canary and Kozicki 1978, pp. 3–39.

Gouldner, Alvin W. 1970, *The Coming Crisis of Western Sociology*, Heinemann, London.

Graham, Gerald S. and R. A. Humphreys (eds) 1962, *The Navy and South America 1807–1820*, Navy Records Society, London.

Graham, Loren, Wolf Lepevies & Peter Weingart (eds) 1983, *The Function and Uses of Disciplinary Histories*, Reidel, Dordrecht.

Green, R. and K. 1968, 'Religious Structures of the Society Islands', *New Zealand Journal of History* 2: 66–89.

Gunson, N. 1963, 'A Note on the Difficulties of Ethnohistorical Writing with Special Reference to Tahiti', *Journal of the Polynesian Society* 72: 415–19.

Halliwell, Stephen 1986, *Aristotle's Poetics*, University of North Carolina Press, Chapel Hill.

Hamilton-Paterson, James 1992, *The Great Deep. The Sea and Its Thresholds*, Henry Holt, New York.

Handler, Richard & William Saxton 1988, 'Dyssimulation: Reflexivity; Narrative and the Quest for Authenticity in "Living History"', *Cultural Anthropology* 3: 242–60.

Haskell, Thomas L. 1977, *The Emergence of Professional Social Science*, University of Illinois Press, Urbana.

Hastrup, Kirsten 1990, 'The Ethnographic Present: A Reinvention', *Cultural Anthropology* 5: 45–61.

Hawkesworth, J. 1772, *An Account of the Voyages Undertaken by the Order of His Present Majesty for Making Discoveries in the Southern Hemisphere*, Strahan and Cadell, London.

Hawthorn, Geoffrey 1976, *Enlightenment and Despair. A History of Sociology*, Cambridge University Press, Cambridge.

Helms, Mary W. 1988, *Ulysses' Sail. An Ethnographic Odyssey of Power, Knowledge and Geographical Distance*, Princeton University Press, Princeton.

Henderson, James 1970, *The Frigates*, Adlard Coles, London.

Henige, David 1982, *Oral Historiography*, Longman, London.

Henry, T. 1928, *Ancient Tahiti*, B. P. Bishop Museum, Honolulu, Bulletin 48.

Hill, Jonathan D. (ed.) 1988, *Re-Thinking History and Myth. Indigenous South American Perspective on the Past*, University of Illinois Press, Urbana.

Himmelfarb, Gertrude 1987, *The New History and the Old*, Belknap Press, Cambridge, Mass.

Historic Epistle 1775, *An Historic Epistle from Omiah to the Queen of Otaheite, being his remarks on the English Natives, with notes by the editor*, T. Evans, London.

Hogan, Charles Beecher 1968, *The London Stage 1660–1800*, Southern Illinois University Press, Carbondale.

Horsman, Reginald 1962, *The Causes of the War of 1812*, A. S. Barnes, New York.

Hudson, Nicholas 1993, *Modern Australian Usage*, Oxford University Press, Melbourne.

Hunt, Lynn (ed.) 1989, *The New Cultural History*, University of California Press, Berkeley.

Huse, W. 1936, 'A Noble Savage on the Stage', *Modern Philology*, 33: 303–16.

Injured Islanders 1779, *The Injured Islanders or the Influence of Art upon the Happiness of Nature. A Poetical Epistle from Oberea of Otaheite to Captain Wallis*, Faulkner, London.

Irwin, Geoffrey 1992, *Prehistoric Exploration and Colonisation of the Pacific*, Cambridge University Press, Cambridge.

James, William 1817, *A Full and Correct Account of the Chief Naval Occurences of the Late War*, T. Egerton, London.

Joppien, R. 1979, 'Philippe Jacques de Loutherbourg's Pantomime 'Omai, or, A Trip Round the World' and the Artists of Cook's Voyages', in *Captain Cook and the South Pacific*, British Museum, London, Yearbook 3.

Judt, Tony 1979, 'A Clown in Regal Purple: Social History and the Historians', *History Workshop*, 7: 66–94.

Kant, Emmanuel 1973, 'What is Enlightenment?', in Peter Gay (ed.), *The Enlightenment: A Comprehensive Anthology*, Simon and Schuster, New York.

Keegan, John 1977, *The Face of Battle*, Cape, New York.

Keller, A. S. 1938, *Creation of Rights of Sovereignty through Symbolic Acts 1400–1800*, Columbia University Press, New York.

Knapp, Mary E. 1961, *Prologues and Epilogues of the Eighteenth Century*, Yale University Press, New Haven.

Kemble, P. H. 1931, 'The USS *Essex* versus HMS *Phoebe*', *United States Naval Institute, Proceedings*, 57: 199–202.

Kuritz, Paul 1988, *The Making of Theatre History*, Prentice-Hall, Englewood Cliffs, NJ.

La Pérouse, Jean Francois de 1799, *A Voyage Round the World Performed in the Years 1785–1788 by the* Boussole *and* Astrolabe, J. Stockdale, London.

Lasch, Christopher 1991, *The True and Only Heaven. Progress and its Critics*, Norton, New York.

Letter from Omai 1780a, *A Letter from Omai to the Right Honourable, the Earl of*******, Bell, London.

——1780b, *A Letter from Omai to the Right Honourable, the Earl of ******, Late—Lord of the—, translated from the Ulaeietean tongue, in which, amongst other things is fairly and irrefragably stated, the Nature of Original Sin: together with a proposal for Planting Christianity in the Islands of the Pacific Ocean*, Bell, London.

Lewis, Charles Lee 1941, *David Glascow Farragut*, USNI, Annapolis.

Lind, Staughton 1969, 'The Historian as Participant', in Robert Allen Skotheim (ed.) 1969, *The Historian and the Climate of Opinion*, Addison-Wesley, Reading, Mass.

Long, David 1970, *Nothing Too Daring*, USNI, Annapolis.

Lovette, Leland Pearson 1939, *Naval Customs, Traditions and Usages*, USNI, Annapolis.

MacAloon, John J. (ed.) 1984, *Rite, Drama, Festival, Spectacle. Rehearsals Toward a Theory of Cultural Performance*, ISHI, Philadelphia.

McCormick, E. H. 1977, *Omai. Pacific Envoy*, University of Auckland Press, Auckland.

Mackaness, G. 1960, 'Extracts from the Logbook of HMS *Providence* Kept by Lt. Francis Godolphin Bond RN', *Royal Australian Historical Society Journal*, 46: 24–66.

Malarde, Y. 1931, 'Attributes Royaux', *Bulletin de la Société des Etudes Océaniennes*, 4: 204–09.

Malin, David 1994, *A View of the Universe*, Cambridge University Press, Cambridge.

Malinowski, Bronislaw 1967, *A Diary in the Strict Sense of the Term*, Harcourt, New York.

Marcuse, Herbert 1978, *The Aesthetic Dimension. Towards a Critique of Marxist Aesthetics*, Beacon Press, Boston.

Marshall, David 1986, *The Figure of Theater*, Columbia University Press, New York.

Marshall, John 1825, *Royal Naval Biography*, London.

Mayer, D. 1969, *Harlequin in his Element. The English Pantomime 1806–1836*, Harvard University Press, Cambridge, Mass.

Merwick, Donna 1991, 'Postmodernism and the Possibilities of Representation', *Australasian Journal of American Studies*, 10: 1–10.

Merrill, A. S. 1940, 'First Contacts in the Glorious Cruise of the Frigate *Essex*', *USNIP* 66: 218–23.

Mimosa. 1779, *Mimosa or the Sensitive Plant. A Poem Dedicated to Kitt Frederick, Duchess of Queensberry Elect*, London.

Montgomery, J. 1831, *Journal of Voyages and Travels by the Rev. Daniel Tyerman and George Bennett*, Westley and Davis, London.

Moore, Sally & Barbara Meyerhoff (eds) 1976, *Symbol and Politics in Communal Ideology*, Cornell University Press, Ithaca.

Morrison, James, 1935, *The Journal of James Morrison*, Golden Cockerell, London.

Morrison, Karl F. 1982, *The Mimetic Tradition of Reform in the West*, Princeton University Press, Princeton.

Newbury, C. 1967a, 'Aspects of Cultural Change in French Polynesia: The Decline of the Arii', *Journal of the Polynesian Society*, 76: 7–26.

——1967b, 'Te Hau Pahu Rahi. Pomare II and the Concept of Interisland Government in Eastern Polynesia', *Journal of the Polynesian Society*, 76: 477–514.

——1980, *Tahiti Nui. Change and Survival in French Polynesia*, University Press of Hawaii, Honolulu.

Nicholl, Allardyce 1927, *A History of Late Eighteenth Century Drama 1750–1800*, Cambridge University Press, Cambridge.

Obeysekere, Gananath 1992, *The Apotheosis of Captain Cook. European Myth-making in the Pacific*, Princeton University Press, Princeton.

O'Brien, Patricia 1989, 'Michel Foucault's History of Culture', in Hunt 1989, pp. 25–46.

O'Keeffe, J. 1785, *Omai, or, A Trip Round the World*, Australian National Library, Canberra, RBq.Misc 1991.

——1826, *Recollections of the Life of John O'Keeffe, Written by Himself*, Colburn, London.

Oliver, Douglas 1974, *Ancient Tahitian Society*, University Press of Hawaii, Honolulu.

Omiah's Farewell 1776, *Omiah's Farewll, Inscribed to the Ladies of\London*, Kearsley, London.

Poetical Epistle 1775, *A Poetical Epistle (Moral and Philosophical) from an Officer at Otaheite to Lady Gr**v*n*r with notes critical and Historical*, Evans, London.

Padfield, Peter 1973, *Guns at Sea*, Hugh Evelyn, London.

Parkin, David (ed.) 1982, *Semantic Anthropology*, Academic Press, London.

Paullin, Oscar 1909, 'Duelling in the Old Navy', *USNIP* 35: 1155–97.

Porter, David 1822, *Journal of a Cruise Made to the Pacific*, 2nd edn, Wiley and Halsted, New York.

Porter, David Dixon 1875, *Memoirs of Commodore David Porter of the United States Navy*, Munsell, Albany.

Price, Richard 1983, *First Time*, Johns Hopkins University Press, Baltimore.

Prown, Jules D. 1982, 'Mind in Matter', *Winterthur Portfolio* 17: 1–20.

Rippy, James F. 1964, *The Rivalry of the United States and Great Britain over Latin America*, Octagon, New York.

Robertson, G. 1948[1766], *The Discovery of Tahiti. A Journal of the Second Voyage of HMS Dolphin Round the World 1766–1768*, Hakluyt Society, 2nd Series, 98, London.

Roderick, Colin 1972, 'Sir Joseph Banks, Queen Oberea and the Satirists', in W. Veit (ed.), *Captain James Cook. Image and Impact*, Hawhorn Press, Melbourne, pp. 67–89.

Roosevelt, Theodore 1882, *The Naval War of 1812*, G. P. Putnam, New York.

Rorty, Richard 1989, *Contingency, Irony and Solidarity*, Cambridge University Press, Cambridge.

Rosaldo, Renato 1984, 'Grief and the Headhunter's Rage: On the Cultural Force of Emotions', in Bruner 1984: 178–198.

——1986, 'Ilongot Hunting as Story and Experience', in Turner and Bruner 1986: 97–138.

Rose, Roger 1978, *Symbols of Sovereignty. Feather Girdles of Tahiti and Hawaii*, B. P. Bishop Museum, Pacific Anthropological Records 28, Honolulu.

Sahlins, Marshall 1976, Culture and Practical Reason, University of Chicago Press, Chicago.

——1981, *Historical Metaphors and Mythical Realities*, University of Michigan Press, Ann Arbor.

——1985, *Islands of History*, University of Chicago Press, Chicago.

——1995, *How "Natives" Think. About Captain Cook For Example*, University of Chicago Press, Chicago.

Said, Edward 1978, *Orientalism*, Random House, New York.

——1989, 'Representing the Colonized: Anthropology's Interlocutors', *Critical Inquiry*, 15: 205–25.

Samuel, Raphael 1981, *People's History and Socialist Theory*, Routledge and Kegan Paul, London.

Schechner, Richard 1985, *Between Theater and Anthropology*, University of Pennsylvania Press, Philadelphia.

——1988, 'Magnitudes of Performance', in Turner and Bruner 1986, pp. 344–69.

Scholte, Bob 1972, 'Toward a Reflexive and Critical Anthropology', in Dell Hymes (ed.) *Re–Inventing Anthropology*, Vintage., New York, pp. 430–58.

——1983, 'Cultural Anthropology and the Paradigm-Concept', in Graham, Loren, Wolf Lepenies & Peter Weingart (eds) 1983, *Functions and Uses of Disciplinary History*, D. Reidel, Dordrecht.

Second Letter n.d., *A Second Letter from Oberea, Queen of Otaheite to Joseph Banks*, Carnegy, London.

Seventeen Hundred 1777, *Seventeen Hundred and Seventy–Seven, or a Picture of the Manners and Character of the Age. In a Poetical Epistle from a Lady of Quality*, Evans, London.

Smith, P. C. F. 1974, *The Frigate* Essex *Papers*, Peabody Museum, Salem.

Sontag, Susan 1967, *Against Interpretation*, Eyre and Spottiswoode, London.

——1979, *On Photography*, Penguin, Harmondsworth.

Stafford, Barbara Maria 1984, *Voyage into Substance. Art, Science and the Illustrated Travel Account 1760–1840*, MIT, Cambridge, Mass.

Stagg, J. C. A. 1976, '"Malcontents": The Political Origins of the War of 1812', *William and Mary Quarterly*, 33: 557–85.

Stallybrass, Peter and Allon White 1986, *The Politics and Poetics of Transgression*, Cornell University Press, Ithaca.

Stanislavski, Constantin 1958, *Stanislavski's Legacy*, Max Reinhardt, London.

Stanner, W. E. H. 1979, *White Man Got No Dreaming. Essays 1938–1973*, ANU Press, Canberra.

Strong, Tracey B. 1978, 'Dramaturgical Discourse and Political Enactments. Toward an Artistic Foundation for Political Space', in Brown & Lyman 1978, pp. 237–60.

Taussig, Michael T. 1980, *The Devil and Commodity Fetishism in South America*, University of North Carolina Press, Chapel Hill.

Thompson, E. P. 1978, *The Poverty of Theory*, Merlin Press, London.

Tillinghast, Pardon E. 1972, *The Spacious Past*, Addison-Wesley, Reading, Mass.

Tobin, George n.d., Sketches, Mitchell Library, PXA 563 ff1–50, Sydney.

——1791, Journal on HMS *Providence* 1791–3, Mitchell Library, MS CY A 562, Sydney.

Toner, Raymond J. 1906, 'A Page from the Old Navy: USF *Essex*', *USNIP* 32: 1136–9.

Turner, Terence 1988, 'Ethno–Ethnohistory: Myth and History in Native American Representations of Contact with Western Society', in Hill 1988, pp. 235–81.

Turner, Victor W. 1974, *Dramas, Fields and Metaphors*, Cornell University Press, Ithaca.

——1977, 'Process and Symbol: A New Anthrpological Synthesis', *Daedalus* 106: 61–80.

——1982, *From Ritual to Theatre*, Performing Arts Journal Publication, New York.

——1986, 'Dewey, Dilthey and Drama: An Essay in the Anthropology of Experience', in Turner & Bruner 1986, pp. 33–44.

——1987, *The Anthropology of Performance*, PAJ Publications, New York.

Turner, Victor W. & Edward M. Bruner (eds) 1986, *The Anthropology of Experience*, University of Illinois Press, Urbana.

Wagner, Roy 1972, *Habu. The Innovation of Meaning in Daribi Religion*, University of Chicago Press, Chicago.

——1981, *The Invention of Culture*, University of Chicago Press, Chicago.

Wallis, Samuel 1776, Logbook of Captain Samuel Wallis, Kept During His Voyage Round the World in Command of HMS *Dolphin* 1766–1768, Mitchell Library Ms., Sydney.

Wesseling, H. L. (ed.) 1978, *Expansion and Reaction. Essays in European Expansion and Reaction in Asia and Africa*, Leiden University Press, Leiden.

White, Hayden 1973, *Metahistory: The Historical Imagination in Nineteenth–Century Europe*, Johns Hopkins University Press, Baltimore.

——1980, 'The Value of Narrativity in the Representation of Reality', *Critical Inquiry* 7: 5–27.

Williams, Raymond 1976, *Keywords. A Vocabulary of Culture and Society*, Fontana, Glascow.

——1981, *Culture*, Fontana, Glascow.

Wilson, Arthur 1972, *Diderot*, Oxford University Press, New York.

Yovel, Yitmiahu (ed.) 1974, *Philosophy of History and Action*, Reidel, Jerusalem.

Zagorin, Perez 1990, 'Historiography and Postmodernism: Reconsiderations', *History and Theory* 29: 263–74.

Zinn, Howard, 1970, *The Politics of History*, Beacon, Boston.

GLOSSARY OF HAWAIIAN (Hwn), TAHITIAN (Tah) AND MARQUESAN (Mq) WORDS

ahu (Mq)	sacred place
aoe (Mq)	stranger, not native to *te henua*
ari'i (Tah)	'chiefs', persons of high status
ari'i rahi (Tah)	highest ranking 'chiefs'
arioi (Tah)	sect of the cult of 'Oro
atua (Tah)	supernatural
akua (Hwn)	supernatural
enata (Mq)	native to *te henua*
haka'iki (Mq)	'chiefs', persons of high status
heiau (Hwn)	place of worship, 'temple'
heiva (Tah)	dance
hula (Hwn)	dance
kapu (Hwn)	prohibition, separated and sacred
Lono (Hwn)	'god' of *makahiki*
makahiki (Hwn)	four months festival of Lono
maohi (Tah)	native-born to Tahitian islands
marae (Tah)	place of worship
maro tea (Tah)	yellow feather girdle of titled *ari'i rahi*
maro ura (Tah)	red feather girdle of titled *ari'i rahi*
'Oro (Tah)	'god' of war and sacrifice
paepae (Mq)	stone platform
pahupu (Hwn)	group of warriors 'cut-in-two' by tattoos
rahui (Tah)	secular prohibition

285

ta'ata meia roa (Tah)	plantain branch proxy for human sacrifice
ta ika (Mq)	'fishing' for sacrificial victims
tapa (Tah)	bark cloth
tapu (Tah)	prohibition, separated and sacred
Taputapuatea (Tah)	place of sacrifice and worship of 'Oro
te henua (Mq)	the land, native name of Marquesas
tiki (Tah)	statue
tohua (Mq)	dance and feast place

INDEX

accuracy: and objectivity, 40; and scientific history, 54; and truth, 49–50, 127
acting: Diderot on, 122; Garrick on, 121; Melville on, 101; paradox of, 121
'Acts', 4, 18; *see also disputatio*
actuality, 60
Adams, Henry, 163–5
Addison, Joseph, as spectator, 107–8
after-meditation, 3; texts as, 17
akua (*atua*, 'gods'), 76–7; European strangers as, 65
Amo (Tahitian chief), 147, 163–4, 165
Anson, Lord, 88
anthropology: dialectic in, 62; discipline of, 221; ethnographic moment in, 195–6; reflexive, 125, 196; fears for, 200
anti-theatre, 19; Barish on, 110; church, 113; Puritan, 112; science, 113
Anzac Day, 225ff; attitudes to, 227
Aotorea (New Zealand), 213
'Application of the Senses', 14–15
archives, 43, 51, 167
ari'i nui (high rank chief), 129, 134
ari'i rahi (highest rank chief), 141
Arii-Tamai (of Pomare dynasty), 163–5
arioi (players), 131, 139
Aristotle: on catharthis, 205; on history, 35; on *mythos*, xv; on mythopoetics, 104; on theatre, xv
Arnold, John, 218
author: death of, xv; presence, 121

Bakhtin, Michail, on the grotesque, 123
Banks, Joseph, 148; satires about, 152–6
Barish, Jonas, on anti-theatre, 110
Barthes, Roland, 62; on erotics, xiv; on language, 116; on readers, 102; on *Spiritual Exercises*, 12; on theatre, 104
battle: description, 90ff; etiquette of, 92, 136–7; nature of, 83–5; Tahitian, 138
beachcombers, 60, 123
Beaglehole, J. C., 162–3; on 'timorodee', 154
Bellagio, 267
Bellarmine, Robert, 22
Belloc, Hilaire, 10, 22
Benjamin, Walter, on history, 111
Benson, Robert Hugh, 10
Bergson, Henri, 8
Berlin, Isaiah, on narrative, 33
Bible, literary forms of, 16
Biersack, Aletta, xii
Bligh, William, 45, 77, 130, 132; after the mutiny, 168–9, 186; bad language, 63; belief in cause of mutiny, 188; draws *maro ura*, 143; portraits of, 171; scandalised by Tahitians, 139; supposed homosexuality, 188; **Plate 8**
Blunden, Edmund, on war, 203
blurred genres, 58
Boas, Franz, 197
Bolt, Robert, 188, 189
Book of Genesis, and Judaeo-Christian songlines, 210

Boon, James, 47, 58, 228
boundaries, 58
Braudel, Fernand, on narrative, 33
Bougainville, Louis Antoine de, 142
Bounty, 45, 168, 169; and anti-slavery, 181–2; cinematics of, xv; mutineers, 132; significance of, 171
Bourdieu, Pierre, on praxis, 119–20
Bourke, William, as 'Fletcher Christian', 170
Brando, Marlon, 172; as fop, 182; 'methodises', 183; reluctant Christian, 182; script for, 183–4, 185–7; **Plate 9**
Brett, Judith, xii
Brown, Richard H., on symbolic realism, 36
Burke, Kenneth, on logology, 270–1
Byrne, Michael (*Bounty* fiddler), 172–3
Byron, Lord (poet), on Fletcher Christian, 181
Byron, Lord (admiral): at Kealakekua, 75; memorial for Cook , **Plate 2**

Calvin, John, 9
Cambridge University: 'Acts' at, 4; Wordsworth's failure at, 3
Campion, Edmund: Jesuit martyr, 8; life and death, 9; quoted, 10
Canisius, Peter, 22
Canisius College, 21
'cargo': museums and, 132, 167; notion of, 43, 46–7; of past to present, 43, 128
carnival, 66
Carr, E. H.: on historical fact, 72; on interpretation, 127
Carrera, Jose Miguel (Chilean revolutionary), 85
Carson, Rachel, on Pacific Basin, 209–10
Centurion, 88
ceremony, and discipline 144; *see also* rituals
Chatwin, Bruce, on songlines, 207, 221
Chauvel, Charles, 172
Chavert, Jean, 214, 221
Cherub, 79, 85, 89ff, **Plate 7**

Chesterton, G. K., 10
Christian, Edward, 181
Christian, Fletcher, 132; Bligh's description, 168; debt to Bligh, 188; Dodd's depiction, 170; family connections, 181–2; gentleman, 181–2; inventions of, 190; Thalberg's creation, 175; **Plate 9**
Clendinnen, Inga, xi
Clerke, Captain Charles, 71, 72
Clio, history's muse, 103–4, 110
Cohn, Barney, 58
Coleridge, Samuel, and Fletcher Christian, 181
Collingwood, R. G., 49, 124
'Composition of Place', 14–15; sources of, 16; stage for meditation, 15
consolation, 13
Cook, Captain James: and Bligh, 171; *Apotheosis*, 158–60, **Plate 3**; arrival in Hawaii, 67; as Lono, 68, 140; as 'discoverer', 218; at Tahiti, 214ff; cultural relativism of, 155, 221; death and historical consciousness, xv, 45, 71; death, reasons for, 73–4; mythologised, 74–5, 77; naming discoveries, 209; portrait, 132–3; property divided, 73; sacrifice of, 72; sees *maro ura*, 143; shipwrecked, 150
Cornford, F. M., on structures of mind, 17
Crook, William Pascoe, 9
Crosby, Alfred W., on ecological imperialism, 78
Cross, Southern (Crux), 217–18; Knights of, 252–3
culture: as map, 120; invention of, 134; modernity and, 223; theatricality in, 109, 113

Daedalus, 3–4
Darby, Madge, on *Bounty* homosexuality, 188
Darnton, Robert, 58
Davis, Natalie Zemon, 58

Dawn Service, rituals of, 226–7, 228
De Certeau, Michel, on the gendered other, 123
deep play, 98
desolation, 13
Dewey, John: on experience, 104; on life as histories, 105
Diderot, Denis, 114, 121; on acting, 122; on sensibility, 121
Dilthey, Wilhelm, 49, 124
'Discernment of Spirits', 13, 14; in performance, 20; Loyola on, 23–4
disciplines: and academic history, 43; as cultural systems, 40; conventionalities of, 39; myths of, 40
Discovery, 67
disputatio, 17–18; as performance, 18, 19
Divino Afflante Spiritu, 16
Doctorow, E. L., on civilisation as metaphor, 105
Dodd, Robert, painting of *Bounty* mutiny, 170
Dollund, John, 218
Dolphin, 133, 135, 136, 139, 140, 141, 147, 165, **Plate 4**
Donaldson, Roger, 172
Douai, 82
double helix, of past and present, 62
Dreamtime, 207
Dudley, Robert Cecil, 8
duels, nature of, 83

Easter Island, *see* Rapanui
effects: notion of, 114; producing, 102, 108
Earnshaw, Thomas, 218
Elizabeth I, Queen, 8
Elton, Geoffrey, on narrative, 33
empowering: histories' force, xv; meaning, 205; of narratives, 34, of the present, 204
enata (Marquesans), 76, 77
encounters, 139; entertainment in, 167; factors at work in, 140; metaphoric understanding in, 139

Endeavour, 214–15
Enlightenment, 107, 108
entertainment: Frye on, 49; Geertz on, 49; in encounters, 167; notion of, 47–8; of academic history, 55–6; of anthropology, 199; of history, 167; of sacred history, 52; Turner on, 48–9
Essex, 79, 81, 82, 85, 88, 89ff; armoury of, 82; mottos of, 80; **Plate 7**
Essex Junior, 82, 89ff, **Plate 7**
ethnographic present, 107, 108
ethnographic moment, 107, 195, 223
ethnography: and otherness, 44; and reification, 23; and social alertness, 27; and teaching history, 30, 226; as cultural reflection, 196; as fiction, 194; Evans-Pritchard's, 193–4; in present participle, 120; Malinowski's, 194–5; Mead's, 196; methodology, 194–5; of an historical act, 62; of Anzac, 225ff; of Christ's life, 16–17; of ethnographic moments, 45; of history, 41; of the actual, 60; of Wordsworth's mind, 3
ethnohistory, 44–5, 58–9; as analysis of consciousness, 44–5
Evans-Pritchard, E. E., 193, 197
'Examination of Conscience', 25
experience: Dewey on, 104; of battle, 83–5, 93–4; reflective, 125; risk in, 118; Turner on, 118

faith, and rationality, 22
Fanon, Franz, 114
Farragut, David: experience of battle, 93–4, 97; memories as history, 96
'Fatal Impact', and cultural memory, 212
Ferris, Tim: on observation, 220; on the Milky Way, 216
fiction, 34; realising the, 117
fighting, naval, 94
films: and cultural literacy, 190; as cultural artefacts, 168; as mythmaker, 173–4
Fitzgerald, Jim, letter from Flanders, 262–3

Flynn, Errol, 173, **Plate 9**
'force': in narrative, 115, 205; of the word, 270
Foucault, Michel, 62; on commenting, 105
Fox, William, 174
Freeman, Derek, 57, 191; in Samoa, 199; on American anthropology, 192
Frye, Northrop, on entertainment, 49
Fuelhop-Miller, René, 12
fundamentalism: changes in, 211; fear of theatre, 101; subversions of, 30
Furneaux, Tobias, 142–3
Fussell, Paul: on battle, 79; on pastoral metaphors, 228

Gable, Clark, 172; American character, 177; reluctant Christian, 175; script for, 176–7
Gabler, Neal, on the invention of Hollywood, 174
Gadamer, H. G., 49
Galapagos Islands, 82, 83
Gallipoli, 225, 226, 229, 247, 250, 264
Gambetta, Archie, on brother's death, 254
Garrick, David: on acting, 121; on theatre, 117–18
Gay, Peter, on style, 116
Geertz, Clifford, 58; on deep play, 80; on entertainment, 49
George III, King, 129, 132, 142, 160
Gibson, Mel, 172, 189
Gilson, Etienne, 22
Goffman, Irving, on total institutions, 24
'going native', 122–3; deference to realism, 124; in history, 124; scandal of, 123
Gooch, William: and Cambridge *mentalité*, 3; death in Hawaii, 4; education at Cambridge, 3–4; historical ethnography of, 61
Gosson, Stephen, on theatre, 112
Green, Roger, 162–3
grotesque, 123, 161, 214
Gunson, Neil, 162–3

Halley, Edmond, 219
Hau'ofa, Epeli, on Oceania, 208
Hawaii: Cook's arrival, 67; ritual cycles, 65–6
heiau (temple): at Kealakekua, 68; of Ku, 72
'Hell', 7, 8, 11
Hawkesworth, Dr John, 149, 151
Hergest, Richard, 4
Herschel, William, on seeing, 219–20
Hexter, J. H., on narrative, 33
Hillyer, Captain James, 79, 82, 89; account of battle, 91–2; on battle etiquette, 87
Himmelfarb, Gertrude, on history, 126
historian, as composer, 102
historical consciousness, in myth, 64
histories: of Cook, 75; present past, 42; types, 37, 49–50
history: academic, 53–4; analytic concept, 36–7; and accuracy, 40, 55; and anthropology, 49, 58, 61; and factual, 40; and irony, 57–8; and memory, 36; and mythic meaning, 51, 78; and paradox of living, 122; and past, 72; as consciousness, xiv, 38; as explanation, 36; as metaphor, 34; as metonymy, 34, 37; as myth, 75; as parable, 52, 101; as social system, 29; cross-cultural, 77–8; defining, 39; discipline of, 221; entertainment, 167; exegesis of exegesis, 61; feeds on meaning, 98; going native to the past, 124; in ceremony, 144; in fluent present, 226; in ordered present, 140; moral force of, 126; of ideas, 192; pantomime as, 156; performance of, xiv, 30; philosophy of, 33, 125–6; politics of, 125; public, 36; realism and, 63; reflective, 15, 125; sacred, 50–1; shaping events, 97; teaching of, 19; theatre of truth, 101; theatricality of, xv; vernacular, 35
Hodges, William, 214
Hollywood: invention of, 174; problem with banal evil, 179

Hopkins, Anthony, 172, 189
Hough, Richard, on the *Bounty* mutiny, 188–9
Howard, Trevor, 172, 182
Hudson, Nicholas, on empowering, 205
Humanae Vitae, 29
Hume, David, 8; on imagination, 102
Hunter, Ced, on death of a friend, 254–6
Husserl, Edmund, on spectacle, 120

imagination, dialogic, 232
Index of Forbidden Books, 7–8
irony: in anthropology, 200; in history, 117, 200; trope, 108
Irwin, Geoffrey, on Pacific voyaging, 213
Isaac, Rhys, xi, 58

James, William, 8
Jansenism, 23
Jesuits (Society of Jesus): and Irish, 23; and Jansenism, 23; and 'real distinction', 23; and risks of scholarship, 22; and theatre, 19; Australian experience, 20–1; novitiate training, 24–5; profession as, 18; spirit of prophecy, 21, 24
John XXIII, Pope, 268
Johnson, Dr Samuel, 150

Kalaniopu'u (high chief of Hawaii), 69; meeting Cook, 69; made hostage, 71; village of, 75
kali'i, conflict ritual, 66
kanaka, 76, 77
Kant, Immanuel, on the enlightened, 107, 216
kapu (*tapu*), 66
Kealakekua: Cook's welcome, 68; description, 68; in 'Omai', 160; **Plate 2**
Keegan, John, on battle, 79, 83–5
Kendall, James, 218
Kepler, Johannes, 219
King, Lt James, 72
Ku (Hawaiian god), 65, 66; images of, 69, 75; season of, 70, 71, 73

Ladurie, Emmanuel Le Roy, on narrative, 33
Laemmle, Carl, 174
Lalor, Joseph Peter, symbolic death, 248–50
Laughton, Charles: conflict with Gable, 175; sadistic Bligh, 171–2; script for, 178–9; **Plate 8**
Le Goff, Jacques, on narrative, 33
Lewis, C. S., 10
Liholiho (Hawaiian king), 75
Lloyd, Frank, 172
Lonergan, Bernard, 22
Longford, Raymond, 172
Lono (Hawaiian god), 65; Cook as, 72; myth and history of, 78; priests of, 69; symbols of, 66, 69, 70
Loughnan, Frank, letter from Lone Pine, 261–2
Loutherbourg, Philippe Jacques de, 157–8, 161; **Plates 1, 5**
Loyola College, 6, 21
Loyola, Ignatius: and discernment of spirits; and rule, 23–4; founder of Society of Jesus, 9; *Spiritual Exercises*, 11

MacLuhan, Marshall, on 'hot' and 'cold', 231
Madison, President, 80, 82
Mahaiatea (Purea's *marae*), 132, 147, 149, 163, 165, 166
Mahan, Alfred T., on naval ceremony, 144
makahiki, 65–7, 70, 73; ceremonies of, 69, 72; procession of, 68
Malin, David, on the Southern Cross, 217–18
Malinowski, Bronislaw, 194–5, 197
maohi (Tahitians), 76, 77 131, 214
Marcuse, Herbert: on forgetting, 203; on reification, 23, 211
Maréchal, Joseph, 22
Maritain, Jacques, 22
maro tea, 130, 164–6
maro ura, 128, 129, 134, 139, 164–6; description of, 129–30

Marquesans, *see enata*
Marquesas Islands, 9, 61, 82; **Plates 6, 12**
Marx, Karl, on consciousness, 38
Maskelyne, Nevil, 3, 218
Matavai, 132, 135, 140, 149, 214–15
Mayer, Louis, 174–5
Mead, Margaret, 57, 191, 197; in Samoa, 197–8
Meagher, Leo, letter from Paschendale, 258–61
Melbourne University Historical Society, 8
Melville, Herman, 60; on acting, 101
memory: and history, 36, 96; in Anzac Day, 230; of battle, 95; of war, 248
Merwick, Donna, xi, xii
metaphor, 34, 271; history as, 104; native and stranger, 65; perceptions and, 139
metonymy, 34, 271; history as, 104
Metro Goldwyn Mayer: archives, 168; Mayer's creation, 174; Mutiny films, 171
Milestone, Lewis, 172, 182
Mill, John Stuart, 8
Miller, Arthur, 47
mimesis, and cloning, 113
Moho, 210
models: and symbols, 40; of disciplines, 40
monuments: and rituals, 228; debate on, 223–4; dialogic imagination and, 232; freezing memory, 225; paradoxes in, 251
Morton, H. V., 16
Muses, 103
museums, 43, 103, 268; of encounters, 167; Tahitian, 133
Musicians' Seamounts, 210
'Mutiny on the Bounty': 1916 film, 172; 1932 film, 172–3; 1935 film, 171–2, 176–80; 1962 film, 183–9; 1984 film, 189–90
Myers, Fred, xii

narrative, 33; as lived experience, 104; deep, 221; formulaic, 231; gospel, 50; producing effects in, 115; tropes of, 34

Native: and Stranger, 64; representation of, 161; *see also* 'going native'
navigation: as progressive science, 216; as school subject, 108
Newbury, Colin, 162–3
neo-marxism, 107
Newport, Father, 6, 7, 8
New Zealand, *see* Aotorea
Nuer, 194

Oahu, 4
Oberea, *see* Purea
Obeysekere, Gananath, 76
objectivism, unreality of, 56
observer: as culture mapper, 120; Ferris on, 220; Herschel on, 219–20; in ethnography, 226; telescopic/microscopic, 220
Oceania: encompassing, 212–13; fashions in the name, 208; Hau'ofa on, 208; naming the sea-bed, 210
oceans, encompassing, 209
O'Keeffe, John, 157–8, 160
Oliver, Douglas, 162–3; on *maro ura*, 165–6; on 'timorodee', 154
'Omai' (pantomime), 156ff
Omai, 158
'Oro (Tahitian god), 141; attracting attention of, 138; god of sacrifice, 130; worship of, 131, 132
Other, 122–3; as grotesque, 123, 161, 214; gendered, 123; inventing, 138, 196

pahupu, 4
pantomime, 155; structures of, 156
Papara (district of Tahiti), 132
parable, 52, 101; history as, 101
paradoxes: and learning history, 30; and religious life, 25; in monuments, 251; of acting, 121; of living, 122
Parkinson, Sydney, 214
participle, 119–20; past, 17, 119; present, 16–17, 119; 'real distinction' and, 23
past: as 'cargo', 43, 46–7; in present, 44; leaves relics, 42, 126; possibilities

reduced, xvi; realism of, xv; texted, 41–3; represented not replicated, xiv; total particularity, xv

performance: ambivalence in meaning, xii; as duty done, xii; attitudes towards, 110; audience and, xiv, 20; consciousness, 30, 121; in *disputatio*, 18; of history, xiv, 30, 75; of scholastic philosophy, 4; public nature of, 20; risk in, 20; spaces of, 116; whole person involved, 20

perspective, geometric vision, 108

Petrach, Francesco, on time, 107, 216

philosophy, scholastic, 22–3

Phoebe, 79, 82, 85; mottos of, 80; **Plate 7**

Picard, George, 23

Pitcairn Island, 173; murders on, 187

Pius XII, Pope, 16

plagiarism: of living, 222; Tomkis on, 105

Plato, and anti-theatre, 113

play: in ritual, 229; scandal of, 113

Pleiades, and *makahiki*, 69

poetics, 35ff; and texts, 36; of orality, 214

Poetua, 221

Poincaré, Jules Henri, on space, 120

Point Venus, 135, 214–15

'Points of Meditation', moments of art, 15

Polynesians 64; myths, 65; 'Problem', 213

Pomare II (Tahitian king), 129, 131–2, 164, 166; ceremonies of investiture, 133

Pomare III (Tahitian king), investiture, 134

Porter, Commodore David Dixon: on courtesies of battle, 92; on rate of fire, 94

Porter, Lt David, 79; at Valparaiso, 85ff; in battle, 91ff; madcap adventurer, 81; on gentlemanly ethics, 87; **Plate 6**

possessions: ceremonies of, 142; of Tahiti, 142

postmodernism, 107

prayer: narrative forms, 13; touches of mysticism, 13

praxis, 38; of culture, 44

Prelude, The, 3

'Preludes': cathartic point of, 15; of *Spiritual Exercises*, 14–15

presence, authorial, 112–13

present: consciousness of things past, xiv; double meaning of, xvi, 34; nothing so civilised as, 124

presentations, 34

presenting: making something now, xiv, xv; staging something, xiv, xv

Price, Richard, 58

prize system, 88; and prisoners, 89

privateering, ambivalence of, 88

processions: left/right handed, 65; *makahiki*, 68; of Lono, 65

prologues, nature of, 111

prophecy, spirit of, 21, 24

Providence, 180

Prynne, William, on theatre, 112

Purea ('Oberea'), 147; inventions of, 148ff, 161ff, 167; object of satire, 153–3; political machinations, 165; represented, 151; **Plate 5**

Raccoon, 82, 89

Rahner, Karl, 22

rahui (secular taboo), 165

Raiatea, origin of 'Oro, 130

'Rainbow', 140, 167; 'Oro's canoe, 131

Ramsden, Jesse, 218

Rapanui (Easter Island), 213

Ratio Studiorum, 21

reading: birth of reader, xv; creative reader, 116; films, 168; roguishness of, 102; vital skills of, 33–4

realism: and performance consciousness, xvi; and multivalency, 127; and process, 43; and style, 118; conspiracies of, 112; deference to, 124; in encounters, 139; of being there, 113; of history, 63; of turgid style, 115; reality effects, 114, 125

reality: effects, 114, 125; not actual, 60; the reductively known, 60

Reed, Carol, 172, 182

reflective history, *see* history

relativism: and anthropology, 194; and belief, 269; and dialectic of process and order, 43; Cook's, 155; sad jokes and, 122; unreality of, 56

religious life: changing symbols, 226; closed nature of, 25–6; penance in, 5; relics of, 5–6; sacrifices and, 11; views in, 11, 26

Resolution, 67, 69, 70, 73, 171, 221

retreats, *see Spiritual Exercises*

Reynolds, Sir Joshua, on 'Omai', 158

Ricoeur, Paul, 49

rituals: of discipline, 144; of investiture, 133–5; of possession, 142–3; of religion, 267; of transformation, 50

Robarts, Edward, 50

Roberts, Michael, xii

Robertson, George, 148

Rockwell, Norman, 174

'Roger Byam', 174, 179–81

Rorty, Richard: on defunct distinctions, 110; on imagination, 106, 205, 122

Roosevelt, Theodore, on War of 1812, 81–2

Rosaldo, Renato, 58; on narrating 'force', 115; on rage in grief, 204

Rose, Roger, 162–3

'Rules of Modesty', 27–8

Rousseau, Jean Jacques, on theatricality of civilisation, 113–14

sacrifices, proxy, 141

Sahlins, Marshall, 58, 72, 76, 140, 147

Said, Edward: on invention of the Orient, 46; on mediating, 124

St Augustine, on wonderment, 107, 216

St John's College, 3

St Louis' School, 21

Salmon, Tati, 164

Samoa: Freeman, on 199; Mead's fieldwork in, 197; sexual practices of, 192

'Schools', 4

Shield, William, 157–8

Shrine of Remembrance: and imagination, 231–2; barren symbols, 227

signs: and models, 39; and symbols, 39; in rituals, 271

Sinclair, Upton, 174

Skinner, Richard (*Bounty*'s barber), 132

Smart, John, drawing of Bligh, 171, **Plate 8**

Society of Jesus, *see* Jesuits

sociology, reflexive, discovery of politics, 125

Socrates, and anti-theatre, 113

soliloquy, ontologically subversive, 111

'songlines', 207; deep-rooted understandings, 11; interlocked, 211–12; of incarnation and redemption, 211; transmission of, 214

Sontag, Susan, on erotics of texts, xiv, 61

sources, primary, 55

Spiritual Exercises, 9, 51; and brainwashing, 12; and decision, 13; and methodology, 13; as spiritual manual, 14; Barthes on, 12; Weeks of, 14; *see also* 'Application of the Senses', 'Composition of Place', 'Discernment of Spirits', 'Points of Meditation'

Stafford, Barbara, on voyaging, 108

Stallybrass, Peter, on theatre of grotesque, 123

Stanner, Bill, on dreaming, 210–11

Stone, Lawrence, on narrative, 33

stranger, and native, 64

Strong, Tracey, on theatre, 106

structuralism, 107

style, 116; and realism, 118

subjunctive, 117, 124; space of theatre, 118

symbols: ambience of, 267; and historical environments, 61; and models, 39; and signs, 39, 271; emptiness of, 128; in history making, 145; in time, 226; of flag and *maro ura*, 165; of missions, ships, 62; of radical dress, 170–1; of religion, 267; of the plantain, 145–6; of the Shrine, 227–8; of the Southern Cross, 217; realism of, 36

ta'ata meia roa, symbol of sacrifice, 145–6

Tahaara, 147

Tahiti: ceremonies at, 128; Cook at, 214ff; 'discovery' of, 107; meaning a 'distant place', 64; possession of, xv, 152

Tahitians, 76; *see also maohi*

Taputapuatea, 141; place of sacrifice, 130; treasure house, 131; **Plate 4**

Tarahoi, 132, 147

Teri-i-reree (son of Purea), 149, 165

texts: different to films, 168; mediate past, 17; past-participled, 17

Thalberg, Irving, 174, 180

theatre: and history learning, 30; Aristotle on, xv; as *thea*, 104; enigmas of, 117; Gosson on, 112; histories as, 48; Jesuit tradition in, 19; of civilising process, 109; of everyday life, 34; of film, 174; of novitiate, 25, 28; of mutiny, 170; of Pacific, 109; of power, 118; of reform, 21–2; of voyaging, 108; poetics of, 48; producing effects in, 102; Prynne on, 112; reinforcing hegemony, 174; threatening, 110; undermines fundamentalism, 101

theatricality: and invention of culture, 114; of civilisation, 113; of cultural actions, 109; of history making, xv, 103ff, 105, 122, 127; narrating paradoxes, 122; Rousseau on, 113–14; threatening notion, 110

theory: and theatre, 104; as mode of consciousness, 107

Thompson, E. P., on theory, 125–6

Thompson, Roger, xii

Thucydides, 17

Tone, Franchot, 174; script for, 179–80

trope, 34; of irony, 57; of understanding, 59

truth: and accuracy, 127; history as theatre of, 101; stage, 122

Truxton, Captain Thomas, 81

Tubuai, 132, 190

Turner, Victor: on entertainment, 48–9; on experience, 118; on the subjunctive, 117

Utu'aihamurau (marae of 'Oro), 132, 149

Valeri, Valerio, 58

Valéry, Paul, on silence, 116

Valparaiso, 81, 83, 85, 89

Vancouver, George, 3

Vatican Council II, 21, 22, 25

Venus, Transit of, 148, 218ff; and politics of knowledge, 219

'vocation': determining, 10; sacrifices and, 10

voyaging, traditional, 213–14

Wagner, Richard, 114

Wagner, Roy: on culture, 57; on events, 106; on impersonation, 104

Waimea, 4

Wakefield, Gilbert, on astronomy, 216

Wallis, Samuel, 107, 133, 135, 141, 144; and Purea, 151; makes history, 145

Walpole, Horace, 150

war: attitudes to, 227; honouring dead, 225; metaphors in song, 240–2; morality of, 246–7; recording, 233

War of 1812, causes, 79–80

Warner, Benjamin, 174

Watman, William, death and burial, 69–70

Watts, Sir James, on Cook's health, 67

Webber, John, 132, 157–8; portrait of Bligh, 171; portrait of Poetua, 221; **Plate 8**

Weber, Max, 49

Wesley, Charles, 9

Wesley, John: on Hawkesworth, 150; on hermeneutics of soul, 51

Wewitzer, Ralph, 159, 170, **Plate 1**

White, Hayden: on perspectives, 105; on reflective history, 35

White, Allon, on theatre of grotesque, 123

White, Peter, xii

Wilder, Brian, xii

Williams, Raymond, on soliloquies, 11

Williamson, Lt John, accused of cowardice, 71, 74

Witherspoon, John, on theatre, 113
women, and Strangers, 137–8
words, with history, 117
Wordsworth, William: and Fletcher Christian, 181; education at Cambridge, 3; spoils family ambitions, 3; *Prelude*, 3
writing: and 'force', 115; creating readers, 116; liminality of, 62–3; reality effects in, 115; sculpted, xiii

Xavier College: and Irish, 242–4; and Public Schools, 235–6; and South African War, 233–5; at war, 233ff; history and anthropology of, 9, 61; honouring the dead, 226; school songs, 239–42; **Plate 10**

Young, Edward, 173

Zukor, Adolph, 174